The Bible In 52 Weeks For Couples

Deepening Love and Faith throughout the Year for Married People

Thank you

Dear Readers,

Thank you for choosing *The Bible in 52 Weeks for Couples*! I am truly honored that you have invited this book into your life and relationship. My hope is that, as you journey through the Scriptures together, you'll find each lesson bringing you closer not only to God but to each other. Each week is crafted with couples in mind—designed to spark meaningful conversations, deepen your bond, and help you discover fresh insights into God's Word as a team.

You've taken a wonderful step in investing in your relationship spiritually, and I'm excited to walk with you through this journey of faith, growth, and love. May this book be a source of encouragement, wisdom, and joy, strengthening you as you build a relationship rooted in faith and purpose.

Thank you again for making this book part of your journey. May it bless your relationship and draw you closer to the life God has planned for you, together.

With gratitude,

Esther W. Dawson

Content

Welcome _____ 8

   How to Approach This Year Together _____ 9

   Why Couples' Bible Study? _____ 10

   Tips for the Journey _____ 11

   A Year of Transformation_____ 11

Week 1 _____ 12

   God's Design for Partnership and Unity __ 12

   Couple for Week 1: Adam and Eve _____ 14

Week 2 _____ 15

   Trust, Commitment, and Faithfulness ____ 15

   Couple for Week 2: Abraham and Sarah __ 17

Week 3 _____ 18

   Reconciliation, Forgiveness, and Trusting in God's Guidance_____ 18

   Couple for Week 3: Isaac and Rebekah ___ 20

Week 4 _____ 21

   Provision, and Humility in Relationships__ 21

   Couple for Week 4: Jacob and Rachel _____ 23

Week 5 _____ 24

   Humility, Patience, and Trust in God's Justice _____ 24

   Couple for Week 5: Boaz and Ruth _____ 26

Week 6 _____ 28

   Obedience, Faith, and Trust in God's Timing _____ 28

   Couple for Week 6: Elkanah and Hannah _ 30

Week 7 _____ 32

God's Covenant, Holiness, and Service in Marriage _____ 32

   Couple for Week 7: Zacharias and Elizabeth _____ 34

Week 8 _____ 36

   God's Presence, Guidance, and Living in His Word _____ 36

   Couple for Week 8: Joseph and Mary ___ 38

Week 9 _____ 41

   Sacrifice, Obedience, and Purity in Marriage _____ 41

   Couple for Week 9: Priscilla and Aquila __ 43

Week 10 _____ 46

   Purification, Holiness, and Commitment in Marriage _____ 46

   Couple for Week 10: Manoah and His Wife _____ 48

Week 11 _____ 51

   God's Faithfulness and Our Response in Marriage _____ 51

   Couple for Week 11: Job and His Wife ___ 53

Week 12 _____ 55

   Obedience and Trust in God's Leadership 55

   Couple for Week 12: David and Bathsheba 57

Week 13 _____ 59

   Commitment and Sacrifice in Marriage __ 59

   Couple for Week 13: Amram and Jochebed _____ 61

Week 14 _____ 63

Trust and Obedience in Marriage _____ 63

Couple for Week 14: Shem and His Wife __ 65

Week 15 _____ 67

Faithful Commitment and Generosity in
Marriage _____ 67

Couple for Week 15: Asa and His Wife ___ 69

Week 16 _____ 71

Faith, Trust, and God's Promises _____ 71

Couple for Week 16: Hezekiah and His
Wife _____ 73

Week 17 _____ 75

Obedience, Renewal, and Trust in God's
Power _____ 75

Couple for Week 17: King Xerxes and
Esther _____ 77

Week 18 _____ 80

Commitment, Faith, and New Beginnings _ 80

Couple for Week 18: Tobiah and Sarah ___ 81

Week 19 _____ 84

Faith, Courage, and the Power of God's
Strength _____ 84

Couple for Week 19: Hosea and Gomer __ 85

Week 20 _____ 88

Faithfulness, Redemption, and New
Beginnings _____ 88

Couple for Week 20: Abraham and
Keturah _____ 89

Week 21 _____ 91

Trusting God's Plan and Growing in
Humility _____ 91

A Team for Week 21: Noah and His Wife 93

Week 22 _____ 95

Forgiveness, Humility, and Trusting in God's
Redemption _____ 95

Couple for Week 22: Micaiah and His Wife 97

Week 23 _____ 99

Repentance, Restoration, and the Power of
the Holy Spirit _____ 99

Couple for Week 23: Samson and His
Wife _____ 101

Week 24 _____ 103

Leadership, Legacy, and the Power of God's
Presence _____ 103

Couple for Week 24: Lot and His Wife __ 105

Week 25 _____ 107

Wisdom, Choices, and Divine Guidance _ 107

Couple for Week 25: Zechariah and
Elizabeth _____ 109

Week 26 _____ 111

Courage, Faith, and God's Unwavering
Presence _____ 111

Couple for Week 26: David and Abigail _ 113

Week 27 _____ 115

Trusting God's Guidance in Uncertain
Times _____ 115

Couple for Week 27: Isaiah and the
Prophetess _____ 116

Week 28 _____ 119

Finding Strength and Courage in God's
Faithfulness _____ 119

Couple for Week 28: Joseph and Asenath 120

Week 29 _____ 123

Righteousness and Restoration _____ 123

Couple for Week 29: Cleopas and His
Wife _____ 124

Week 30 _____ 127

God's Unfailing Love and Transformation 127

Couple for Week 30: Nabal and Abigail _ 128

Week 31 _____ 131

    Unity, Humility, and God's Sovereign
Faithfulness _____ 131

    Couple for Week 31: Aaron and Elisheba 133

Week 32 _____ 135

    Wisdom, Dedication, and God's Eternal
Perspective _____ 135

    Couple for Week 32: Tamar and Judah __ 137

Week 33 _____ 139

    Embracing Wisdom, Love, and Worship _ 139

    Couple for Week 33: Phinehas and His
Wife _____ 142

Week 34 _____ 145

    Strength in Faith, Wisdom in Leadership, and
Hope in Resurrection _____ 145

    Couple for Week 34: The Levite and His
Wife _____ 148

Week 35 _____ 150

    Restoration, Renewal, and the Call to
Reconciliation _____ 150

    Couple for Week 35: Esau and Judith ___ 152

Week 36 _____ 155

    God's Judgment and Mercy _____ 155

    Couple for Week 36: Jacob and Leah ____ 158

Week 37 _____ 160

    Trust in God's Deliverance and Strength _ 160

    Couple for Week 37: Ahab and Jezebel __ 163

Week 38 _____ 166

    God's Faithfulness in Restoration and
Salvation _____ 166

    Couple for Week 38: Rehoboam and
Naamah _____ 168

Week 39 _____ 171

    Living in the Light of God's Glory and
Calling _____ 171

    Couple for Week 39: Ananias and
Sapphira _____ 174

Week 40 _____ 176

    Responding to God's Call in Times of
Struggle and Faithfulness _____ 176

    Couple for Week 40: Herod and Herodias 178

Week 41 _____ 181

    Staying Faithful in the Midst of Trials and
Hope in God's Promise _____ 181

    Couple for Week 41: Naaman and His
Wife _____ 183

Week 42 _____ 186

    Living Out Faith in the Midst of Adversity 186

    Couple for Week 42: Lamech and His
Wives _____ 188

Week 43 _____ 190

    God's Justice and Faithfulness in Troubling
Times _____ 190

    Couple for Week 43: Elimelech and
Naomi _____ 192

Week 44 _____ 195

    Hope in God's Mercy and Strength ____ 195

    Couple for Week 44: Jehoiada and
Jehosheba _____ 197

Week 45 _____ 200

    God's Righteousness and the New
Covenant _____ 200

    Couple for Week 45: Jehoram and
Athaliah _____ 202

Week 46 _____ 205

    Walking by Faith and Living in God's
Promises _____ 205

    Couple for Week 46: David and Michal _ 207

Week 47 _____ 210

   God's Restoration and Living in Holiness 210

   Couple for Week 47: King Ahasuerus and Vashti _____212

Week 48 _____ 215

   Trusting God in Times of Trial and His Sovereignty_____215

   Couple for Week 48: Solomon and Pharaoh's Daughter _____217

Week 49 _____ 219

   God's Sovereignty and His Promise of Restoration_____219

   Couple for Week 49: King Saul and Ahinoam _____221

Week 50 _____ 224

   God's Faithfulness and the Triumph of His Kingdom _____224

   Couple for Week 50: King Solomon and Naamah _____ 226

Week 51 _____ 229

   Returning to God's Presence and the Victory of Christ _____ 229

   Couple for Week 51: Tamar and Er_____ 231

Week 52 _____ 234

   A Year of Restoration and Hope in Christ's Return _____ 234

   Couple for Week 52: Abraham and Hagar 236

Conclusion _____ 239

   Looking Back at What You've Gained __ 239

   Moving Forward: How to Continue Nurturing Your Faith and Marriage ____ 240

   Closing Blessing_____ 241

Welcome

Dear Couples,

Welcome to a year of exploration, discovery, and growth—a year designed to deepen your bond with one another while also drawing closer to God. This journey through the Bible is crafted with you in mind: a couple seeking to live out your faith together, to strengthen your relationship, and to establish a foundation that can weather all of life's seasons. Here, you will find tools, stories, and guidance meant to uplift your marriage and nurture your walk with God, step by step, week by week.

This book isn't merely a reading plan. It's an invitation to make your marriage a living reflection of God's love and design. In a world that often rushes by, filled with distractions and challenges, creating intentional time with your spouse can be transformative. Committing to a year of weekly Bible exploration as a couple allows you to grow in both understanding and grace, equipping you with the wisdom, patience, and faith to walk together in unity. Throughout the coming year, each week will bring you a new theme, a collection of Scripture passages, and practical ways to infuse these lessons into your lives.

How to Approach This Year Together

This journey is built to be both enriching and manageable, structured with busy lives in mind. Each week features several key elements designed to help you engage with the Bible in a way that feels personal, interactive, and meaningful. Let's take a closer look at each part:

1. Weekly Theme

Each week focuses on a central theme, carefully chosen to speak to your journey as a couple. Themes like "God's Design for Partnership and Unity," "Embracing Forgiveness," or "Building a Legacy of Faith" will guide you and provide a framework for your discussions. These themes anchor your reading and reflection, helping you to see how the Word applies to real areas in your marriage. By keeping the theme in mind, you'll find new insights and encouragement that go beyond daily life and into the heart of a strong, enduring relationship.

2. Daily Reading Plan

The daily reading plan is structured to guide you through a thoughtful blend of Old and New Testament passages, accompanied by Psalms or Proverbs. Each day's readings are designed to be manageable—providing a consistent rhythm that keeps you engaged without feeling overwhelming. As you read together, listen to God's voice in the stories of Scripture. Some days may reveal new insights, while others may reinforce values or truths you hold dear. By the end of the year, you'll have journeyed through significant portions of the Bible, gaining a broader understanding of God's plan and purpose for couples.

3. Weekly Reflection

At the end of each week, take time to pause and reflect on what you've read. The weekly reflections will guide you in applying the messages of Scripture to your relationship. Think of this reflection time as a gentle prompt, inviting you to look at the ways in which God's Word speaks directly to the joys, challenges, and growth points within your marriage. Use this time to discuss how the Scriptures resonate with each of you and where you feel called to grow as a couple. Reflection is powerful; it opens up pathways for growth, understanding, and renewed commitment.

4. Discussion Prompts

We've included thought-provoking discussion prompts to facilitate honest and meaningful conversations. These prompts are designed to foster a deeper understanding of each other's hearts and minds and to inspire you to talk openly about important aspects of your relationship. Think of these prompts as a way to draw closer, creating a space where both of you can express thoughts, fears, dreams, and hopes. Over time, these discussions can deepen your connection, enhance your communication, and remind you of the blessings of sharing your lives with one another.

5. Couple Activity

Each week includes a joint activity, allowing you to put what you're learning into practice. These activities are intentionally varied, offering you opportunities to connect in different ways—from creating a "marriage covenant" to writing down shared goals, to planning a prayer walk together. By engaging in these exercises, you build habits of love, respect, and intentionality that will strengthen your bond. These activities are intended to be simple yet impactful, creating memories and habits that affirm your commitment to each other.

6. Weekly Couple Spotlight

Every week, you'll meet a new couple from the Bible. Their stories offer rich insights into both the blessings and trials of marriage. Whether you're learning from Adam and Eve's journey of trust, Priscilla and Aquila's example of partnership, or Ruth and Boaz's story of loyalty, these couples will inspire you with their resilience, faith, and dedication. Their lives are reminders that God works through every kind of relationship—whether it's steady and faithful, filled with trials, or even marked by mistakes. Each couple's story will give you a fresh perspective on your own marriage and the ways God can work through your relationship.

Why Couples' Bible Study?

Marriage is a calling, one that involves both immense joy and a dedication to growth. The Bible reveals that marriage is meant to be a sacred partnership, mirroring God's love, commitment, and faithfulness. This year-long journey offers you the chance to explore that calling deeply and intentionally. You'll find that the stories of Scripture reflect the many stages of marriage: from the excitement of new love to the challenges of enduring hardships together, to the beauty of building a legacy that outlasts you. As you read, you'll uncover the tools you need to build a marriage that can thrive in any season.

This book is a guide, but it's also an invitation: an invitation to see your marriage as a vital part of God's greater plan. By dedicating yourselves to this study, you're choosing to nurture a love that reflects Christ's love, a love that is patient, forgiving, and anchored in faith. You'll learn how to pray together, how to seek wisdom from God's Word, and how to honor each other as precious gifts from God. Let each day's reading, each reflection, and each conversation remind you that marriage is a divine journey—a journey that is not meant to be walked alone but with God at the center.

Tips for the Journey

1. Create a Rhythm: Set aside time each day to read together. Whether it's in the morning over coffee or in the evening after a long day, find a rhythm that works for both of you.

2. Stay Open and Vulnerable: Approach each discussion prompt and activity with an open heart. Be willing to listen, share, and grow together. Vulnerability is a powerful tool for deepening trust.

3. Celebrate the Small Moments: Each time you share a new insight, overcome a challenge, or complete an activity, take a moment to celebrate it. Marriage is made up of these small, beautiful moments that strengthen your bond.

4. Pray Together and for Each Other: At the end of each day or week, take a moment to pray together. Praying for one another strengthens your spiritual bond and reminds you of the sacredness of your commitment.

5. Be Patient and Persistent: Not every week will feel easy, and not every reading will spark immediate insight. Trust that the process itself is part of the growth.

A Year of Transformation

As you begin this journey, remember that the most profound transformations often happen quietly, over time. Let this book be a gentle guide, a source of inspiration, and a means to build a marriage rooted in love and faith. Know that each page is here to support, encourage, and empower you to create a marriage that not only endures but thrives.

Marriage is a gift, a mystery, and a beautiful commitment that reflects the very heart of God. May this year bring you closer to each other and to the One who brought you together. We pray that *The Bible in 52 Weeks for Couples* enriches your love, inspires your faith, and leaves a lasting imprint on your hearts.

Let the journey begin.

Week 1

God's Design for Partnership and Unity

Weekly Readings:

Day 1- Genesis 1, Genesis 2:1-17; Matthew 1:1-25; Psalm 1:1-6
Day 2- Genesis 2:18-25, Genesis 3, Genesis 4:1-16; Matthew 2:1-18; Psalm 2:1-12
Day 3- Genesis 4:17-26, Genesis 5, Genesis 6; Matthew 2:19-23, Matthew 3; Psalm 3:1-8
Day 4- Genesis 7, Genesis 8, Genesis 9:1-17; Matthew 4:1-22; Proverbs 1:1-7
Day 5- Genesis 9:18-29, Genesis 10, Genesis 11:1-9; Matthew 4:23-25, Matthew 5:1-20; Psalm 4:1-8
Day 6- Genesis 11:10-32, Genesis 12, Genesis 13; Matthew 5:21-42; Psalm 5:1-12
Day 7- Genesis 14, Genesis 15, Genesis 16; Matthew 5:43-48, Matthew 6:1-24; Psalm 6

Weekly Reflection:

This week's passages introduce us to the beauty and purpose of God's creation, particularly in the context of human relationships and marriage. From the very beginning, God designed marriage as a union built on mutual support, companionship, and a shared purpose. In Genesis, we see the creation of humanity, where God brings Adam and Eve together to complement and support one another. This reflects the divine intention for a marriage marked by unity, trust, and love.

As we move through the early stories of the Bible, we encounter both the blessings and challenges that come with relationships. Adam and Eve's story highlights not only the joy of companionship but also the vulnerability that can arise when we face trials. The stories of Cain and Abel, Noah, and Abraham further show us the importance of family, legacy, and obedience to God, reminding us that every marriage will have its seasons of growth, struggle, and renewal.

In the New Testament, Matthew's Gospel recounts the genealogy of Jesus, emphasizing the importance of family lineage and faith. This invites us to reflect on the heritage we are building as a couple, the values we are cultivating, and the legacy we want to leave. Jesus' teachings in the Sermon on the Mount also guide us to live out our faith and love with integrity and compassion, both within and beyond our marriage.

This week, let each day's readings be a reminder of God's presence in your partnership. Embrace the calling to support and uplift each other, even as you navigate life's challenges together. Celebrate the unique qualities you bring to each other, and find ways to deepen your connection through shared prayer, open communication, and small acts of love. Marriage is a journey of faith, one where you walk hand in hand with each other and with God, growing stronger together in His love.

Weekly Discussion Prompts:

1. Reflect on Creation Together: How does knowing God created marriage with a purpose encourage you in your relationship?

2. Overcoming Challenges: Share a challenge you've faced together. How did overcoming it strengthen your bond?

3. Building Your Legacy: What values or traits would you like to define your relationship and pass on to others?

4. Commitment in Small Acts: Discuss simple ways you can fulfill promises to each other this week.

5. Strengthening Communication: Identify an area where you could enhance your communication and build unity.

6. Taking a Leap of Faith Together: What new goal or experience could you embark on as a couple?

7. Renewing Your Commitment: Reflect on what commitment means to you and how you can honor it daily.

Joint Couple Activity:

"Our Covenant in Love": End the week by creating a "covenant" together. Write down a few promises that you commit to honoring in your marriage, such as showing patience, offering encouragement, or supporting each other's goals. Pray together, asking God to help you fulfill these promises and to strengthen your bond. Display your covenant somewhere meaningful as a reminder of your commitment.

Couple for Week 1: Adam and Eve

Adam and Eve were the first human couple created by God. Adam was formed from the dust of the earth, and Eve was created from one of Adam's ribs. They were placed in the Garden of Eden to live in harmony with God and each other, enjoying a paradise without sin. God gave them freedom to enjoy the garden but commanded them not to eat from the tree of the knowledge of good and evil. However, Eve was tempted by the serpent (Satan), ate the forbidden fruit, and gave it to Adam. Together, they disobeyed God, and as a result, sin entered the world, bringing pain, suffering, and separation from God. They were cast out of Eden and had to face the consequences of their actions.

Lessons for Couples:

1. Trust in God's Guidance: Adam and Eve's disobedience stemmed from a lack of trust in God's commands. Couples can learn the importance of following God's guidance and trusting in His plan for their lives and relationships.

2. Communication is Key: While Eve was tempted, Adam's silence and failure to protect his wife played a role in their fall. Couples should communicate openly, support one another, and take responsibility for their actions in the relationship.

3. Dealing with Consequences Together: After the fall, Adam and Eve faced the consequences of their actions. They had to work hard and live with the consequences of their sin. This teaches couples the importance of facing challenges and mistakes together, seeking redemption, and growing through difficulties.

4. Forgiveness and Redemption: Though Adam and Eve were punished, God still showed them grace by providing for them and promising a future redemption through the seed of the woman (a reference to Jesus Christ). Couples can find hope in God's forgiveness and grace, even when they fall short.

Week 2

Trust, Commitment, and Faithfulness

Weekly Readings:

Day 8- Genesis 17, Genesis 18; Matthew 6:25-34, Matthew 7:1-23; Proverbs 1:8-19
Day 9- Genesis 19, Genesis 20:1-18; Matthew 7:24-29, Matthew 8:1-22; Psalm 7:1-9
Day 10- Genesis 21, Genesis 22, Genesis 23; Matthew 8:23-34, Matthew 9:1-13; Psalm 7:10-17
Day 11- Genesis 24:1-67; Matthew 9:14-38; Psalm 8:1-9
Day 12- Genesis 25, Genesis 26; Matthew 10:1-31; Proverbs 1:20-33
Day 13- Genesis 27, Genesis 28:1-22; Matthew 10:32-42, Matthew 11:1-15; Psalm 9:1-6
Day 14- Genesis 29, Genesis 30; Matthew 11:16-30; Psalm 9:7-12

Weekly Reflection:

In this week's readings, we encounter moments that test the faith, trust, and commitment of the figures in Scripture. In Genesis, Abraham and Sarah receive the promise of a son in their old age, showing us that God's timing often defies human expectation but always fulfills His plans. Their story is a reminder of how trust and patience are essential in marriage, especially when facing uncertainties or waiting on promises to be fulfilled.

We also see the marriage of Isaac and Rebekah in Genesis 24, a beautiful depiction of a relationship grounded in faith and prayer. Abraham's servant seeks God's guidance to find a wife for Isaac, resulting in a union blessed by God. This story invites us to reflect on how seeking God's will can lead to stronger, more intentional partnerships. In the New Testament, Jesus' teachings in Matthew encourage us to build our lives on a solid foundation of faith, a call to establish our marriages with God at the center.

Throughout the Psalms and Proverbs, we are reminded to seek wisdom and avoid the pitfalls of fear, pride, or judgment. Trusting each other and God in all aspects of our journey allows a couple to deepen their bond and grow closer, no matter what challenges they face. Just as Abraham and Sarah trusted God's promises, couples today are called to trust and uplift each other, building a marriage grounded in faith, love, and patience.

Let this week's reflection guide you both to focus on trust, understanding, and commitment in your relationship. Embrace the call to support each other through every season, to seek God's guidance in your decisions, and to build a foundation that withstands any challenge.

Weekly Discussion Prompts:

1. Trust and Patience: Reflect on a promise or goal you're currently waiting on as a couple. How can you support each other in patience and trust?

2. Seeking God's Will Together: Like Abraham's servant, how can you invite God's guidance into your relationship and decisions?

3. Building on a Solid Foundation: What aspects of your marriage can you strengthen to ensure a foundation built on faith and love?

4. Facing Challenges with Faith: Share a time when you faced a difficult situation and found strength through each other and through prayer.

5. Living Out Commitment Daily: In what small ways can you show commitment to each other this week, honoring your love and promises?

6. Avoiding Judgment: In Matthew 7:1-23, Jesus warns against judgment. Discuss any tendencies you may have to judge and how you can approach each other with more understanding and grace.

7. Reflecting God's Love: How can you show each other unconditional love this week, reflecting the love that God has for us?

Joint Couple Activity:
"Faith and Foundations": This week, find a quiet moment to pray together for a specific area in your life where you want God's guidance. Write down your prayer together, asking God for wisdom, patience, and faith to walk through any uncertainties with grace. Display this prayer somewhere you can see as a reminder of your faith in God's promises and each other.

Couple for Week 2: Abraham and Sarah

Abraham (initially Abram) and Sarah (initially Sarai) are known as the patriarch and matriarch of Israel. God called Abraham to leave his homeland and travel to a new land, promising to make him the father of many nations. Though initially childless, Abraham and Sarah struggled with the promise of having a son. In their impatience, Sarah suggested that Abraham have a child with her maidservant, Hagar, leading to the birth of Ishmael. However, God remained faithful and, despite their old age, promised Sarah would bear a son, Isaac. Sarah laughed at this promise because of their advanced years, but God fulfilled His promise, and Isaac was born. Later, God tested Abraham's faith by asking him to sacrifice Isaac. Abraham obeyed, but God provided a ram as a substitute, reaffirming His covenant with Abraham.

Lessons for Couples:

1. Trust in God's Timing: Abraham and Sarah's story teaches couples that God's promises may take time to be fulfilled, and waiting patiently on God's timing is essential. They had to trust God despite their doubts and delays. Couples can learn to lean on God's faithfulness when facing delays or uncertainties in their own lives.

2. Patience in God's Promises: Abraham and Sarah's impatience led them to take matters into their own hands by having a child with Hagar. This caused complications and strife. Couples should avoid rushing ahead of God's plan and learn to wait for His promises to unfold in their lives, knowing His ways are perfect.

3. Faith in Difficult Times: When God asked Abraham to sacrifice Isaac, Abraham's faith was tested. Couples can learn from Abraham's obedience and unwavering trust in God, even when the circumstances seem difficult or unclear. Trusting in God's plan, even during times of testing, strengthens relationships.

4. God's Faithfulness: Despite their mistakes, God remained faithful to Abraham and Sarah. Couples can find comfort in knowing that even when they fail or falter, God's covenant of love and faithfulness endures. His grace and promises are unshakable.

5. Partnership and Support: Although they faced many trials, Abraham and Sarah were partners in the journey. They supported each other in moments of doubt and need. Couples can learn from their example to walk together, support one another, and trust in God's plans for their relationship and family.

Week 3

Reconciliation, Forgiveness, and Trusting in God's Guidance

Weekly Readings:

Day 15- Genesis 31:1-55; Matthew 12:1-21; Psalm 9:13-20
Day 16- Genesis 32, Genesis 33; Matthew 12:22-45; Proverbs 2:1-11
Day 17- Genesis 34, Genesis 35; Matthew 12:46-50, Matthew 13:1-17; Psalm 10:1-11
Day 18- Genesis 36, Genesis 37; Matthew 13:18-35; Psalm 10:12-18
Day 19- Genesis 38, Genesis 39; Matthew 13:36-58; Psalm 11:1-7
Day 20- Genesis 40, Genesis 41:1-40; Matthew 14:1-21; Proverbs 2:12-22
Day 21- Genesis 41:41-57, Genesis 42; Matthew 14:22-36, Matthew 15:1-9; Psalm 12:1-8

Weekly Reflection:

This week's readings bring us to moments of reconciliation, forgiveness, and trust in God's guidance. In Genesis, we see Jacob's journey to make peace with his estranged brother Esau. Their reconciliation shows us the healing power of forgiveness and the courage it takes to mend relationships. Jacob's fear and humility remind us that even in marriage, vulnerability and humility are essential for growth and healing. Esau's willingness to forgive Jacob reflects the grace that strengthens a marriage when both partners are willing to let go of past hurts.

We also witness Joseph's story, beginning with his betrayal by his brothers. His journey serves as a reminder of how faith in God can turn even the hardest situations into opportunities for growth and redemption. This is a call for couples to trust God's plan, especially during difficult times, and to stay united even in moments of betrayal or misunderstanding. In the New Testament, Jesus teaches in parables, revealing truths about the Kingdom of Heaven and calling His followers to trust in God's wisdom and guidance, just as we are called to trust Him within our marriage.

In marriage, reconciliation, forgiveness, and a reliance on God's wisdom are vital to nurturing a strong and loving partnership. This week, embrace opportunities to offer forgiveness, express humility, and grow together in trust and unity. Just as God is faithful, let this week's reflection inspire you to lean into His guidance, finding ways to strengthen your bond through love, patience, and understanding.

Weekly Discussion Prompts:

1. Forgiveness and Reconciliation: Are there any unresolved issues that need to be addressed in your relationship? How can you approach these with humility and grace?

2. Facing Challenges Together: Like Jacob's journey to make peace, what steps can you take together to bring healing to areas of tension or misunderstandings?

3. Unity in Faith: How can trusting in God's plan bring peace to any uncertainties you face as a couple?

4. Learning from the Past: Reflect on moments of betrayal or misunderstanding in your relationship. How have these times helped you grow as a couple?

5. Embracing God's Wisdom: As you read the parables in Matthew, consider how God's wisdom can guide you to make wise choices in your marriage. What decisions can you make this week to bring you closer?

6. Acting in Humility: Take time to consider areas where you can serve each other more selflessly. How can you show each other more compassion and understanding?

7. Gratitude and Trust: Thank God for His faithfulness in your relationship. Share ways in which you've seen His hand guiding your marriage and reflect on how this strengthens your faith in each other.

Joint Couple Activity:
"A Heart of Forgiveness": This week, create a "forgiveness list." Each of you writes down areas where you may still hold onto hurt or areas where you seek forgiveness from each other. Share this list in a gentle, open-hearted conversation, and pray together for God to help you let go of past hurts, renew your commitment to forgiveness, and bring peace to your relationship.

Couple for Week 3: Isaac and Rebekah

Isaac, the son of Abraham and Sarah, married Rebekah, who was chosen by Abraham's servant in a divinely orchestrated encounter. Abraham sent his servant to his homeland to find a wife for Isaac, as he wanted to ensure Isaac married within his family line. The servant prayed for God's guidance, asking for a sign to show him the right woman, and God answered by leading him to Rebekah, who graciously offered him water and water for his camels. Rebekah agreed to marry Isaac without hesitation, leaving her family to travel to Isaac. Isaac and Rebekah's marriage was blessed by God, though they faced challenges, including infertility. Isaac prayed to God on behalf of Rebekah, and God answered by giving them twins, Esau and Jacob. Their relationship was tested later by conflicts over their sons, but they remained committed to God's promises.

Lessons for Couples:

1. Trust God's Guidance in Relationships: Isaac and Rebekah's story shows that God is involved in the process of choosing a life partner. Couples can learn to seek God's will and trust His guidance in their decisions, particularly when it comes to marriage and choosing a spouse.

2. God's Timing and Patience: Rebekah's willingness to leave her family and marry Isaac without delay teaches couples the value of obedience and trust in God's timing. Isaac and Rebekah's story highlights that sometimes, even in waiting or uncertainty, God is orchestrating something beautiful in His perfect time.

3. Praying Together for Family Needs: Isaac's prayer for Rebekah when she was unable to conceive is an example of a husband's spiritual leadership in the family. Couples can learn from Isaac's intercession for his wife and remember to pray together for their family's needs, trusting in God's power to intervene.

4. Commitment in Adversity: Despite challenges in their relationship, such as infertility and family conflicts, Isaac and Rebekah's marriage remained intact. Couples can learn from their perseverance that challenges are a part of life, but God's promises stand firm, and commitment to one another and to God is key to overcoming adversity.

5. The Importance of Communication and Cooperation: Though Isaac and Rebekah faced tensions regarding the future of their sons, their story teaches the importance of clear communication and mutual cooperation. Even in difficult moments, working together and seeking God's guidance can bring peace and harmony to a marriage.

Week 4

Provision, and Humility in Relationships

Weekly Readings:

Day 22- Genesis 43, Genesis 44; Matthew 15:10-39; Psalm 13:1-6
Day 23- Genesis 45, Genesis 46, Genesis 47:1-12; Matthew 16:1-20; Psalm 14:1-7
Day 24- Genesis 47:13-31, Genesis 48; Matthew 16:21-28, Matthew 17:1-13; Proverbs 3:1-10
Day 25- Genesis 49, Genesis 50; Matthew 17:14-27, Matthew 18:1-9; Psalm 15:1-5
Day 26- Job 1, Job 2, Job 3; Matthew 18:10-35; Psalm 16:1-11
Day 27- Job 4, Job 5, Job 6, Job 7; Matthew 19:1-15; Psalm 17:1-5
Day 28- Job 8, Job 9, Job 10; Matthew 19:16-30; Proverbs 3:11-20

Weekly Reflection:

This week's readings highlight family reconciliation, God's abundant provision, and the call for humility and patience. In Genesis, Joseph's reunion with his brothers is a powerful story of forgiveness and restoration, showing that God can bring peace and healing even to deeply fractured relationships. As a couple, this is a reminder that forgiveness and a spirit of reconciliation are essential to a lasting, joyful marriage. Reflect on areas where you may need to extend grace, even in difficult circumstances, and trust that God's love can renew your relationship.

In Matthew, Jesus performs miracles, demonstrating His compassion and reminding us that God is the provider of all our needs. Couples can draw strength from this by turning to God together in moments of need or uncertainty, trusting Him to supply wisdom, patience, and unity. Jesus also teaches humility and service, challenging His followers to avoid pride and to embrace a servant heart—qualities essential in a thriving partnership.

In the Book of Job, we encounter suffering, patience, and a relentless trust in God. Job's trials remind us that faith is not always easy, and marriage can face seasons of hardship. However, by supporting each other through challenges and remaining steadfast in faith, couples can find deeper strength and closeness. This week is an invitation to rely on God, not only for provision but also for the patience and understanding needed to love one another in every season.

Weekly Discussion Prompts:

1. The Power of Reconciliation: Reflect on Joseph's forgiveness toward his brothers. Are there any past wounds or misunderstandings that need reconciliation in your marriage?

2. Trusting God's Provision: In what areas of life do you feel called to rely on God's provision as a couple? How can you support each other in trust and patience?

3. Practicing Humility: Jesus speaks of humility and serving others. How can you each take steps to serve each other more selflessly in your relationship?

4. Facing Hardships Together: Like Job, who endured great suffering, how can you strengthen each other's faith during difficult times? What practical steps can you take to stay grounded in God's love and patience?

5. Extending Grace: When conflict arises, how can you work toward reconciliation and extend grace to one another?

6. Building a Foundation of Faith: Reflect on a specific time when God provided for your needs as a couple. How can recalling His faithfulness help you trust Him with the future?

7. Trust and Patience: Patience is an essential theme in this week's readings. How can you practice patience in small ways this week to strengthen your relationship?

Joint Couple Activity:
"Gratitude and Provision Journal": This week, begin a shared journal where you record moments of gratitude for God's provision and faithfulness in your lives. Each day, take turns writing something you are grateful for, focusing on how God has been present in your marriage. Use this as a reminder of His faithfulness, especially when challenges arise.

Couple for Week 4: Jacob and Rachel

Jacob, the son of Isaac and Rebekah, fell in love with Rachel, the younger daughter of Laban, when he met her at a well. Jacob agreed to work for seven years to marry Rachel, but Laban deceived him by substituting his older daughter Leah on the wedding night. Jacob then worked another seven years to marry Rachel, his true love. The couple's relationship faced challenges, including rivalry with Leah, who bore Jacob many children, while Rachel struggled with infertility. Eventually, God opened Rachel's womb, and she gave birth to Joseph and Benjamin, two of the twelve tribes of Israel. Despite the challenges, Jacob loved Rachel deeply, and their story is one of love, sacrifice, and faith in God's timing.

Lessons for Couples:

1. Love and Sacrifice: Jacob's willingness to work fourteen years to marry Rachel demonstrates sacrificial love. Couples can learn that true love often requires sacrifice, whether in time, effort, or personal comfort. A strong marriage is built on a foundation of selflessness and devotion to one another.

2. Trusting God's Timing: Rachel's struggles with infertility teach couples to trust in God's timing. Though she longed for children and faced disappointment, God eventually blessed her with two sons. This highlights the importance of patience and faith when facing challenges in marriage or starting a family.

3. Overcoming Rivalry and Jealousy: The rivalry between Rachel and Leah teaches couples the dangers of jealousy and comparison. Instead of competing for Jacob's affection, they could have supported each other. Couples can learn from their story to avoid unhealthy comparisons and focus on mutual love and respect in their relationship.

4. Faith Through Challenges: Jacob and Rachel faced numerous obstacles in their relationship, from deception to infertility. Yet, they continued to rely on God. Couples can learn that even through struggles, faith in God's provision and trust in His plans can bring about blessings in their relationship.

5. Communication in Marriage: Jacob and Rachel's marriage, though deeply rooted in love, was complicated by outside pressures and family dynamics. Their story encourages couples to communicate openly with each other, to seek understanding, and to stand together when faced with external challenges. Strong marriages thrive on trust and honest dialogue.

Week 5

Humility, Patience, and Trust in God's Justice

Weekly Readings:

Day 29- Job 11, Job 12, Job 13, Job 14; Matthew 20:1-19; Psalm 17:6-12
Day 30- Job 15, Job 16, Job 17, Job 18; Matthew 20:20-34; Psalm 17:13-15
Day 31- Job 19, Job 20, Job 21; Matthew 21:1-17; Psalm 18:1-6
Day 32- Job 22, Job 23, Job 24; Matthew 21:18-32; Proverbs 3:21-35
Day 33- Job 25, Job 26, Job 27, Job 28, Job 29; Matthew 21:33-46, Matthew 22:1-14; Psalm 18:7-15
Day 34- Job 30, Job 31, Job 32; Matthew 22:15-46; Psalm 18:16-24
Day 35- Job 33, Job 34; Matthew 23:1-39; Psalm 18:25-36

Weekly Reflection:

This week's readings dive into deep questions of suffering, justice, and trust in God's timing. The Book of Job presents a man in deep anguish and confusion, yet ultimately trusting in God's wisdom and justice. Job's response to suffering challenges us to reflect on how we approach hardship in our own lives and marriages. When facing difficulties, it's easy to question God's goodness or feel overwhelmed, but Job's story reminds us that God is present even in our darkest times. As a couple, it's important to support each other through trials, remaining grounded in faith that God will bring justice and restoration, even when we cannot understand the circumstances.

In the Gospel of Matthew, Jesus teaches about the kingdom of heaven and the importance of humility. The parable of the workers in the vineyard reminds us that God's grace is not something we can earn through deeds but is freely given to all who seek it. This extends to our relationships as well—grace, forgiveness, and humility are essential in building strong marriages. It is not about who is "right" or "wrong" in a conflict but about approaching each other with a spirit of humility and love, seeking reconciliation and peace.

This week, reflect on areas where you may need to practice humility, trust God's justice, or rely on His timing. Whether it's facing personal struggles or relational challenges, let Job's perseverance and the teachings of Jesus inspire you to walk in faith and patience, trusting that God will work all things together for good.

Weekly Discussion Prompts:

1. Handling Suffering Together: Job's story is one of deep suffering, but also trust in God. How do you support each other when facing hardships, and how can you grow together in faith during tough times?

2. Humility in Marriage: Jesus teaches humility in the Gospel of Matthew. In what ways can you embrace humility as a couple, especially in conflicts or disagreements?

3. Grace Over Competition: Reflect on the parable of the workers in the vineyard. How does God's grace, given freely to all, shape how you interact with one another in your marriage?

4. Trusting God's Justice: Job struggled with understanding God's justice. Have there been times in your marriage when you've questioned God's timing or fairness? How did you navigate those moments together?

5. God's Wisdom in Difficult Times: Job's friends offered their opinions, but ultimately God's wisdom prevailed. How can you encourage each other to seek God's wisdom in decision-making and challenges?

6. Seeking Peace and Reconciliation: Reflect on the areas where you might need to seek reconciliation in your marriage. How can humility and grace help you restore peace in these areas?

7. Faith and Patience: In moments of struggle, what are some practical ways you can strengthen each other's faith and patience as a couple?

Joint Couple Activity:
"Grace-filled Reflection": This week, set aside time for a prayer walk or quiet moment together, reflecting on God's grace in your lives. Discuss how grace has shown up in your relationship, especially in areas of conflict or struggle. Pray for more patience and humility in your marriage and ask God for strength to endure challenges with faith, trusting that He is working in both of you.

Couple for Week 5: Boaz and Ruth

The story of Boaz and Ruth is one of love, loyalty, and redemption. Ruth, a Moabite widow, had married into an Israelite family. After the death of her husband and her father-in-law, she chose to stay with her mother-in-law, Naomi, rather than return to her own people. Ruth's faithfulness to Naomi and her commitment to God led her to Bethlehem, where she gleaned in the fields of Boaz, a wealthy relative of Naomi's late husband. Boaz, noticing her kindness and work ethic, showed her favor and protection. After Naomi's counsel, Ruth approached Boaz to seek his protection as a kinsman-redeemer, a tradition where a relative marries a widow to continue the family line. Boaz, impressed by Ruth's loyalty and virtue, agreed to marry her, redeeming her family and ensuring their future. Their union led to the birth of Obed, the grandfather of King David, making Ruth an ancestor of Jesus.

Lessons for Couples:

1. Loyalty and Commitment: Ruth's loyalty to Naomi and her commitment to God set the stage for the eventual blessing of her marriage to Boaz. Couples can learn from Ruth that loyalty—both to their spouse and to God—is foundational in a strong, lasting relationship. Love is not only about attraction but also about deep commitment and faithfulness, especially through life's challenges.

2. Respect and Integrity: Boaz's response to Ruth reflects the importance of integrity and respect in a relationship. He honored Ruth's decision to seek him as a kinsman-redeemer and treated her with kindness and dignity. Couples can learn that mutual respect, especially when making important decisions, strengthens the bond between spouses.

3. Providence and Trusting God's Plan: The way Boaz and Ruth's story unfolded is a testimony to God's providence. Though Ruth could have returned to her homeland after her husband's death, she trusted in God's plan for her life. Couples can learn that trusting in God's direction for their lives, even in uncertainty, leads to blessings in ways they may not expect.

4. Generosity and Selflessness: Boaz showed generosity by ensuring Ruth's safety and providing extra grain for her, even before he knew she would be his wife. His actions were rooted in kindness and a desire to serve others. Couples can learn that generosity, whether in time, resources, or love, deepens their connection and fosters a spirit of service to one another.

5. Support and Guidance in Marriage: Naomi played a key role in guiding Ruth to seek Boaz's protection, offering wise counsel during a time of uncertainty. This highlights the importance of mutual support, both from within the marriage and from trusted loved ones. Couples can learn that seeking and providing wise counsel, whether from

each other or from trusted mentors, can be a great help in making decisions that affect their relationship.

6. God's Redemption: The story of Boaz and Ruth is ultimately about redemption. Ruth, a foreigner, was redeemed and brought into the family of Israel. Their story is a reminder to couples that God's grace and redemption can restore broken situations. Couples can take comfort in knowing that no matter their past, God's redemptive love can bring new life to their marriage.

Week 6

Obedience, Faith, and Trust in God's Timing

Weekly Readings:

Day 36- Job 35, Job 36, Job 37; Matthew 24:1-31; Proverbs 4:1-9
Day 37- Job 38, Job 39, Job 40:1-2; Matthew 24:32-51, Matthew 25:1-13; Psalm 18:37-42
Day 38- Job 40:3-24, Job 41, Job 42; Matthew 25:14-46; Psalm 18:43-50
Day 39- Exodus 1, Exodus 2, Exodus 3; Matthew 26:1-30; Psalm 19:1-6
Day 40- Exodus 4, Exodus 5, Exodus 6:1-12; Matthew 26:31-46; Proverbs 4:10-19
Day 41- Exodus 6:13-30, Exodus 7, Exodus 8; Matthew 26:47-68; Psalm 19:7-14
Day 42- Exodus 9, Exodus 10; Matthew 26:69-75, Matthew 27:1-10; Psalm 20:1-9

Weekly Reflection:

This week's readings bring together profound lessons on trust in God's sovereignty, the need for obedience to His calling, and the patience required as we wait on His timing. In the Book of Job, we witness God's powerful response to Job's suffering, affirming that God is in control of all things and that His understanding far surpasses ours. As couples, this teaches us to trust God even when we don't understand the circumstances. Just as Job's faith was refined through trials, so too can our marriages be strengthened when we place our trust in God's plan, even in times of difficulty.

In the Gospel of Matthew, Jesus speaks about the coming of the Kingdom and the importance of being ready for His return. These passages challenge couples to be vigilant in their faith, maintaining a heart of obedience and readiness to serve. The parable of the talents (Matthew 25:14-46) invites us to reflect on how we use the gifts God has given us in marriage—how can we steward our relationship, time, and resources for His glory?

The early chapters of Exodus bring us into the story of Moses, highlighting God's call and the resistance Moses faced in accepting his mission. Just as Moses questioned his ability to follow God's call, we too might doubt ourselves at times. However, God equips those He calls. Couples are invited to consider how they are responding to God's calling in their marriage and whether they are trusting Him to provide what is needed to fulfill His purposes.

Weekly Discussion Prompts:

1. Trusting God in Times of Doubt: In Job's story, God answers Job with powerful reminders of His sovereignty. Have you ever had a moment of doubt or confusion in your marriage? How can you strengthen each other's faith in those moments?

2. Obedience in Relationships: The story of Moses' call to lead God's people requires obedience, even when the path is unclear. How can you practice obedience to God's calling for your marriage, even when you don't have all the answers?

3. God's Timing: Job's story teaches us to trust God's timing. How do you navigate moments of waiting or uncertainty in your marriage? How can you support each other in trusting God's perfect timing for your lives?

4. Being Ready for God's Call: In Matthew 25:14-46, the servants are asked to be faithful with what they've been given. How can you as a couple ensure that you're being good stewards of the gifts God has entrusted to you, such as your relationship, finances, and talents?

5. Facing Challenges Together: Moses' initial reluctance in answering God's call shows that stepping out in faith is not always easy. What are some challenges you face in your marriage, and how can you encourage one another to persevere, trusting that God is equipping you for the journey?

6. Reaching Beyond Your Comfort Zone: Exodus shows Moses struggling to step into God's plan. In what ways can you stretch beyond your comfort zones as a couple, trusting that God will provide everything you need to succeed?

7. Reflecting on God's Faithfulness: As you reflect on this week's readings, how have you seen God's faithfulness in your marriage? Take time to share moments where you've seen Him move in your relationship.

Joint Couple Activity:

"Vision Board of Faith": This week, create a vision board as a couple, reflecting on your marriage's journey and what God is calling you to do together. Consider how God has called you to serve, grow, and steward the resources He has given you. On the board, write down your marriage goals, prayers, and dreams for the future, asking God for clarity, strength, and obedience as you walk forward together.

Couple for Week 6: Elkanah and Hannah

The story of Elkanah and Hannah is one of deep faith, prayer, and trust in God's timing. Elkanah was a man who had two wives, Peninnah and Hannah. Peninnah had children, but Hannah was unable to conceive, which caused her great sorrow. Despite this, Elkanah loved Hannah dearly and treated her with kindness, but her inability to have children caused her pain and distress, especially as Peninnah taunted her. In her grief, Hannah prayed earnestly to the Lord at the temple, vowing that if He gave her a son, she would dedicate him to the Lord's service for his entire life. God answered her prayer, and she gave birth to Samuel. True to her vow, Hannah brought Samuel to the temple once he was weaned and left him there to serve God under the priest Eli. Hannah's faith and obedience were rewarded with additional children, and she praised God for His faithfulness.

Lessons for Couples:

1. Faith and Patience: Hannah's journey teaches couples the importance of trusting God's timing. Despite her years of barrenness, she remained faithful and did not give up on God. For couples, especially those struggling with infertility or other difficult circumstances, this story serves as a reminder to remain patient and trust that God has a plan for their lives, even when things seem impossible.

2. The Power of Prayer: Hannah's prayer was an honest, heartfelt cry to God. She didn't hide her pain or frustration but laid her desires before the Lord. Couples can learn the power of sincere prayer in their marriage, especially in moments of difficulty. When facing challenges, bringing concerns to God together as a couple strengthens the relationship and fosters spiritual intimacy.

3. Sacrificial Love: Hannah's vow to dedicate her son, Samuel, to the Lord is an example of sacrificial love. She did not hold onto Samuel for herself but gave him back to God. This teaches couples the importance of surrendering their desires and plans to God, recognizing that all blessings are ultimately from Him. It also demonstrates that sometimes, love involves selflessness and letting go for a higher purpose.

4. Trusting God with Deep Desires: Hannah's struggle with infertility highlights how couples may face deeply personal struggles that are beyond their control. She teaches that even in our most personal desires and hurts, we can trust God to meet our needs and to work things out for our good. Couples can learn that God is trustworthy with the desires of their hearts and that His plans for them are greater than they can imagine.

5. The Blessing of Obedience: Hannah's obedience in fulfilling her vow to God by dedicating Samuel to the Lord demonstrates her faithfulness and obedience. For couples, obedience to God's will, even when it involves sacrifice, brings blessings and

deep fulfillment. This story reminds couples that obedience to God's calling, whether big or small, leads to peace and purpose in their marriage.

6. Celebrating God's Faithfulness: After Samuel's birth, Hannah offered a prayer of praise to God, acknowledging His greatness and faithfulness. This is an important example for couples to celebrate the victories and blessings in their relationship and to continually praise God for His goodness. In marriage, taking the time to acknowledge God's faithfulness builds gratitude and strengthens the couple's bond with each other and with God.

7. The Role of Supportive Partnership: While Elkanah's love for Hannah was evident, he also recognized her distress and encouraged her to seek God. Couples can learn that mutual support is essential in times of hardship. Elkanah showed understanding by providing emotional support and comforting her in her pain, illustrating the importance of being there for each other in times of trial.

Week 7

God's Covenant, Holiness, and Service in Marriage

Weekly Readings:

Day 43- Exodus 11, Exodus 12; Matthew 27:11-44; Psalm 21:1-7
Day 44- Exodus 13, Exodus 14; Matthew 27:45-66; Proverbs 4:20-27
Day 45- Exodus 15, Exodus 16; Matthew 28:1-20; Psalm 21:8-13
Day 46- Exodus 17, Exodus 18; Mark 1:1-28; Psalm 22:1-11
Day 47- Exodus 19, Exodus 20; Mark 1:29-45, Mark 2:1-17; Psalm 22:12-21
Day 48- Exodus 21, Exodus 22; Mark 2:18-27, Mark 3:1-30; Proverbs 5:1-14
Day 49- Exodus 23, Exodus 24; Mark 3:31-35, Mark 4:1-29; Psalm 22:22-31

Weekly Reflection:

This week's readings focus on the themes of covenant, deliverance, holiness, and the servant heart. In the Book of Exodus, we see God's covenant with His people and His powerful deliverance from Egypt. This covenant is a symbol of God's faithfulness and the promise of His presence and blessing. For couples, this is a beautiful reminder of the commitment you make to each other in marriage—just as God makes a covenant with His people, so too do you make vows to one another, vowing to be faithful, loving, and supportive through the highs and lows of life.

Exodus 12, which recounts the Passover, reminds us of God's protection and deliverance. The blood of the lamb marked the doorposts to spare the firstborn, which parallels Christ's sacrifice on the cross for our salvation. In marriage, the love of Christ and His sacrificial love are the model for how we should love and serve each other.

The Gospel readings from Matthew and Mark highlight Jesus' ministry of healing, teaching, and ultimately His sacrificial death and resurrection. The call to service, humility, and sacrifice in marriage is clear—just as Jesus served His disciples and laid down His life for them, so too should you serve one another with love, humility, and commitment.

As you reflect on these passages, consider how you can deepen your covenant with each other, honor God in your relationship, and serve one another with the same selflessness that Jesus demonstrated.

Weekly Discussion Prompts:

1. God's Covenant and Marriage: In Exodus, God establishes His covenant with the Israelites. How does the covenant of marriage mirror this divine covenant? In what ways can you grow in commitment to each other as you reflect on God's faithfulness?

2. The Power of Sacrificial Love: Reflect on Jesus' sacrifice for us, as seen in Matthew 27. How can you practice sacrificial love in your marriage, laying down your own preferences or comforts for the sake of your spouse?

3. Serving One Another: In Mark 1:1-28, Jesus serves others selflessly. How can you serve your spouse in practical ways this week? What specific act of service can you offer to demonstrate your love?

4. Responding to God's Deliverance: Exodus 14 recounts the miraculous parting of the Red Sea. In what ways have you experienced God's deliverance in your marriage? How can you express gratitude to God for His faithfulness?

5. Living Out Holiness in Marriage: The Ten Commandments (Exodus 20) give us a model for living holy lives. How can you incorporate these principles into your marriage to foster peace, love, and respect?

6. The Role of Forgiveness: Jesus' teachings in Mark 2:1-17 emphasize forgiveness. How do you handle conflict in your marriage? How can you practice forgiveness as a couple and strengthen your relationship through grace?

7. Building a Strong Foundation: Reflect on Proverbs 4:20-27. What principles can you incorporate into your marriage to build a strong, lasting relationship centered on God's word?

Joint Couple Activity:

"Covenant Renewal Ceremony": This week, take time as a couple to renew your commitment to one another. This could be done in a simple ceremony where you reaffirm your vows, thank God for His faithfulness, and ask for His continued guidance in your relationship. You could write down new promises to each other based on the lessons you've learned this week from the Bible and from one another.

Couple for Week 7: Zacharias and Elizabeth

Zacharias and Elizabeth were a righteous and devout couple who lived during the time of King Herod. Elizabeth was from the priestly line of Aaron, and Zacharias was a priest. Despite their faithful lives, they had no children because Elizabeth was barren, and they were both advanced in age. This brought them much sorrow, as having children was considered a blessing and a sign of favor from God.

One day, while Zacharias was serving in the temple, an angel appeared to him and announced that his prayers had been answered and that his wife would bear a son, who would be named John. This child, the angel said, would be filled with the Holy Spirit even before birth and would prepare the way for the coming Messiah. Zacharias, though righteous, doubted the angel's message, asking how it could happen given their old age. As a result of his doubt, he was struck mute until the child was born.

True to the angel's word, Elizabeth conceived and gave birth to a son. When it came time to name the child, Elizabeth insisted on naming him John, as instructed by the angel. Zacharias confirmed her choice by writing on a tablet, and immediately his speech was restored. Zacharias then praised God for His faithfulness, and prophecy about the future role of John the Baptist in preparing the way for Jesus was spoken.

Lessons for Couples:

1. Faith in God's Timing: Zacharias and Elizabeth's story teaches couples the importance of trusting God's timing, even when it seems impossible or too late. Though they had prayed for a child for many years, God answered their prayer when the time was right. Couples can learn that God's plans are perfect, even if they don't align with our own timeline or expectations.

2. Trusting God Despite Doubts: Zacharias' initial doubt when the angel announced the coming of his son shows that even the faithful can struggle with disbelief. Yet, despite his doubt, God still fulfilled His promise. Couples can learn that while doubts may arise in difficult seasons, God's promises are trustworthy, and His plans will come to fruition regardless of our temporary uncertainties.

3. The Power of Prayer: Zacharias and Elizabeth were known for their righteousness and devotion to God. Even though they had not seen the fruit of their prayers for a child, they continued to pray faithfully. This teaches couples the importance of perseverance in prayer. Even when the answers don't come immediately, continuing to pray with faith and trust in God is key to receiving His blessings.

4. God Can Use Any Season for His Purposes: Although Zacharias and Elizabeth were advanced in age, God chose them to fulfill a significant role in His redemptive plan: the birth of John the Baptist. This shows that God can use us at any stage of life to carry out

His purposes, no matter how old or young we are. Couples can learn that no matter the season, God still has a purpose for their marriage and can work through them to impact His kingdom.

5. Faithful Obedience Leads to Blessings: Elizabeth's obedient acceptance of God's plan for her to name her child John is a powerful example of faithfulness. She trusted God's plan and followed His instructions, even when it defied cultural norms. Couples can learn the importance of being obedient to God's commands, even when they don't fully understand the reasons. Obedience often leads to unexpected blessings and fulfillment.

6. Celebrating God's Faithfulness Together: After the birth of John, Zacharias and Elizabeth praised God for His faithfulness. Couples can take a lesson from this and make it a point to celebrate the goodness of God together. In times of blessing, it is important to praise God as a couple, recognizing His work in your lives and strengthening your bond in gratitude and faith.

7. The Role of Support and Encouragement: Zacharias' role in the birth of John also reflects the importance of supporting one another. Though he had been temporarily silenced by God due to his doubt, he stood by Elizabeth in her time of joy and difficult moments. For couples, this is a reminder that mutual support and encouragement are key in strengthening the marriage and helping each other grow in faith, even through challenging times.

8. God's Miracles Are Possible: Zacharias and Elizabeth's story is a testimony of God's miraculous power. Even in old age, God made the impossible possible. For couples facing challenges or seemingly insurmountable obstacles, this story encourages them to believe that God is able to do the impossible in their lives, whether that's in starting a family, overcoming hardships, or achieving a dream together.

Week 8

God's Presence, Guidance, and Living in His Word

Weekly Readings:

Day 50- Exodus 25, Exodus 26; Mark 4:30-41, Mark 5:1-20; Psalm 23:1-6
Day 51- Exodus 27, Exodus 28; Mark 5:21-43, Mark 6:1-6; Psalm 24:1-10
Day 52- Exodus 29, Exodus 30; Mark 6:7-29; Proverbs 5:15-23
Day 53- Exodus 31, Exodus 32, Exodus 33:1-6; Mark 6:30-56; Psalm 25:1-7
Day 54- Exodus 33:7-23, Exodus 34; Mark 7:1-30; Psalm 25:8-15
Day 55- Exodus 35, Exodus 36; Mark 7:31-37, Mark 8:1-13; Psalm 25:16-22
Day 56- Exodus 37, Exodus 38; Mark 8:14-38, Mark 9:1; Proverbs 6:1-11

Weekly Reflection:

This week, we focus on the presence and guidance of God in our lives, particularly in our relationships. The Book of Exodus continues to emphasize God's instructions for His people, showing that He desires to dwell among them. For couples, this is a reminder that God wants to be present in your relationship, guiding and strengthening you as you walk together through life.

The presence of God is not just a comfort but a calling. In Exodus 25-27, God gives detailed instructions for the building of the Tabernacle, where His presence would dwell among the Israelites. For couples, this underscores the importance of creating space for God in your marriage. Just as God provided specific instructions for His dwelling place, He also calls you to invite Him into your relationship through prayer, worship, and obedience to His word.

Mark's Gospel reveals the power of Jesus over nature and demons, reminding us that when we face challenges in our marriage or life, we can trust in His power and presence. Psalm 23 beautifully expresses the assurance that God, as our Shepherd, will lead us, restore us, and guide us through life's journey—just as He will do in your marriage.

In Exodus, we also see God's instructions for holy living and the importance of sanctification. For couples, this means living in a way that honors God—by being loving, kind, patient, and sacrificial with one another. Proverbs 5:15-23 calls us to be faithful and avoid temptation. In marriage, this is a challenge to remain true to your vows and trust in God's design for your relationship.

Weekly Discussion Prompts:

1. Inviting God Into Your Marriage: Reflecting on Exodus 25 and Exodus 26, how can you make space for God in your daily lives and in your marriage? What are some practical ways to invite His presence into your relationship?

2. God as Our Shepherd: In Psalm 23, God is described as our Shepherd. How have you seen God's guidance in your marriage? How can you rely on His wisdom and care more in your relationship?

3. The Importance of Holiness: Exodus 29-30 talks about the sanctification of the Israelites. What does it mean to you as a couple to live a holy and sanctified life? How can you encourage each other in this pursuit?

4. Faith Over Fear: Mark 4:30-41 shows how Jesus calms the storm. How can you apply the lessons from this passage when facing difficulties or challenges in your marriage? What steps can you take to face challenges with faith rather than fear?

5. Commitment to Faithfulness: Proverbs 5:15-23 calls us to remain faithful in our relationships. In what areas do you need to strengthen your commitment to one another? How can you grow in faithfulness, both to each other and to God?

6. Dealing with Disagreements: Reflecting on Mark 7:1-30, Jesus emphasizes the importance of inner purity. How can you handle disagreements in your marriage with respect and purity, focusing on understanding and reconciliation rather than conflict?

7. Obedience to God's Word: Exodus 35 and Exodus 36 emphasize the Israelites' obedience to God's instructions. How can you encourage each other to obey God's word in your marriage? What areas of obedience can you focus on this week?

Joint Couple Activity:

"Building Your Marriage Tabernacle": This week, as a couple, take time to create a "tabernacle" in your home—a designated space where you can pray, worship, and seek God's presence together. It could be a quiet corner with a Bible, candles, or worship music. Spend time in this space together each day, inviting God to guide and strengthen your marriage through prayer and reflection on His word.

Couple for Week 8: Joseph and Mary

Joseph and Mary are one of the most well-known couples in the Bible, chosen by God to be the earthly parents of Jesus Christ. Mary, a young woman from Nazareth, was betrothed to Joseph, a carpenter. One day, Mary was visited by the angel Gabriel, who told her that she would conceive a child by the Holy Spirit and give birth to the Son of God. Though initially troubled by the message, Mary accepted God's will with humility and faith, saying, "I am the Lord's servant. May your word to me be fulfilled."

When Joseph learned that Mary was pregnant, he initially planned to divorce her quietly, as they were not yet married in the full sense. However, an angel appeared to him in a dream and reassured him that Mary's pregnancy was by the Holy Spirit and that he should marry her. Joseph obeyed the angel's message, took Mary as his wife, and cared for her and the child, Jesus, as his own.

The couple faced many challenges, including the journey to Bethlehem for a census, where Mary gave birth to Jesus in a humble stable because there was no room for them in the inn. Afterward, they received visits from shepherds and later from wise men, confirming that Jesus was the promised Messiah. Joseph and Mary's lives continued to be marked by divine intervention, including a warning in a dream to flee to Egypt to escape King Herod's plot to kill the infant Jesus. They eventually returned to Nazareth after Herod's death, where Jesus grew up.

Throughout their lives, Joseph and Mary remained faithful to God's calling, raising Jesus with love and devotion, while trusting in His plans even when the future seemed uncertain or difficult.

Lessons for Couples:

1. Trusting God's Plan, Even When It's Unfamiliar: Joseph and Mary were both asked to trust God with an extraordinary and unexpected plan. For Mary, this meant accepting the miraculous conception of Jesus, and for Joseph, it meant trusting his fiancée despite the circumstances. Couples can learn that God's plan for their lives may not always be what they envisioned, but faith and trust in His direction are essential to walking together in His will.

2. Obedience to God's Will: Joseph's quick and unquestioning obedience to the angel's message shows the importance of obedience in marriage. When God calls us to a specific action, as a couple, we must be willing to follow His guidance, even when it's difficult or doesn't make sense. Joseph's example teaches couples that obedience to God is vital in fulfilling His purposes in their lives.

3. Unity in Facing Challenges: Throughout their journey, from the uncomfortable journey to Bethlehem to fleeing to Egypt, Joseph and Mary faced hardships. Yet, they remained

united and committed to God's plan for their lives and their family. For couples, this highlights the importance of supporting each other in challenging times and remaining unified in faith, trusting that God will provide and guide them through every difficulty.

4. Humble Service in Marriage: Both Joseph and Mary showed humility in their service to God and one another. Mary humbly accepted her role as the mother of Jesus, while Joseph accepted the responsibility of caring for and raising the Messiah, despite the challenges. Couples can learn the value of serving one another with humility and recognizing the divine purpose in their relationship.

5. Faith in the Face of Uncertainty: When Joseph and Mary first received the news about Jesus' birth and the events surrounding it, there was much uncertainty. They didn't know what the future held, but they trusted in God's direction. This teaches couples that life together may involve uncertainty and even fear, but having faith in God's plan can bring peace and assurance.

6. Sacrificial Love: The love between Joseph and Mary is marked by self-sacrifice. Joseph risked his reputation by marrying a pregnant woman, and Mary accepted the responsibility of being the mother of the Savior of the world. Their actions were sacrificial and selfless. Couples can learn that a successful marriage requires sacrificial love, putting each other's needs before their own and being willing to make difficult decisions for the good of the relationship and family.

7. Strengthening Faith Together: Joseph and Mary's story shows that a marriage rooted in faith will provide strength and resilience. They faced challenges, but together they relied on God's faithfulness and protection. Couples can learn that growing in faith together as a couple is vital in building a strong foundation for marriage and in navigating life's ups and downs.

8. Protection and Care for One Another: Joseph was deeply protective of Mary and Jesus, responding to God's warnings to flee to Egypt to escape Herod's wrath. His actions exemplify how spouses should protect and care for one another in every circumstance. For couples, this means being there for each other emotionally, spiritually, and physically, ensuring the safety and well-being of their partner and family.

9. Commitment to Raising Children in Faith: Joseph and Mary were dedicated to raising Jesus according to God's will, even though they didn't fully understand His divine nature or mission. This shows the importance of parents guiding their children in faith, supporting their spiritual growth, and setting a godly example in their home. Couples can learn the importance of nurturing their children's faith, prayerfully guiding them toward a relationship with God.

10. God's Timing and Purpose: The birth of Jesus and the couple's role in His life demonstrates that God's timing and purposes are always perfect, even when we don't

understand them. For couples, this reinforces the importance of trusting God with their lives and believing that He is working in their marriage and family, even when the journey ahead seems unclear.

Week 9

Sacrifice, Obedience, and Purity in Marriage

Weekly Readings:

Day 57- Exodus 39, Exodus 40; Mark 9:2-32; Psalm 26:1-12
Day 58- Leviticus 1, Leviticus 2, Leviticus 3; Mark 9:33-50, Mark 10:1-12; Psalm 27:1-6
Day 59- Leviticus 4, Leviticus 5:1-13; Mark 10:13-31; Psalm 27:7-14
Day 60- Leviticus 5:14-19, Leviticus 6, Leviticus 7:1-10; Mark 10:32-52; Proverbs 6:12-19
Day 61- Leviticus 7:11-38, Leviticus 8; Mark 11:1-27; Psalm 28
Day 62- Leviticus 9, Leviticus 10; Mark 11:28-33, Mark 12:1-12; Psalm 29
Day 63- Leviticus 11, Leviticus 12; Mark 12:13-27; Psalm 30:1-7

Weekly Reflection:

This week's focus is on sacrifice, obedience, and purity—key elements that not only define the relationship between God and His people but are essential to a thriving marriage. The readings from Exodus and Leviticus provide us with a deep understanding of how sacrifices were made to God, emphasizing the cost of obedience and the need for purity. These themes serve as profound lessons for couples, highlighting how marriage is a sacred covenant requiring mutual sacrifice, unwavering obedience to God's commands, and a commitment to live in purity.

In Exodus 39-40, we see the final preparations for the Tabernacle and the importance of obedience to God's instructions. For couples, this is a reminder that building a strong marriage involves following God's plan for unity, love, and mutual respect. Just as the Israelites were obedient to God in their work on the Tabernacle, couples are called to obey God's will in their relationship, ensuring that their marriage is built on His word.

The readings from Leviticus emphasize the importance of holiness and sacrifice. Leviticus outlines the different types of offerings that the Israelites brought before God, illustrating that God desires sacrifices that are pure and offered with the right heart. For couples, this points to the idea that marriage requires sacrifices—small and large—that are made with a heart of love and reverence for God. Each act of selflessness is a sacrifice offered to God, deepening the bond of marriage.

In Mark's Gospel, Jesus teaches His disciples about humility and servitude, values that are essential in marriage. In Mark 9:33-50, Jesus calls His followers to be servants of one another, which mirrors the sacrificial love that should define a couple's relationship. True love in marriage is sacrificial—it means putting each other's needs before your own, serving one another, and forgiving one another.

Psalm 27 and Psalm 28 provide encouragement and trust in God's protection and guidance. In marriage, trusting in God's protection and leading is crucial, especially during difficult seasons. This trust builds a foundation of faith in your spouse and in God's ability to lead you both as a couple.

Weekly Discussion Prompts:

1. Sacrifice in Marriage: Reflecting on the sacrificial offerings in Leviticus, how can you make daily sacrifices to show love for one another? What are some small sacrifices you can make to put your spouse's needs first this week?

2. Obedience to God's Word: The Israelites followed God's detailed instructions for the Tabernacle (Exodus 39-40). How can you as a couple better follow God's instructions for your marriage? Are there areas where you can align more closely with His word?

3. Purity and Holiness in Marriage: Leviticus talks about purification and sanctification. How can you encourage each other to live a pure and holy life together, both individually and as a couple?

4. Serving One Another: In Mark 9:33-50, Jesus teaches that greatness is found in serving others. How can you serve one another better in your marriage? What is one way you can show your spouse sacrificial love this week?

5. Trusting God in Marriage: Psalm 27 speaks of trusting in God's protection. In what ways do you rely on God for strength in your marriage? How can you build a stronger trust in God's leading during difficult times?

6. Forgiveness and Grace: Reflecting on Mark 10:32-52, where Jesus heals a blind man, what does it mean for you as a couple to forgive one another? How can you practice grace and forgiveness in your relationship?

7. Commitment to Each Other: Leviticus 6 speaks of the importance of commitment. How can you show greater commitment to each other in your relationship? What practical steps can you take to nurture your marriage this week?

"Offerings of Love": Inspired by the sacrificial offerings described in Leviticus, each of you will take time to write down three offerings or sacrifices you can make for one another in the coming week. These could be small things—like giving your spouse extra time, serving them when they are tired, or offering words of encouragement. Share your offerings with each other and commit to carrying them out during the week. At the end of the week, revisit them and reflect on how these sacrifices helped to strengthen your bond.

Couple for Week 9: Priscilla and Aquila

Priscilla and Aquila were a married couple who played a significant role in the early Christian church. They are mentioned several times in the New Testament, particularly in the Acts of the Apostles and the letters of Paul. Both were tentmakers by trade, and they are often highlighted for their dedication to Christ, their hospitality, and their partnership in ministry.

Priscilla and Aquila first met Paul in Corinth during his second missionary journey. Paul, being a tentmaker himself, stayed with them and worked alongside them. This partnership soon extended beyond their trade to ministry. They became avid supporters and companions in spreading the gospel. When Paul left Corinth for Ephesus, Priscilla and Aquila went with him and continued their work in the early church.

One of their most notable contributions to the church was their involvement in teaching the gospel to Apollos, an eloquent and knowledgeable preacher, but who only knew of the baptism of John. When they heard him preach in Ephesus, Priscilla and Aquila invited him into their home and explained to him the way of God more accurately, filling in the gaps in his understanding of Jesus Christ and the Holy Spirit.

Priscilla and Aquila's commitment to the gospel and their hospitality helped establish strong Christian communities in several cities, including Corinth and Ephesus. They are seen as a model of teamwork in marriage, mutual support in ministry, and a deep dedication to God's mission.

Lessons for Couples:

1. Partnership in Ministry: Priscilla and Aquila demonstrate the power of working together as a couple in ministry. Their shared dedication to spreading the gospel and supporting Paul's work shows that couples can make a significant impact for God's kingdom when they serve together. Couples today can learn to use their skills, resources, and time as a team in ministry, whether through formal ministry or acts of service within their community.

2. Hospitality and Welcoming Others: One of the key aspects of Priscilla and Aquila's ministry was their open home. They welcomed Paul and later Apollos, offering

hospitality and teaching. Their home became a place of spiritual growth and discipleship. Couples can learn the importance of offering hospitality and creating spaces for others to learn, grow, and experience the love of Christ. Whether hosting small groups, Bible studies, or offering a listening ear, hospitality is a way to serve God and others.

3. Supporting Each Other's Gifts: Priscilla and Aquila worked together in their tentmaking business, and later in ministry. Their relationship shows how couples should support and encourage each other's gifts and talents. Priscilla was often mentioned first, indicating that she might have had a prominent role in teaching and ministry, yet Aquila worked alongside her in all aspects. Couples can learn to respect and uplift one another's strengths, recognizing that God has gifted each person uniquely.

4. Mentoring and Discipleship: Priscilla and Aquila did not keep their knowledge of the gospel to themselves; they invested in others. Their mentoring of Apollos, helping him to understand the full gospel, exemplifies the power of discipleship. Couples can learn the importance of not only growing in their faith but also mentoring others, helping them understand Scripture more deeply and encouraging spiritual maturity in others.

5. Flexibility and Adaptability in Serving God: Throughout their story, Priscilla and Aquila demonstrated flexibility in their ministry, moving from place to place as God led them. They went from Corinth to Ephesus, following Paul's mission but continuing to work and serve wherever they were called. Couples can learn that serving God may involve changes in location, occupation, or ministry, but being adaptable and open to God's leading is an essential part of faithfully following Him.

6. Spiritual Unity and Teamwork in Marriage: Priscilla and Aquila's relationship was a model of teamwork, both in their marriage and in their service to God. They worked side by side in their trade and ministry, supporting each other through both challenges and successes. Couples can learn the importance of unity in their marriage, ensuring that they are aligned in their faith, values, and goals as they serve together in God's mission.

7. Perseverance in Ministry: The couple's commitment to spreading the gospel, despite the challenges they faced, is a powerful example of perseverance. Whether facing opposition or moving to new locations, they remained steadfast in their mission. Couples can learn that ministry is not always easy and that perseverance is key. Supporting one another through difficult times and remaining focused on God's purpose can strengthen both the marriage and the work they are doing together.

8. Humility and Teaching with Love: Priscilla and Aquila did not seek recognition for their role in teaching Apollos but were humble in their approach to discipleship. They taught him in love and patience, without condemning his lack of understanding. Couples can learn that when offering correction or guidance to others, especially in a teaching or

mentoring role, it should be done with kindness, humility, and a desire to build up, not tear down.

9. Commitment to God's Work Beyond the Family: While marriage is a sacred covenant, Priscilla and Aquila's story shows that God's work extends beyond the family to the wider community. They did not limit their devotion to one another but extended their love and service to the church and the world. Couples can learn that their relationship is a foundation for ministry, but they are also called to serve and love others in the larger body of Christ.

10. Faithful Witness to the Gospel: Ultimately, Priscilla and Aquila's legacy is a testimony of their faithfulness to the gospel and to God's call on their lives. They didn't live for their own comfort or success but devoted themselves to God's mission. Couples can learn the value of being faithful witnesses to Christ in every area of their lives, prioritizing His kingdom over personal gain or worldly success.

Week 10

Purification, Holiness, and Commitment in Marriage

Weekly Readings:

Day 64- Leviticus 13:1-59; Mark 12:28-44; Proverbs 6:20-29
Day 65- Leviticus 14:1-57; Mark 13:1-31; Psalm 30:8-12
Day 66- Leviticus 15, Leviticus 16; Mark 13:32-37, Mark 14:1-16; Psalm 31:1-8
Day 67- Leviticus 17, Leviticus 18; Mark 14:17-42; Psalm 31:9-18
Day 68- Leviticus 19, Leviticus 20; Mark 14:43-72; Proverbs 6:30-35
Day 69- Leviticus 21, Leviticus 22; Mark 15:1-32; Psalm 31:19-24
Day 70- Leviticus 23, Leviticus 24; Mark 15:33-47; Psalm 32

Weekly Reflection:

This week, the readings from Leviticus invite us to reflect on the importance of purification and holiness in our relationship with God and with one another. Leviticus highlights rituals for purification, laws concerning holiness, and the requirements for living a life that is set apart. These passages are a reminder for couples to cultivate a marriage that is purified and sanctified through God's word, actively working toward a relationship that reflects His holiness.

In Leviticus 13, we read about the purification of those with leprosy. While physical cleansing is central to these instructions, the spiritual lessons are profound. Just as lepers were required to be separated from the community, we too must be mindful of things that separate us from God and one another in our marriages. It is a reminder to cleanse our hearts and our relationships through confession, forgiveness, and the pursuit of purity.

Leviticus 14 continues the theme of purification, detailing the cleansing rituals after leprosy. In marriage, we may encounter moments of brokenness, hurt, or sin. It is essential to understand that just as the Israelites went through a purification process, marriages also require effort and intentionality to heal, restore, and maintain their sanctity. Purification in marriage doesn't happen automatically—it requires open communication, grace, and the willingness to rebuild.

Leviticus 15 and 16 speak of bodily and spiritual purification, stressing the importance of living in a state of holiness before God. This week, as a couple, consider how you can maintain spiritual cleanliness in your relationship. Holiness is not a passive state—it involves actively pursuing God's will, honoring Him in all things, and committing to live out the values of His kingdom.

The teachings in Mark 12:28-44 about loving God and loving others are pivotal. Jesus clarifies that the greatest commandment is to love God with all our heart, soul, and mind, and the second is to love our neighbor as ourselves. For couples, this commandment must govern their relationship. In practice, this means loving one another unconditionally, forgiving each other, and prioritizing each other's well-being above personal desires.

In Proverbs 6:20-29, we are reminded of the importance of wisdom and fidelity. This passage speaks of the dangers of temptation, urging us to cling to wisdom and stay committed to our vows. In marriage, it is essential to safeguard the relationship, protect it from external influences, and prioritize faithfulness in thought, word, and action.

Weekly Discussion Prompts:

1. Purification in Marriage: Reflecting on Leviticus 13 and 14, how can you purify your marriage? Are there areas where you need to ask for forgiveness or restore broken trust?

2. Holiness and Commitment: Leviticus 16 stresses the importance of holiness before God. How can you pursue holiness together in your marriage? What does holiness look like in your daily interactions?

3. Loving Each Other Like Jesus Loves Us: In Mark 12:28-44, Jesus teaches us to love one another as ourselves. What does this kind of sacrificial love look like in your marriage? How can you better love each other selflessly?

4. Guarding Against Temptation: Proverbs 6:20-29 speaks about guarding against temptation. Are there areas in your marriage where you need to protect yourselves from negative influences, such as external relationships or unhealthy habits?

5. Healing and Restoration: Just as lepers were cleansed, marriages can be healed through forgiveness. Is there anything in your relationship that needs healing or restoration? How can you work together to restore wholeness to your marriage?

6. Faithfulness and Fidelity: What practices can you put in place to ensure that your marriage remains strong and faithful, even during difficult seasons?

7. Commitment to Each Other: Leviticus 19:1-2 urges us to be holy as God is holy. How can you demonstrate a deeper commitment to each other this week? What actions can you take to show love, respect, and honor in your relationship?

Joint Couple Activity:
"Cleansing Rituals for Marriage": Inspired by the purification rituals in Leviticus, take time together to cleanse your marriage by letting go of any bitterness, hurt, or misunderstandings. Sit down and share one area where you have hurt each other, followed by a prayer for forgiveness and restoration. Exchange vows of commitment to one another, reaffirming your love and the sacredness of your marriage. As you pray together, ask God to purify your relationship and help you both live in harmony with His will.

Couple for Week 10: Manoah and His Wife

Manoah and his wife are the parents of Samson, one of the most famous judges of Israel. Their story is found in the Book of Judges, primarily in chapters 13 and 14. Manoah's wife is initially unnamed, but she is an important figure in the biblical narrative. The couple's story is one of divine intervention, faith, and obedience.

The couple lived in the region of Zorah during a time when Israel was under the oppression of the Philistines. Manoah's wife was barren and had no children, but one day, an angel of the Lord appeared to her, announcing that she would conceive a son who would begin to deliver Israel from the Philistines. The angel instructed her to live a life of dedication to God during her pregnancy, including not drinking wine or eating unclean food, as her son was to be a Nazirite—a person consecrated to God from birth.

Manoah's wife, after receiving the angel's message, told her husband, but he was skeptical and prayed for God to send the angel again to confirm the message. God answered Manoah's prayer, and the angel reappeared to his wife. This time, Manoah also spoke with the angel and received more instructions. Manoah offered a sacrifice to God, and when the angel ascended in the flame of the altar, Manoah and his wife realized they had encountered God Himself.

The child born to them was Samson, who would later grow up to become a judge of Israel, known for his incredible strength and his tumultuous life, which included struggles with his faithfulness to God's calling.

Lessons for Couples:

1. Faith in God's Promises: Manoah and his wife displayed faith and trust in God's promises, even when the circumstances seemed improbable. Manoah's wife believed the angel's message that she would bear a son despite her barrenness. Couples can

learn from this story to trust in God's promises, especially in times when their circumstances seem impossible. God is faithful, and He fulfills His word in His timing.

2. Prayer and Seeking God's Will: Manoah's prayer for confirmation shows the importance of seeking God's will, especially when faced with major decisions or challenges. Instead of acting on his own understanding, he prayed for God to clarify the message. Couples can learn the value of seeking God in prayer, particularly when they face important decisions that affect their marriage or family. God is always willing to guide those who earnestly seek Him.

3. Obedience to God's Instructions: After receiving the angel's message, Manoah and his wife were careful to follow the instructions regarding their son's consecration. This included the Nazarite vow, which required both spiritual and practical discipline. Couples can learn the importance of obedience to God's guidance, especially when it comes to raising children or following God's plans for their lives. Obedience leads to blessing and fulfillment of God's purposes.

4. Supporting Each Other in Faith: Throughout the story, Manoah and his wife work together in faith, especially when they seek confirmation of God's message. They supported one another in prayer, and the wife communicated the angel's message with clarity and conviction. Couples can learn from this how to support each other in their spiritual walk, sharing faith, praying together, and reinforcing each other's trust in God.

5. Hospitality and Reverence for God: When Manoah offered the sacrifice to the Lord, he displayed reverence and worship. The couple showed their commitment to God by honoring Him with an offering. In their hospitality to the angel, they displayed humility and reverence for God's presence. Couples can learn to practice hospitality not just toward people, but also in reverence to God, by creating an environment of worship and honor in their homes.

6. Embracing God's Plan for the Family: Manoah and his wife's story highlights God's purpose for their family, which was to bring forth a child who would help deliver Israel. They accepted God's plan for their lives, even though it was unconventional and challenging. Couples can learn to embrace God's plan for their family, whether it's having children or fulfilling a unique purpose in ministry, trusting that God's plans are always for their good and for His glory.

7. God's Timing Is Perfect: The announcement of Samson's birth came at the appointed time when God's people needed deliverance. Though Manoah and his wife had likely prayed for children for many years, they trusted God's timing. Couples can learn to wait on God's perfect timing, especially in situations where they are waiting for answers or hoping for change. Patience and trust in God's timing can bring about His perfect will.

8. Reverence for God's Messengers: When the angel appeared to Manoah's wife, she received the message with reverence, and when Manoah saw the angel himself, he offered a sacrifice in worship. The couple demonstrated respect for God's messengers. Couples can learn to honor God's word and those He sends to deliver His messages. Respect for God's commands and messengers strengthens both the marriage and the faith journey.

9. The Power of Divine Intervention: Manoah and his wife experienced a miraculous intervention when God chose them to be the parents of Samson. Their story shows how God can intervene in extraordinary ways in the lives of ordinary people. Couples can learn that God's intervention in their lives can lead to great things, and even when their situation seems hopeless, God can bring about miraculous outcomes.

10. Joy in the Gift of Children: Finally, Manoah and his wife were blessed with a child who would play a key role in Israel's history. While their journey to parenthood was filled with divine intervention, it also showed the joy and responsibility that comes with the gift of children. Couples can learn to cherish and care for the children God gives them, seeing them as part of God's greater plan. Raising children is both a privilege and a responsibility that requires faith, love, and dedication.

Week 11

God's Faithfulness and Our Response in Marriage

Weekly Readings:

Day 71- Leviticus 25, Leviticus 26:1-13; Mark 16:1-20; Psalm 33:1-11
Day 72- Leviticus 26:14-46, Leviticus 27; Luke 1:1-25; Proverbs 7:1-5
Day 73- Numbers 1, Numbers 2:1-9; Luke 1:26-38; Psalm 33:12-22
Day 74- Numbers 2:10-34, Numbers 3; Luke 1:39-56; Psalm 34:1-10
Day 75- Numbers 4, Numbers 5:1-10; Luke 1:57-80; Psalm 34:11-22
Day 76- Numbers 5:11-31, Numbers 6:1-27; Luke 2:1-20; Proverbs 7:6-20
Day 77- Numbers 7:1-65; Luke 2:21-40; Psalm 35:1-10

Weekly Reflection:

This week's readings from Leviticus and Numbers emphasize God's covenantal faithfulness, His divine laws, and the calling He places upon His people. We see God's deep care for His people in how He sets forth instructions for them to live holy lives, honor Him, and maintain order in their communities. These readings, when applied to marriage, remind us that God is faithful to His promises, and as couples, we are called to respond in faith, commitment, and obedience to His Word.

Leviticus 25 introduces the concept of the Year of Jubilee, a time when all debts were forgiven and land was returned to its rightful owners. This practice reflects God's heart for restoration and renewal. In marriage, there are times when couples experience struggles and debts— whether emotional, financial, or relational. The Year of Jubilee can serve as a reminder that God offers us a fresh start in our relationships. Through His grace, we can experience healing, forgiveness, and restoration.

Leviticus 26 stresses the importance of obedience to God's commandments. God promises blessings for obedience and discipline for disobedience. In marriage, obedience to God's commands leads to peace, joy, and unity. When couples honor God's Word in their relationship, they position themselves to receive His blessings. It's crucial to reflect on how both partners can honor God through their actions, words, and attitudes.

In Mark 16, we read about the resurrection of Jesus and the Great Commission. Jesus' victory over death gives hope for all relationships, including marriage. Just as Christ has triumphed over sin and death, marriages can overcome struggles and difficulties through His power. Jesus' command to go and make disciples can also be a call for couples to live out their faith together, sharing the gospel and demonstrating the love of Christ in their home and in their community.

Luke 1:1-25 and the story of Zechariah and Elizabeth serve as a powerful reminder of God's faithfulness in fulfilling His promises. Despite their old age, God blessed them with a child—John the Baptist—because of His promise. Zechariah's initial doubt and eventual faith in God's timing are relatable for couples. In marriage, we often experience waiting for God's promises to be fulfilled, whether in our personal lives or in the growth of our relationship. Patience and trust in God's timing are key to navigating challenges together.

In Luke 1:26-38, we read about Mary's faithful response to the angel's announcement of Jesus' birth. Mary's willingness to accept God's plan is a beautiful example of how couples can respond to God's calling in their lives. In marriage, saying "yes" to God's will requires trust and surrender. Couples must be open to God's plans for them, even when they may not fully understand them.

Weekly Discussion Prompts:

1. Restoration in Marriage: Reflecting on Leviticus 25 and the Year of Jubilee, are there areas in your marriage where you need restoration or a fresh start? How can you create space for healing and renewal?

2. Obedience and Blessing: Leviticus 26 outlines the blessings that come with obedience. How can you as a couple commit to obeying God's commands together? What blessings have you experienced as a result of this obedience?

3. Overcoming Challenges Together: Mark 16 speaks of Christ's victory over death. How can you draw strength from Christ's resurrection power to overcome obstacles in your marriage?

4. Faith in God's Timing: Zechariah and Elizabeth waited for many years for their promised child. Are there areas in your marriage where you are waiting for God to fulfill a promise? How can you strengthen your faith and trust in His perfect timing?

5. Saying "Yes" to God's Plan: Mary's "yes" to God's plan was a pivotal moment in salvation history. Are there areas in your marriage where you need to say "yes" to God's will, even if it's difficult or uncertain? How can you support each other in this decision?

6. Living the Great Commission: Jesus commands us to go and make disciples. How can you as a couple share your faith with others? What actions can you take to live out the gospel together?

7. Faithfulness and Commitment: Throughout this week's readings, we see examples of God's faithfulness. How can you demonstrate that same faithfulness to your spouse? Are there ways you can deepen your commitment to each other?

Joint Couple Activity:

"A Commitment to Restoration": Inspired by the Year of Jubilee, take time together to identify any debts (emotional or relational) that need to be forgiven or restored. Write down the areas where you want to experience renewal and restoration, and pray together for God's healing power in those areas. Commit to working together toward a stronger, more unified marriage, free from past hurts and full of hope for the future.

Couple for Week 11: Job and His Wife

Job's story, primarily found in the Book of Job, is one of intense suffering and steadfast faith. Job was a wealthy man, blessed with a large family, many possessions, and a strong faith in God. Satan challenged Job's faith, claiming that Job only worshiped God because of his blessings. In a divine test, God allowed Satan to take away Job's wealth, children, and health. Job's wife is mentioned only briefly, yet her reaction to their misfortunes gives insight into the overwhelming grief and despair they both endured.

After witnessing their children's deaths, the loss of their possessions, and seeing Job suffer from painful boils, Job's wife famously said to him, "Do you still hold fast your integrity? Curse God and die!" (Job 2:9). In her anguish, she encouraged Job to end his suffering by abandoning his faith. Job, however, responded with patience, gently reminding her that they must accept both good and adversity from God. While Job's wife does not reappear in the rest of the story, Job's faith eventually led to a divine encounter with God, who restored his health, blessed him with twice the wealth he had before, and gave him new children.

Lessons for Couples:

1. Support Each Other in Times of Suffering: Job's wife expressed her pain and frustration, perhaps as a way of coping with the unimaginable loss they endured. Couples can learn from this story to offer support and empathy in times of suffering. Instead of giving in to despair, couples can seek comfort and encouragement from each other, praying for strength to endure hardship together.

2. Avoid Bitterness and Despair: In her suffering, Job's wife became bitter and lost sight of her faith. While her reaction was human, it shows the danger of allowing despair to cloud our judgment. Couples can learn to be aware of this tendency and strive to support each other in staying hopeful and trusting God even when times are bleak.

3. Enduring Faith Amidst Trials: Job's faithfulness despite intense trials teaches couples about the importance of endurance. Job's commitment to God, even when his life seemed destroyed, demonstrates how a foundation of faith can help couples weather the worst storms. Holding onto faith allows couples to find strength beyond their own, trusting God's purpose, even in situations they don't understand.

4. Patience with One Another's Reactions: Job did not respond harshly to his wife's suggestion; instead, he reminded her that God gives both blessings and trials. Job's response shows patience and understanding, even though his wife spoke in anger and hurt. Couples can learn to approach one another's reactions with empathy, recognizing that pain can cause momentary lapses in faith or hope.

5. Accepting Good and Bad from God's Hand: Job's response emphasizes an important principle: to accept both blessings and hardships as part of life's journey. Couples can learn to view both prosperity and adversity as opportunities to grow together in faith, trusting that God has a purpose for every season of their lives.

6. The Importance of Forgiveness: Although Job's wife's words were harsh, Job did not hold them against her, understanding that she was in pain. Couples can learn to forgive one another for hurtful words spoken in moments of anger or sorrow, extending grace to each other in times of distress.

7. Finding Restoration and Renewal: Ultimately, God restored Job's fortunes and blessed him again with children and abundance. This reminds couples that even after deep suffering, God can bring restoration and joy. Couples can be hopeful that after seasons of hardship, there is often a season of renewal, where they can experience healing and even greater blessings.

8. Praying Together During Hardship: Though the Book of Job does not detail this, it's evident that Job was a man of prayer. Couples can learn from Job's example to pray together in times of hardship, bringing their fears and grief to God. Prayer can serve as a refuge and bring peace, helping couples find strength to endure difficult times.

9. Compassion Over Judgment: While it may be easy to judge Job's wife for her response, her words came from a place of profound grief. Couples can remember the importance of compassion over judgment when their partner is hurting. Recognizing that suffering affects people differently can help foster an atmosphere of empathy and understanding in the relationship.

10. Building Resilience in Faith as a Couple: Job's story, though painful, is ultimately one of resilience. Couples can learn to grow in their faith together, striving to build resilience that enables them to stand firm in the face of adversity. By fostering spiritual growth together, couples can create a strong foundation that supports them through life's inevitable challenges.

Week 12

Obedience and Trust in God's Leadership

Weekly Readings:

Day 78- Numbers 7:66-89, Numbers 8, Numbers 9:1-14; Luke 2:41-52; Psalm 35:11-18
Day 79- Numbers 9:15-23, Numbers 10, Numbers 11:1-3; Luke 3:1-22; Psalm 35:19-28
Day 80- Numbers 11:4-35, Numbers 12, Numbers 13:1-25; Luke 3:23-38, Luke 4:1-13; Proverbs 7:21-27
Day 81- Numbers 13:26-33, Numbers 14; Luke 4:14-37; Psalm 36:1-12
Day 82- Numbers 15, Numbers 16:1-35; Luke 4:38-44, Luke 5:1-16; Psalm 37:1-9
Day 83- Numbers 16:36-50, Numbers 17, Numbers 18; Luke 5:17-32; Psalm 37:10-20
Day 84- Numbers 19, Numbers 20, Numbers 21:1-3; Luke 5:33-39, Luke 6:1-11; Proverbs 8:1-11

Weekly Reflection:

This week's readings from Numbers explore the journey of the Israelites through the wilderness and their interactions with God. We see God's provision, His guidance, and the challenges His people face when they struggle with obedience. In marriage, just as the Israelites were called to trust in God's leadership, couples are also called to surrender their lives and relationships to His guidance.

In Numbers 7:66-89, we see the leaders of Israel offering their gifts to the Lord for the dedication of the altar. Each act of obedience was significant, showing the importance of honoring God with what they had. This is a powerful reminder for couples to honor God with their gifts, talents, and resources, no matter how big or small. By doing so, we not only honor God but also build a foundation of trust and mutual respect in our marriages.

Numbers 8 speaks about the consecration of the Levites, setting them apart for the work of the Lord. Similarly, couples are called to set their relationship apart for God's glory. When a marriage is consecrated to God, it becomes a powerful witness to His love, grace, and faithfulness.

Numbers 9 recounts how the Israelites were led by the cloud of God's presence by day and the fire by night. For couples, this represents the need for God's guidance in every aspect of life. There will be times of uncertainty, but God promises to lead those who trust in Him. Couples are called to seek God's direction in their decisions, whether they're navigating career changes, financial decisions, or family dynamics.

In Luke 2:41-52, the story of the boy Jesus in the temple demonstrates Jesus' awareness of His identity and mission at a young age. Mary and Joseph's response of seeking and trusting in God's plan provides a beautiful model for married couples. Even when faced with unexpected challenges or confusion, couples should seek the Lord together and trust that He is leading them on the right path.

Luke 3:1-22 and the baptism of Jesus emphasize the importance of obedience to God's calling. Jesus' baptism marks the beginning of His ministry, and He models for us the importance of submitting to God's will. In marriage, this submission to God is essential. Couples must surrender their plans, dreams, and desires to God's will, trusting that He has a perfect plan for them.

The Israelites struggled with trust and obedience throughout their journey, as seen in Numbers 13:26-33 and Numbers 14. They faced giants in the land and allowed fear to overtake their faith. In marriage, there will be moments of doubt and fear—whether it's in dealing with personal challenges or external pressures. Yet, like Joshua and Caleb, who trusted God's promise, couples are called to stand firm in faith, even in the face of adversity.

Weekly Discussion Prompts:

1. Consecrating Your Marriage: Reflecting on the Israelites' offering in Numbers 7, how can you consecrate your marriage to God this week? What steps can you take to honor God with your relationship?

2. Trusting God's Guidance: Just as the Israelites were led by the cloud and fire, how can you invite God to lead your marriage? Are there areas where you need to trust God's direction more fully?

3. Obedience in Difficult Times: In Luke 3:1-22, Jesus models obedience to the Father's will. How can you practice obedience in your marriage, even when it's difficult or uncertain?

4. Handling Fear Together: In Numbers 13, the Israelites allowed fear to take over. Are there areas in your marriage where fear is hindering your trust in God's plan? How can you face those fears together and trust God for the future?

5. Seeking God's Presence: Mary and Joseph sought God's presence when they lost Jesus in the temple. How can you as a couple intentionally seek God's presence this week? What does that look like in your daily lives?

6. Building Mutual Trust: Reflect on how trust in God helped the Israelites through the wilderness. How can you build deeper trust in your marriage, relying on God's faithfulness?

7. Responding to Challenges with Faith: The Israelites complained and doubted when faced with challenges. How can you respond to challenges in your marriage with faith and trust in God's provision?

Joint Couple Activity:

"Faith and Obedience in Action": This week, identify one area of your marriage where you need to practice greater obedience or trust in God's guidance. Take intentional steps to obey God together in that area. Whether it's through prayer, making a decision together, or offering something to God, commit to walking in faith as a couple. Afterward, share how you experienced God's leading and how it strengthened your bond.

Couple for Week 12: David and Bathsheba

The story of David and Bathsheba is one of love, sin, repentance, and redemption. King David, captivated by Bathsheba's beauty, committed adultery with her while her husband, Uriah, was away in battle. When Bathsheba became pregnant, David attempted to cover up his sin by bringing Uriah home, hoping he would be with his wife. However, Uriah's loyalty to his fellow soldiers kept him from enjoying any comforts while they were at war. In desperation, David arranged for Uriah to be placed in the front lines of battle, where he was killed. After Uriah's death, David took Bathsheba as his wife, but their actions displeased God.

The prophet Nathan confronted David, leading him to recognize the weight of his sin. David expressed sincere repentance, and God forgave him, though he still faced painful consequences. Bathsheba gave birth to their child, but the child soon died. Despite the tragic beginning of their relationship, David and Bathsheba's story continued, and they later had a son, Solomon, who would become one of Israel's greatest kings and a direct ancestor of Jesus.

Lessons for Couples:

1. The Importance of Accountability and Transparency: David's actions show the risks of secrecy and deception. Couples can learn to practice honesty, accountability, and transparency with each other, avoiding secret actions or choices that could harm the relationship.

2. The Power of Repentance and Forgiveness: After David's sin was exposed, he showed sincere repentance, and God granted him forgiveness. Couples can learn from this that, while mistakes are inevitable, a humble heart and genuine repentance can lead to

healing. Being open to forgiving one another is essential for maintaining a healthy relationship.

3. Recognizing the Consequences of Poor Choices: David and Bathsheba's story illustrates that choices have consequences, even when forgiveness is granted. Couples can learn the importance of making wise decisions and considering the potential impact of their actions on each other and their families.

4. Seeking God's Guidance Before Acting: David's impulsive decisions with Bathsheba stemmed from acting on desire without seeking God's guidance. Couples can take this as a reminder to involve God in their decisions, especially when they face strong emotions, pressures, or temptations.

5. Working Through Difficult Beginnings: Despite a difficult start, David and Bathsheba's relationship eventually stabilized, and they went on to parent Solomon, whose lineage was essential in fulfilling God's promises. This shows that, through God's grace, couples can overcome even the most challenging beginnings or past mistakes to build a strong future together.

6. God's Grace for Imperfect Couples: David and Bathsheba were both imperfect, yet God's grace was evident in their story. They were blessed with another son, Solomon, who became a key figure in Israel's history. This teaches couples that, despite human failures, God's grace can bring healing, purpose, and blessings.

7. The Role of Correction and Support: Nathan's role as a prophet was critical, as he helped David realize his error and take steps toward repentance. Couples can seek mentors, friends, or spiritual guides who lovingly provide support and correction when needed, encouraging growth in their faith and relationship.

8. Humility and Ownership in Relationships: David didn't shift the blame for his actions; he accepted full responsibility. Couples can learn to own up to their actions and avoid blaming each other. Admitting faults with humility strengthens trust and encourages a culture of mutual respect.

9. Making the Most of Redemption: God used David and Bathsheba's union to fulfill a greater purpose, eventually leading to the birth of Jesus through Solomon's line. This is a reminder that God can use even broken situations for good. Couples can trust that their relationship, when surrendered to God, has the potential to fulfill a purpose beyond their expectations.

10. Supporting One Another in Loss and Renewal: David and Bathsheba faced the sorrow of losing their child, which could have strained their relationship. However, they went through the grieving process together and found renewal in God's continued blessings. Couples can support each other through losses and struggles, allowing these experiences to strengthen their bond.

Week 13

Commitment and Sacrifice in Marriage

Weekly Readings:

Day 85- Numbers 21:4-35, Numbers 22:1-20; Luke 6:12-36; Psalm 37:21-31
Day 86- Numbers 22:21-41, Numbers 23:1-26; Luke 6:37-49, Luke 7:1-10; Psalm 37:32-40
Day 87- Numbers 23:27-30, Numbers 24, Numbers 25; Luke 7:11-35; Psalm 38:1-11
Day 88- Numbers 26, Numbers 27:1-11; Luke 7:36-50; Proverbs 8:12-21
Day 89- Numbers 27:12-23, Numbers 28, Numbers 29:1-11; Luke 8:1-18; Psalm 38:12-22
Day 90- Numbers 29:12-40, Numbers 30, Numbers 31:1-24; Luke 8:19-39; Psalm 39:1-13
Day 91- Numbers 31:25-54, Numbers 32; Luke 8:40-56, Luke 9:1-9; Psalm 40:1-8

Weekly Reflection:

As we continue reading through the Book of Numbers, we see God instructing His people on their commitment to Him and the sacrifices required for living in covenant with Him. The sacrifices, both physical and spiritual, remind us that in a marriage, commitment and sacrifice are vital for a lasting and fruitful relationship.

In Numbers 21:4-35, we see the Israelites journeying through the wilderness and facing the consequences of their disobedience, yet God in His mercy provides a way for their healing and redemption. In marriage, there will be times when couples face difficulties, misunderstandings, and disappointments. It's in these moments that commitment to one another and to God becomes essential. Couples must be willing to sacrifice their selfish desires and strive for reconciliation and healing, just as the Israelites were healed when they looked to the bronze serpent in the wilderness.

Numbers 22:1-20 highlights the story of Balaam and his encounter with God. Despite Balaam's intentions, God intervened, showing His sovereignty over every situation. In marriage, it's important to recognize that God has authority over our relationship. Even when things seem to be going off course, couples must trust in God's leading and surrender to His will. Balaam's story reminds us that God's plans will always prevail, and couples should seek His will in every decision they make.

In Luke 6:12-36, Jesus teaches about the importance of love, humility, and forgiveness. His message challenges couples to love one another unconditionally, even when it's difficult. Jesus calls His followers to go beyond what is easy and to love even those who hurt or wrong them. For couples, this means extending grace and forgiveness, even in moments of tension or conflict. It also involves serving one another selflessly, reflecting Christ's love in their marriage.

Luke 7:1-10 speaks of the faith of the centurion, who believed that Jesus could heal his servant without even being physically present. This level of faith challenges couples to trust that God can work in their marriage, even in unseen ways. Couples must learn to trust God's timing and methods, knowing that He is always at work, even when they don't fully understand the situation.

In Numbers 26, the census of the Israelites reminds us of the importance of honoring God's design and plan for our lives. For couples, it's a reminder that marriage is part of God's greater plan. Couples should honor their vows and their commitment to one another as a sacred part of God's purpose. As they walk through life together, they are fulfilling His purpose for their lives.

Weekly Discussion Prompts:

1. Commitment in the Wilderness: Reflecting on the Israelites' journey, are there areas in your marriage where you've faced "wilderness" moments? How can you commit to trusting God more fully during challenging times?

2. Sacrifice in Marriage: Just as the Israelites had to make sacrifices to God, what sacrifices can you make for your spouse this week? How can you serve your spouse with a spirit of humility and love?

3. Seeking God's Will Together: In the story of Balaam, God intervened to show His will. How can you as a couple seek God's will together in your decisions? Are there areas where you need to surrender your plans to Him?

4. Unconditional Love and Forgiveness: Jesus teaches about loving and forgiving those who wrong us. How can you practice unconditional love and forgiveness in your marriage this week? Are there past hurts that need healing through forgiveness?

5. Faith in God's Timing: In the story of the centurion, faith was shown in trusting Jesus' power to heal. How can you trust God's timing and methods in your marriage? Are there situations where you need to trust that God is working, even if you can't see it?

6. Honoring Your Vows: The census in Numbers 26 is a reminder of God's faithfulness. How can you honor your vows and commitment to your spouse? What steps can you take this week to strengthen the foundation of your marriage?

7. Serving One Another: Jesus calls His followers to serve others. How can you serve your spouse this week, not out of obligation, but out of love and gratitude?

Joint Couple Activity:

"A Sacrificial Act of Love": This week, plan and carry out a sacrificial act for your spouse. It could be something as simple as taking on a chore or responsibility your spouse normally handles, or it could involve setting aside time to listen and support them in a way that reflects Christ's love. Afterward, discuss how the act made both of you feel and how it deepens your connection.

Couple for Week 13: Amram and Jochebed

Amram and Jochebed were the parents of Moses, Aaron, and Miriam. Living as slaves in Egypt, they faced the oppression of Pharaoh's cruel decree that all Hebrew baby boys be killed. When Moses was born, Jochebed saw he was a beautiful child and courageously hid him for three months. When she could hide him no longer, she made a small ark, placed Moses in it, and set it afloat on the Nile River, trusting God to protect him. Her faith and bravery were rewarded when Pharaoh's daughter found Moses and adopted him, unknowingly hiring Jochebed as his nurse. Through Jochebed and Amram's faith and God's providence, Moses was saved and eventually became the leader who would deliver Israel from Egypt.

Lessons for Couples:

1. Faith in Adversity: Jochebed and Amram had deep faith in God, trusting Him even amid terrifying circumstances. Couples can draw strength from their example, facing challenges together with faith in God's plan and protection.

2. Working Together in Crisis: Amram and Jochebed united in their efforts to protect their child. Couples can learn to work as a team, especially during crises, supporting each other in creating solutions, and sharing responsibilities.

3. Sacrifice for Family: Jochebed was willing to let go of her son, placing him in God's hands, which was an act of immense sacrifice. This teaches couples the importance of selfless love and putting family needs above personal desires, trusting that God will take care of the rest.

4. Trust in God's Providence: By placing Moses in the Nile, Jochebed entrusted her son to God's care, believing He would protect him. Couples can find peace in difficult decisions by surrendering them to God and trusting His providential care.

5. Fostering Strong Values in Children: Though Moses spent his early years with Pharaoh's daughter, he learned about his Hebrew heritage and faith in God from his family. Amram and Jochebed's influence shaped his early faith. Couples are reminded that the values they instill in their children are powerful and can guide them, even in challenging environments.

6. Supporting Each Other's Faith: Together, Amram and Jochebed relied on each other's faith to carry out a plan as risky as hiding their child. Couples can take courage from each other's faith, supporting one another in trusting God even when the path is uncertain.

7. God's Protection and Purpose: God not only protected Moses but also had a plan for him to deliver Israel. Amram and Jochebed's faith was part of a larger divine purpose. Couples can trust that their struggles and faith-filled actions may be part of a greater story in God's plan.

8. The Power of Parental Influence: Though they had limited time with Moses, Amram and Jochebed's influence left a lasting impact. This reminds couples that even short-lived but intentional time with their children can leave a lifelong impression of faith, strength, and resilience.

9. Encouraging Bravery and Trust: Despite the dangers, Amram and Jochebed's bravery saved Moses and allowed God's will to unfold. Their example encourages couples to live bravely and make choices that honor God, trusting that their faithfulness can lead to greater things.

10. Hope Amid Trials: Amram and Jochebed's story shows that God's plans can emerge even through oppression and struggle. Couples can hold onto hope and stay faithful, believing that God can work powerfully even in life's darkest moments.

Week 14

Trust and Obedience in Marriage

Weekly Readings:

Day 92- Numbers 33, Numbers 34; Luke 9:10-27; Proverbs 8:22-31
Day 93- Numbers 35, Numbers 36:1-12; Luke 9:28-56; Psalm 40:9-17
Day 94- Deuteronomy 1, Deuteronomy 2:1-23; Luke 9:57-62, Luke 10:1-24; Psalm 41:1-6
Day 95- Deuteronomy 2:24-37, Deuteronomy 3, Deuteronomy 4:1-14; Luke 10:25-42, Luke 11:1-4; Psalm 41:7-13
Day 96- Deuteronomy 4:15-49, Deuteronomy 5; Luke 11:5-32; Proverbs 8:32-36
Day 97- Deuteronomy 6, Deuteronomy 7, Deuteronomy 8; Luke 11:33-54; Psalm 42:1-6
Day 98- Deuteronomy 9, Deuteronomy 10; Luke 12:1-34; Psalm 42:7-11

Weekly Reflection:

In Numbers 33 and 34, we observe the Israelites retracing their journey from Egypt, a record that reminds them of God's guidance and provision every step of the way. As a couple, reflecting on the journey you've shared—both the blessings and challenges—can reinforce the importance of trusting in God's guidance. Just as God brought the Israelites through each stage, He is present in each chapter of your marriage, leading and sustaining you.

In Numbers 35 and 36, we encounter the establishment of cities of refuge and the inheritance laws for Israel. These instructions underscore God's commitment to justice, protection, and legacy. In marriage, fostering a sense of refuge and safety for one another is crucial. It's a reminder to create a home that is a safe haven, where both partners can find peace, comfort, and unwavering support. Furthermore, God's attention to inheritance and legacy invites couples to consider the legacy of love, faith, and values they are building together.

The Book of Deuteronomy begins with Moses recounting Israel's history and encouraging them to obey God's commandments. In marriage, reflecting on how God has faithfully brought you together can inspire obedience and devotion to His will. When couples focus on God's ways, they strengthen the foundation of their marriage, growing in unity and purpose. In

Deuteronomy 6:5, the command to "love the Lord your God with all your heart, soul, and strength" can inspire couples to love God first, finding the source of love for each other in Him.

In Luke 10, Jesus sends out the seventy-two disciples, instructing them to rely on God's provision and guidance. This scene teaches couples to trust in God's timing and provision, even when they feel vulnerable. Marriage often requires stepping out in faith, trusting that God will provide strength, patience, and love to sustain each other.

Weekly Discussion Prompts:

1. Reflecting on God's Faithfulness: Just as the Israelites remembered their journey, reflect on your own journey together. How has God guided and provided for your marriage? In what ways can you express gratitude for His faithfulness?

2. Creating a Refuge: Numbers 35 speaks about cities of refuge. How can you make your home a place of safety and peace? Are there ways to communicate better or make each other feel more valued and secure?

3. Obedience to God's Commands: Deuteronomy emphasizes obedience to God's commands. How does following God's guidance impact your marriage? Are there specific areas where you feel called to grow in obedience as a couple?

4. Trusting God's Provision: In Luke 10, Jesus sends His disciples out with few resources. How can you trust in God's provision in your marriage, especially during uncertain times? Are there areas where you need to release control and trust that He will provide?

5. Legacy and Inheritance: In Numbers, inheritance laws are established to honor the next generation. What legacy do you hope to leave as a couple? How can you start building that legacy through your actions, values, and love for one another?

6. Loving God First: Deuteronomy 6:5 commands us to love God wholeheartedly. How can prioritizing your relationship with God enhance your marriage? Are there practices you can implement together to deepen your faith?

7. Faith in the Unseen: Psalm 42 speaks of longing for God in times of trouble. How can you draw closer to each other and God during difficult times? How can you remind each other of His presence and promises?

"Journey Mapping": Together, create a visual map of your relationship journey so far. Start from the time you met, marking key moments, blessings, challenges, and times when you felt God's guidance. Use symbols, drawings, or words to represent these points. Reflect together on how God has brought you through each phase, and discuss how you can continue to trust Him in the future.

Couple for Week 14: Shem and His Wife

Shem was one of Noah's three sons, and he, along with his wife, was among the eight people saved on the ark during the Great Flood. Following God's instructions, Noah built the ark to preserve his family and representatives of the world's animals as humanity faced destruction due to widespread sin and corruption. After the floodwaters receded, Shem and his wife, along with the rest of Noah's family, embarked on a new beginning, responsible for repopulating and restoring humanity. Shem's descendants would eventually lead to the line of Abraham and ultimately to Jesus Christ, highlighting the spiritual legacy that began with Shem's faithfulness to God.

Lessons for Couples:

1. Faithful Obedience Together: Shem and his wife supported Noah's obedience to God's command to build the ark. Couples can learn the importance of working together in faith and obedience, even if they don't fully understand God's plan at the time.

2. Starting Anew with Faith: As survivors of the flood, Shem and his wife were tasked with helping rebuild humanity. Their example teaches couples the value of stepping into new beginnings with hope, faith, and a commitment to honoring God.

3. Building a Spiritual Legacy: Shem's lineage would become the foundation of Israel, from whom the Messiah would come. This reminds couples of the potential for their lives, decisions, and faith to impact future generations in profound, godly ways.

4. Enduring Life's Storms Together: As a couple who survived the Great Flood, Shem and his wife's endurance and unity through the ordeal serve as a model for couples today. Their example encourages spouses to weather life's challenges together, trusting that God has a purpose even in the storms.

5. Trust in God's Covenant Promises: After the flood, God established a covenant with Noah and his family, promising never to destroy the earth by water again. This promise was a sign of hope and stability for Shem and his wife. Couples are reminded to trust in God's promises, which bring hope and assurance in uncertain times.

6. Patience and Perseverance in Isolation: The time on the ark likely tested the family's patience and endurance. Shem and his wife demonstrate the strength that couples can find in supporting each other through seasons of isolation, trusting God's timing and outcome.

7. Embracing New Responsibilities Together: As the world began anew, Shem and his wife had the responsibility of helping guide the next generation. Their story encourages couples to embrace shared responsibilities with purpose, working together to lead, guide, and nurture those around them.

8. Unity in Purpose: Shem and his wife were united in the mission God had given their family—to survive, rebuild, and trust in His plan for humanity's future. This unity in purpose shows how shared faith and values can strengthen couples as they pursue God's purposes together.

9. Remaining Faithful in an Unfaithful World: Living in a time of widespread wickedness, Shem and his family stayed faithful to God, which spared them from destruction. Couples today can be inspired by their example to uphold their values and faith, even when surrounded by challenges and temptations in the world.

10. Hope for Future Generations: Through Shem and his wife, God began a lineage that would lead to the nation of Israel. Couples are reminded that, even if they don't see immediate results, their faith and obedience can positively shape their family's future for generations.

Week 15

Faithful Commitment and Generosity in Marriage

Weekly Readings:

Day 99- Deuteronomy 11, Deuteronomy 12; Luke 12:35-59; Psalm 43:1-5
Day 100- Deuteronomy 13, Deuteronomy 14; Luke 13:1-30; Proverbs 9:1-12
Day 101- Deuteronomy 15, Deuteronomy 16:1-20; Luke 13:31-35, Luke 14:1-14; Psalm 44:1-12
Day 102- Deuteronomy 16:21-22, Deuteronomy 17, Deuteronomy 18; Luke 14:15-35; Psalm 44:13-26
Day 103- Deuteronomy 19, Deuteronomy 20; Luke 15:1-32; Psalm 45:1-9
Day 104- Deuteronomy 21, Deuteronomy 22; Luke 16:1-18; Proverbs 9:13-18
Day 105- Deuteronomy 23, Deuteronomy 24, Deuteronomy 25:1-19; Luke 16:19-31, Luke 17:1-10; Psalm 45:10-17

Weekly Reflection:

In Deuteronomy 11 and 12, God reminds the Israelites of His promise and their need to follow His commands in order to receive His blessings. This week's readings underscore the significance of faithful commitment in both faith and marriage. For a couple, remaining committed to each other and to God's ways is foundational for a lasting and fulfilling relationship. Just as God instructed the Israelites to choose His ways wholeheartedly, couples are encouraged to make conscious choices that nurture and strengthen their marriage.

Luke 12:35-59 speaks of readiness, with Jesus urging His followers to remain vigilant for His return. In marriage, vigilance can mean being attentive to each other's needs, staying emotionally connected, and being intentional in nurturing love daily. As partners, staying "ready" and responsive to each other's emotional, physical, and spiritual needs helps build a relationship that can withstand life's trials.

In Deuteronomy 15 and 16, God commands generosity and compassion, particularly toward the needy. These passages can inspire couples to embrace generosity not only toward others but also toward each other. Generosity in marriage extends beyond material gifts; it includes giving your time, attention, patience, and understanding. When you're generous in giving of yourself to one another, your bond deepens, and the love you share becomes an outpouring of God's love in action.

Luke 15 brings us the parables of the lost sheep, lost coin, and prodigal son, illustrating God's grace and mercy toward those who repent. As a couple, reflecting on God's forgiveness can encourage you to practice forgiveness in your relationship. Relationships often require patience and grace, especially during conflicts or misunderstandings. Embracing forgiveness as God does strengthens the unity and compassion within your marriage.

Weekly Discussion Prompts:

1. Renewing Commitment: Reflect on Deuteronomy 11, where God calls His people to remain faithful. What does faithfulness mean to each of you in your marriage? Are there any specific commitments you want to renew or strengthen?

2. Vigilance in Love: In Luke 12, Jesus speaks about readiness. How can you be more attentive and responsive to each other's needs? Are there practical steps you can take this week to nurture your relationship?

3. Practicing Generosity: Deuteronomy 15 encourages generosity. In what ways can you be more generous toward each other, whether in time, words, or actions? How does being generous in your relationship benefit both of you?

4. Grace in Conflict: Reflect on the parables of forgiveness in Luke 15. How can you practice forgiveness more readily within your relationship? Are there past grievances that you can let go of, moving forward in unity?

5. Standing Together in Trials: Psalm 43 expresses a desire for God's light and truth in dark times. How can you better support each other when one of you is going through a challenging time? In what ways can you invite God's presence into your struggles?

6. Building a Strong Foundation: Proverbs 9 emphasizes wisdom. What wisdom have you gained from your journey together? How can you apply this wisdom to strengthen your marriage as you grow older together?

7. Reflecting God's Love: Psalm 45 describes a beautiful love. How can your marriage be a reflection of God's love to others around you? Are there specific ways to serve others as a couple?

"Generosity Challenge": This week, practice intentional acts of generosity toward one another. Each day, surprise your partner with a small, thoughtful gesture—whether it's a note of encouragement, doing an unexpected task, or spending quality time together. At the end of the week, reflect on how these gestures impacted your connection.

Couple for Week 15: Asa and His Wife

Asa was a king of Judah who ruled for 41 years, and his reign is primarily noted for his dedication to reforming the nation and restoring worship of the true God. Asa removed idols, destroyed pagan altars, and urged the people to seek the Lord wholeheartedly. While his wife (or wives) are not specifically named in the Bible, we do know that he acted firmly even against his family when they opposed his commitment to God; for example, he removed his grandmother Maachah from her influential role as queen mother because she had made an idol. Although Asa later faltered in his faith by relying on alliances instead of God, his early years were marked by devotion, and his reforms led Judah into a season of peace and spiritual renewal.

Lessons for Couples:

1. Spiritual Leadership and Accountability: Asa demonstrated courage in leading his kingdom back to God, taking drastic measures to ensure that worship was centered on the Lord alone. Couples can learn from his commitment, understanding that creating a God-centered home may require making hard decisions and holding each other accountable.

2. Standing Up for Godly Values in the Family: Asa didn't hesitate to stand against idolatry, even when it involved family members. Couples can take inspiration to uphold godly values and be willing to lovingly confront anything—even within their family—that might compromise their faith.

3. Building a Faith-Filled Legacy: Asa's reforms set an example for future generations in Judah. Couples today can commit to building a faith-based legacy that encourages those around them to seek God and to live with integrity, leaving a positive spiritual impact.

4. Importance of Staying Faithful Over Time: Asa's initial years were filled with zeal for the Lord, but in his later years, he began to rely more on human alliances and strategies rather than on God. Couples can learn from his story the importance of maintaining faith and dependence on God throughout all stages of life, avoiding the drift toward self-reliance.

5. Commitment to Righteousness Despite Opposition: Asa's efforts to restore Judah's faith in God were met with resistance, yet he persevered. Couples can take this lesson to heart, staying committed to doing what's right even when facing challenges or external opposition.

6. Praying for Guidance in Times of Trouble: Asa's early reign showed a reliance on God in times of conflict. Couples today are reminded to pray together for God's wisdom and guidance during trials, trusting that He is more powerful than any earthly alliance or strategy.

7. Removing Negative Influences in the Relationship: Just as Asa removed idols and ungodly influences from Judah, couples can be encouraged to remove any behaviors, attitudes, or influences that hinder their spiritual growth together, focusing on practices that draw them closer to God.

8. Modeling Faith for Those Around Them: Asa's reforms were a powerful testimony to those under his rule. Couples can be a witness to their friends, family, and community, showing others what a Christ-centered relationship looks like through their example of faith, prayer, and love.

9. Humility in Success: Asa's early success and peace were blessings from God, yet he later struggled to keep his reliance on God. Couples can be encouraged to practice humility, acknowledging God's role in their successes and blessings, and staying dependent on Him in every season.

10. Seeking Repentance and Renewal: Asa's life demonstrates the importance of returning to God when mistakes are made. Couples should remember that repentance and renewal are always available and can bring spiritual refreshment, allowing them to move forward in faith and unity.

Week 16

Faith, Trust, and God's Promises

Weekly Readings:

Day 106- Deuteronomy 26, Deuteronomy 27, Deuteronomy 28:1-14; Luke 17:11-37; Psalm 46:1-11
Day 107- Deuteronomy 28:15-68; Luke 18:1-30; Psalm 47:1-9
Day 108- Deuteronomy 29, Deuteronomy 30:1-10; Luke 18:31-43, Luke 19:1-10; Proverbs 10:1-10
Day 109- Deuteronomy 30:11-20, Deuteronomy 31:1-29; Luke 19:11-44; Psalm 48:1-8
Day 110- Deuteronomy 31:30, Deuteronomy 32; Luke 19:45-48, Luke 20:1-26; Psalm 48:9-14
Day 111- Deuteronomy 33, Deuteronomy 34:1-12; Luke 20:27-47, Luke 21:1-4; Psalm 49:1-20
Day 112- Joshua 1, Joshua 2; Luke 21:5-38; Proverbs 10:11-20

Weekly Reflection:

This week's readings bring us to the end of Deuteronomy, where God, through Moses, urges the Israelites to choose obedience and life by following His commands. These passages highlight the blessings that follow those who trust in God and the consequences for turning away from His ways. As a couple, these readings can inspire you to consider how trust and obedience to God play a role in your relationship. By following God's ways together, you can receive His blessings and face life's challenges with confidence.

In Luke 17:11-37, we read the story of the ten lepers and how only one returned to give thanks. Gratitude and appreciation are crucial in marriage. Being intentional about expressing gratitude for each other can bring joy and contentment, even during difficult times. This week, make an effort to openly express thanks for your partner's efforts and qualities that bless your life.

Deuteronomy 30:11-20 offers a poignant choice between life and death, blessings and curses, reminding us that God's ways are not burdensome but rather a pathway to a blessed life. As a couple, choosing God's path can mean seeking His wisdom in decision-making and committing to treat each other with love and respect. When challenges arise, turn to prayer together and seek God's direction.

In Joshua 1, God tells Joshua, "Be strong and courageous," encouraging him to lead with faith. For couples, embracing courage may mean supporting one another during life's uncertainties. Trusting in God's promises can help you overcome fears, trusting that He will guide you as you step forward together.

Weekly Discussion Prompts:

1. Blessings in Marriage: Reflect on the blessings listed in Deuteronomy 28. What blessings have you both experienced as a result of your faith? How does walking in God's ways impact your relationship?

2. Gratitude for Each Other: The story of the ten lepers reminds us of gratitude. What are three specific things you're grateful for about your partner? Share them with each other and discuss ways to show appreciation more regularly.

3. Choosing Life: In Deuteronomy 30, God urges His people to "choose life." What choices can you make in your relationship that bring "life" and joy? Are there areas where you need to let go of negative patterns to embrace God's way?

4. Trust in God's Plan: Psalm 46 calls us to trust in God, even in tumultuous times. Are there areas where you both need to trust more in God's guidance and provision? How can you strengthen each other's faith during challenging seasons?

5. Reflecting God's Love: Consider the example of Zacchaeus in Luke 19, where Jesus's love leads to transformation. In what ways can your love for each other be a reflection of God's unconditional love, inspiring growth and positive change?

6. Strength and Courage: Joshua was told to be "strong and courageous" in God's mission. How can you encourage and strengthen each other to face life's uncertainties? Share any fears or anxieties with each other and pray for courage.

7. Committing to God's Word: Proverbs 10 speaks of the wisdom of the righteous. How can studying God's Word together build wisdom in your marriage? Make a plan to incorporate more spiritual growth as a couple this week.

"Gratitude and Blessings List": Create a list of blessings you've experienced in your marriage and things you're thankful for about each other. Display the list somewhere visible in your home as a reminder of God's goodness and your love for one another.

Couple for Week 16: Hezekiah and His Wife

King Hezekiah of Judah was a righteous king who earnestly sought God and led a major reform to restore true worship in Jerusalem. He destroyed idols, reopened the temple, and called the people back to celebrate Passover, which had been neglected. Hezekiah trusted God wholeheartedly, even when threatened by the powerful Assyrian army, and his prayers for deliverance were answered. Though not much is detailed about his wife in the Bible, we know they had a son, Manasseh, who later ruled Judah. Hezekiah's faith and dedication left a profound impact on Judah, even though his later years saw some pride and a lapse in judgment.

Lessons for Couples:

1. Trusting God Together in Adversity: Hezekiah's unwavering trust in God during the Assyrian siege shows the power of leaning on God in times of crisis. Couples can learn to pray together and strengthen each other's faith in facing life's challenges, finding unity in trusting God's guidance and deliverance.

2. Spiritual Leadership in the Home: Hezekiah's dedication to reforming the spiritual practices of Judah can inspire couples to create a home environment rooted in worship, prayer, and godly values. Supporting each other in spiritual growth can help couples nurture a home focused on honoring God.

3. Making Prayer a Priority: Hezekiah's life shows how prayer can be a powerful tool in times of need. Couples can incorporate prayer into their daily routine, seeking God's wisdom and strength together, which can be a source of comfort and a foundation of their relationship.

4. Standing Firm Against Negative Influences: Hezekiah's reforms required him to take a stand against idolatry and ungodly practices. Similarly, couples can strive to keep their relationship free from influences that lead away from God, focusing on values that bring them closer to each other and to Him.

5. Acknowledging God's Blessings and Staying Humble: Hezekiah was blessed by God with prosperity and deliverance, yet he struggled with pride in his later years. Couples can learn the importance of staying humble and recognizing God as the source of their blessings, remembering to give Him the glory.

6. Supporting Each Other's Spiritual Callings: Hezekiah's leadership was essential to Judah's revival, and his wife's support, while not explicitly recorded, would have been valuable to his mission. Couples can strive to encourage and support each other's unique callings, working together to fulfill God's purposes in their lives.

7. Repentance and Renewal: When Hezekiah faced consequences for his pride, he turned back to God in repentance. Couples can learn the importance of humbly seeking forgiveness when they stumble, allowing renewal and growth in their relationship.

8. Passing on Faith to the Next Generation: Although Hezekiah's son Manasseh did not follow his example initially, Hezekiah's commitment to faith serves as a reminder of the importance of imparting godly values to the next generation. Couples can prioritize passing down their faith, setting an example of devotion and integrity for their children.

9. Seeking God's Guidance in Big Decisions: Hezekiah consulted God when faced with difficult decisions, reminding couples to seek God's guidance together, especially in significant matters. Making decisions in prayerful unity can lead to peace and strengthen their partnership.

10. Living Out Faith as a Witness to Others: Hezekiah's faith and dedication became a powerful testimony to the people of Judah. Couples can strive to let their love, faith, and commitment to God shine as a witness to others, inspiring those around them to seek a deeper relationship with God.

Week 17

Obedience, Renewal, and Trust in God's Power

Weekly Readings:

Day 113- Joshua 3, Joshua 4, Joshua 5:1-12; Luke 22:1-38; Psalm 50:1-15
Day 114- Joshua 5:13-15, Joshua 6, Joshua 7; Luke 22:39-62; Psalm 50:16-23
Day 115- Joshua 8, Joshua 9:1-15; Luke 22:63-71, Luke 23:1-25; Psalm 51:1-9
Day 116- Joshua 9:16-27, Joshua 10; Luke 23:26-56; Proverbs 10:21-30
Day 117- Joshua 11, Joshua 12; Luke 24:1-35; Psalm 51:10-19
Day 118- Joshua 13, Joshua 14; Luke 24:36-53; Psalm 52:1-9
Day 119- Joshua 15, Joshua 16; John 1:1-28; Psalm 53:1-6

Weekly Reflection:

This week, as we enter the final chapters of Joshua, we observe God's guidance for the Israelites as they prepare to claim the Promised Land. Their journey involves trust, obedience, and miraculous moments as God leads them. Joshua's courage and faith serve as a powerful example for couples, inspiring you both to rely on God's power and guidance in your relationship.

In Luke 22, Jesus shares the Last Supper with His disciples and encourages them to remain strong. His example of humility, even in the face of betrayal, is a profound reminder of love's endurance. As a couple, consider how you can cultivate a love that endures difficult seasons, drawing strength from Christ's example.

Psalm 51 offers a moving prayer of repentance and renewal. Reflect on this together: Are there any burdens or misunderstandings between you that need to be cleared? Seeking forgiveness, both from God and from each other, can bring healing and renewal to your relationship.

In Joshua 4, the Israelites set up stones of remembrance to mark God's faithfulness. As a couple, consider ways you can "set up stones" of remembrance to celebrate God's blessings in your life. Keeping a journal or creating a scrapbook of significant moments may remind you both of God's faithfulness and deepen your gratitude.

Weekly Discussion Prompts:

1. Reflecting on Obedience: In Joshua's story, obedience to God brings victory. Are there areas in your marriage where you feel God is calling you to greater obedience? How can you support each other in this?

2. Love's Endurance: Jesus, at the Last Supper, exemplifies enduring love. In what ways can you nurture a love that remains steadfast even during challenges? Discuss practical ways to support each other's growth and resilience.

3. Setting Stones of Remembrance: Consider your relationship journey. What "stones" of remembrance can you set up to mark God's faithfulness? Share some ways you can tangibly remember and celebrate His blessings.

4. Forgiveness and Renewal: Psalm 51 speaks of the joy of forgiveness and cleansing. Are there past hurts or misunderstandings that you both need to let go of? How can forgiveness create a fresh start in your relationship?

5. Facing Challenges Together: Like the Israelites, God often calls us to confront challenges with faith. Are there "walls" in your life that seem insurmountable? Pray together, asking God for strength and courage to face these walls with unity.

6. Trust in God's Plans: Jesus trusted God's plan despite the difficulties ahead. Reflect on God's plans for your marriage. What dreams or goals do you both feel God is calling you toward?

7. Spiritual Renewal as a Couple: As the disciples experienced renewal through Jesus's resurrection, how can you renew your commitment to each other and to your faith? Share ways to grow spiritually together.

Joint Couple Activity:

"Remembrance Journal": Start a journal together, recording key moments where you've seen God's faithfulness in your lives. Include events, answered prayers, or instances where you've felt God's guidance. Over time, this journal will serve as a testament to God's presence and blessings in your marriage.

Couple for Week 17: King Xerxes and Esther

King Xerxes and Esther are the central figures in the biblical book of Esther. Their story unfolds in the Persian Empire, where Esther, a Jewish woman, rises to become queen and uses her position to save her people from destruction. The relationship between King Xerxes (also known as Ahasuerus in some translations) and Esther teaches profound lessons about courage, providence, and the importance of standing up for what is right in the face of adversity.

The Story of King Xerxes and Esther:

- Xerxes' Search for a Queen: King Xerxes ruled the Persian Empire and held a grand feast to celebrate his reign. After deposing his previous queen, Vashti, for her disobedience, Xerxes sought a new queen. The king ordered a beauty contest, and young women from across the empire were brought to the palace to compete for the title of queen (Esther 2:1-4).

- Esther's Selection: Esther, a Jewish orphan raised by her cousin Mordecai, was among the women chosen to appear before the king. Esther's beauty, grace, and wisdom caught the king's eye, and she was selected to become his queen. Despite her new role, Esther kept her Jewish identity a secret, as Mordecai advised her to do (Esther 2:5-20).

- Mordecai's Warning and Haman's Plot: After Esther became queen, a man named Haman was elevated to a high position in the king's court. Haman, filled with pride, sought to destroy the Jewish people when Mordecai, Esther's cousin, refused to bow to him. In response, Haman convinced Xerxes to issue a decree to annihilate all the Jews in the Persian Empire (Esther 3:1-15).

- Esther's Courageous Action: Upon learning of the plot, Mordecai sent word to Esther, urging her to use her position as queen to intervene. He reminded her that her royal status may have been part of God's plan to save her people. Esther, though initially fearful of the king's law that no one could approach the king without being summoned, resolved to act. She fasted and prayed for strength, then approached Xerxes, risking her life (Esther 4:13-16).

- Esther's Request to the King: When Esther approached the king, he extended his scepter to her, signifying that she was welcome. She invited him and Haman to a banquet, where she subtly began to reveal her true identity and the threat to her people. At a second banquet, Esther finally revealed Haman's plot to the king and disclosed that she, too, was Jewish. The king, enraged by Haman's treachery, ordered Haman's execution and reversed the decree to destroy the Jews (Esther 5-7).

- The Salvation of the Jews: Xerxes granted Esther and Mordecai the authority to protect the Jews, and they were able to defend themselves against their enemies. The Jews' salvation led to the institution of the Jewish festival of Purim, which celebrates their deliverance (Esther 8-9).

Lessons for Couples from the Story of King Xerxes and Esther:

1. The Power of Courage and Advocacy: Esther's bravery in the face of danger serves as a powerful lesson for couples. In times of crisis, it is crucial for both partners to support and encourage one another to do what is right, even when it involves risk or personal sacrifice. Esther's willingness to act on behalf of her people, despite the possible consequences, demonstrates how couples can stand up for justice and righteousness together.

2. The Importance of Communication and Trust: Throughout the story, Esther communicates closely with Mordecai, following his guidance even when it required great courage. In a marriage, clear communication and trust between partners are essential for navigating challenges. Just as Mordecai played a key role in advising Esther, couples should support one another by sharing wisdom, encouragement, and counsel in times of decision-making.

3. Divine Providence: One of the most significant themes in the story of Esther and Xerxes is the concept of divine providence. While God's name is never mentioned in the book, His hand is evident throughout the narrative. Esther's rise to queenship and her subsequent actions to save the Jews reveal that God can work through even the most difficult and unlikely circumstances. Couples can take comfort in knowing that God is at work in their lives, even when they do not immediately see His plan.

4. Acting with Wisdom and Discernment: Esther's actions were marked by wisdom and discernment. She didn't rush to reveal the truth to the king but carefully planned her approach, first inviting him to banquets and gradually revealing Haman's plot. Couples can learn from Esther that wisdom in timing and decision-making is key. Sometimes, it is important to take time, pray, and seek God's guidance before taking action in important matters.

5. The Role of Humility and Servant Leadership: Despite being queen, Esther never let her position of power make her arrogant or distant. She remained humble and, as a servant of her people, used her position to protect and advocate for them. In marriage, humility is vital. Even when one partner might be in a position of leadership or authority, it is essential to serve and protect the other, acting in their best interests rather than out of selfish gain.

6. Shared Purpose and Mission: The relationship between Esther and Mordecai illustrates the importance of a shared sense of mission and purpose. While Esther was the queen, it was Mordecai's guidance and support that helped her make the difficult decision to act. Couples who share a common vision and mission can work together more effectively, supporting one another in fulfilling their individual and collective purposes.

7. Faith in Action: Esther's story is a reminder that faith requires action. While she prayed and fasted, she also took the necessary steps to confront the king and save her people. In marriage, faith should be active. Both partners can support one another in living out their faith, trusting God's provision while also taking practical steps to fulfill His will in their lives.

8. Facing Challenges Together: Xerxes and Esther's story ultimately shows how two people—though facing different challenges—can work together to overcome them. Esther faced an incredible challenge, but with the support of her cousin Mordecai, she was able to act in faith and fulfill her purpose. Couples can take this as a lesson to face challenges together, encouraging and supporting one another in times of difficulty.

Week 18

Commitment, Faith, and New Beginnings

Weekly Readings:

Day 120- Joshua 17, Joshua 18; John 1:29-51; Proverbs 10:31-32, Proverbs 11:1-8
Day 121- Joshua 19, Joshua 20, Joshua 21:1-19; John 2:1-25; Psalm 54:1-7
Day 122- Joshua 21:20-45, Joshua 22; John 3:1-21; Psalm 55:1-11
Day 123- Joshua 23, Joshua 24; John 3:22-36; Psalm 55:12-23
Day 124- Judges 1, Judges 2:1-5; John 4:1-26; Proverbs 11:9-18
Day 125- Judges 2:6-23, Judges 3; John 4:27-42; Psalm 56:1-13
Day 126- Judges 4, Judges 5; John 4:43-54, John 5:1-15; Psalm 57:1-6

Weekly Reflection:

This week, we transition from the leadership of Joshua to the era of the Judges. Joshua's final chapters remind us of his commitment to God's covenant and his challenge to the Israelites to remain faithful in the Promised Land. This commitment encourages couples to choose a life centered on God, even when faced with distractions or challenges. Reflect together on how you can make choices that keep God at the heart of your marriage.

In John 2, Jesus performs His first miracle, turning water into wine at a wedding in Cana. This setting beautifully emphasizes how Jesus' presence transforms and elevates marriages. As you reflect on this miracle, consider how Christ's presence can enhance and deepen your relationship, bringing new joy and purpose.

The Book of Judges opens with Israel facing tests of faith and obedience. Though they occasionally falter, God remains merciful, providing leaders to guide them. In your marriage, consider how God's mercy has been present, even during times of struggle, and discuss how you can grow in trust and reliance on His guidance.

Weekly Discussion Prompts:

1. Choosing Commitment: Joshua asks the Israelites to choose whom they will serve. Discuss how you can regularly renew your commitment to each other and to God. What small actions or rituals could remind you of this commitment?

2. Inviting Jesus into Your Marriage: Jesus' first miracle was at a wedding. How can you invite Jesus into your relationship in a deeper way? Consider praying together regularly or including Him in your decision-making.

3. Building a Faithful Legacy: Joshua's legacy was one of steadfast faith. How can you, as a couple, create a legacy of faith for your family or community? Talk about ways to serve together, or set goals for growing in faith as a couple.

4. Facing Trials with Faith: In Judges, Israel faced many trials. Discuss any trials you're currently facing and how you can support each other in faith. How can God's faithfulness help you both find strength and courage?

5. Strengthening Communication: In John 4, Jesus speaks with the Samaritan woman with honesty and compassion. How can you improve your communication with each other, sharing openly but with respect and love?

6. Relying on God's Strength: Psalm 57 reflects a reliance on God during times of distress. How can you, as a couple, turn to God during hard times, drawing strength from prayer and trust in His plan?

7. Renewal and New Beginnings: The people of Israel entered a new chapter in Judges, just as Jesus brings renewal. Are there ways in which your relationship needs a fresh start or a new perspective? Pray together, asking God to guide you in renewing your love and commitment.

Joint Couple Activity:
"Wedding Vows Renewal": Take some time to revisit your wedding vows. Write down ways you've seen each other grow in fulfilling those promises. Then, create a small, private ceremony to renew those vows, thanking God for His presence in your journey.

Couple for Week 18: Tobiah and Sarah

The story of Tobiah and Sarah is found in the Book of Tobit, an ancient Jewish narrative included in the Catholic and Orthodox Bibles. Sarah, a young woman, had been married seven times, but each husband died on their wedding night, cursed by the demon Asmodeus. Tobiah, the son of Tobit, a devout and faithful Israelite, was guided by the angel Raphael to Sarah's town. Despite the tragic fate of Sarah's previous marriages, Tobiah loved her and, with courage and trust in God, married her. Before their wedding night, they prayed together for God's protection, and through God's intervention, the demon was banished. Their marriage was blessed, and they went on to have a life filled with faith and devotion to God.

Lessons for Couples:

1. The Power of Prayer Together: Tobiah and Sarah's story demonstrates the importance of couples coming together in prayer, especially during challenges. Praying together strengthened their bond and invited God's protection and blessings into their marriage.

2. Trusting in God's Plan: Despite Sarah's tragic past and the fears associated with her previous marriages, Tobiah trusted in God's guidance. Couples can learn from this by placing their trust in God, even when facing difficulties or when things seem uncertain.

3. Relying on God for Protection: Tobiah and Sarah's decision to pray on their wedding night acknowledges that God is the ultimate protector. This teaches couples to rely on God's protection over their relationship, entrusting Him with any struggles or fears they face together.

4. Breaking Free from the Past: Sarah's past seemed cursed, yet Tobiah did not let it define their future. Couples can take inspiration from this, understanding that with faith, past wounds or fears can be healed, and a fresh, hopeful future can begin.

5. Support and Compassion for One Another's Burdens: Tobiah supported Sarah, showing compassion and understanding for her difficult experiences. Couples can learn the value of empathy and kindness toward each other, especially when facing personal struggles or past traumas.

6. Facing Challenges with Courage: Tobiah's marriage to Sarah, despite the ominous history of her previous marriages, teaches the importance of courage. Couples can be encouraged to face challenges together, believing in the strength of their love and in God's power to help them overcome obstacles.

7. Inviting God's Blessing on the Marriage from the Start: Tobiah and Sarah began their marriage by seeking God's blessing, emphasizing the importance of inviting God into a relationship from the very beginning. This teaches couples to build their relationship on a foundation of faith and mutual devotion to God.

8. Healing through God's Presence: Sarah's life, once marred by sorrow and loss, was transformed by her union with Tobiah and God's intervention. This teaches couples that God's presence can bring healing, hope, and new beginnings, no matter the hardships endured in the past.

9. The Role of Faithful Companions: Tobiah was guided by the angel Raphael, who led him to Sarah. Couples can learn the importance of surrounding themselves with faithful friends and mentors who encourage them to grow spiritually and make wise decisions.

10. Committing to Love with Selflessness and Patience: Tobiah's acceptance of Sarah, despite her tragic history, reveals a love that is patient, understanding, and selfless. Couples can take this example to heart, committing to love each other with understanding, grace, and the patience to overcome difficulties together.

Week 19

Faith, Courage, and the Power of God's Strength

Weekly Readings:

Day 127- Judges 6, Judges 7:1-8; John 5:16-30; Psalm 57:7-11
Day 128- Judges 7:8-25, Judges 8; John 5:31-47; Proverbs 11:19-28
Day 129- Judges 9; John 6:1-24; Psalm 58:1-11
Day 130- Judges 10, Judges 11; John 6:25-59; Psalm 59:1-8
Day 131- Judges 12, Judges 13; John 6:60-71, John 7:1-13; Psalm 59:9-19
Day 132- Judges 14, Judges 15; John 7:14-44; Proverbs 11:29-31, Proverbs 12:1-7
Day 133- Judges 16, Judges 17; John 7:45-53, John 8:1-11; Psalm 60:1-4

Weekly Reflection:

This week's readings bring us into the stories of Gideon, Jephthah, and Samson—figures who embody strength, faith, and courage in unique ways. Each faced challenges that seemed insurmountable, yet God used their weaknesses to showcase His power. In marriage, there are moments when we may feel weak or inadequate, but like these judges, we can find strength through God's presence and purpose.

In John 6, Jesus speaks of being the "bread of life," offering Himself as the sustenance we need. As a couple, this is a reminder of the importance of nourishing your spiritual lives together. Pray for one another and reflect on the ways you can support each other's faith journey, encouraging each other to draw closer to God.

The story of Samson's strength in Judges 16 highlights both human strength and human weakness. This story can remind us to lean on God in our relationship, recognizing that while we may falter, God remains faithful. Reflect together on how you can rely on God's strength to sustain your love and support for one another.

Weekly Discussion Prompts:

1. Finding Strength in God: Like Gideon, who felt inadequate, have you ever felt weak or unsure in your marriage? Discuss how you can encourage each other to rely on God for the strength you need.

2. Trusting God's Plan: Reflect on the story of Jephthah's faith in God's guidance. How do you trust God with your marriage, especially in uncertain times? Share ways you can grow in trust as a couple.

3. Nourishing Each Other: Jesus calls Himself the "bread of life." How can you provide spiritual "nourishment" to each other? Consider setting aside time for joint prayer, Bible study, or spiritual activities.

4. Overcoming Weaknesses Together: Samson's story shows both strength and weakness. Are there weaknesses in your relationship that need God's healing? Talk openly and seek ways to grow stronger together.

5. Forgiveness and Patience: Judges showcases moments of human failing and divine patience. How can you show each other greater patience or forgiveness? Discuss ways to cultivate these qualities in your marriage.

6. Stepping Out in Faith: Each judge acted in faith, despite personal shortcomings. Are there areas in your life or relationship where God may be calling you to take a step of faith? Encourage each other to take that step.

7. Recognizing God's Faithfulness: This week's psalms remind us of God's unwavering faithfulness. Share moments when you felt God's support in your marriage, and thank Him together for His enduring love.

Joint Couple Activity:

"Faith Wall": Choose a spot in your home and create a "Faith Wall" where you post scriptures, answered prayers, or faith reminders. As the week progresses, add notes on how God's strength and love have touched your relationship, building a visual testament to His faithfulness in your journey together.

Couple for Week 19: Hosea and Gomer

The story of Hosea and Gomer is one of the most striking portrayals of steadfast love and redemption in the Bible, found in the Book of Hosea. Hosea, a prophet, was instructed by God to marry Gomer, a woman who would be unfaithful to him. Despite Gomer's infidelity, which led her away from their home and into ruin, Hosea continually showed her love and forgiveness. He even went to the extent of buying her back from slavery to bring her home. Hosea's marriage to Gomer was a symbol of God's unwavering love for Israel, despite the nation's repeated unfaithfulness.

Lessons for Couples:

1. Unconditional Love and Forgiveness: Hosea's enduring love for Gomer, despite her infidelity, reflects the powerful message of unconditional love. Couples can learn from Hosea's example to extend grace and forgiveness in times of hardship, striving to love one another without conditions, as God loves His people.

2. Healing through Commitment: Hosea's commitment to Gomer, despite her wandering, shows that committed love can bring healing and transformation. In marriage, unwavering commitment can be a powerful force, helping couples to rebuild trust and intimacy even after significant struggles.

3. God's Redemption in Relationships: Hosea's story with Gomer illustrates that God's love is redemptive, healing even the most broken parts of a relationship. Couples can find hope in knowing that, with God's help, brokenness can lead to transformation and renewal.

4. Choosing to Restore Rather than Condemn: Hosea chose to restore his marriage rather than reject or condemn Gomer. This teaches couples the value of choosing reconciliation and working through issues rather than giving up, even when it is challenging.

5. Faithfulness to One's Promises: Hosea's loyalty reflects the importance of staying faithful to one's vows, even when circumstances are painful or disappointing. In marriage, being true to one's promises, even through tough times, is a powerful testament to commitment.

6. Recognizing the Value of Each Person: Despite Gomer's past and mistakes, Hosea valued her and sought her out, even buying her freedom. Couples can learn the importance of valuing each other, seeing past flaws, and cherishing each other's worth.

7. Embodying God's Grace in Marriage: Hosea's story with Gomer was meant to mirror God's grace and steadfast love for His people. This teaches couples to model God's grace in their marriage, showing patience, love, and compassion as God does with us.

8. Learning from Failures without Holding Grudges: Hosea's choice to bring Gomer back shows the importance of moving past mistakes without holding onto grudges. Couples can apply this by working through difficulties, letting go of resentment, and fostering an atmosphere of acceptance.

9. Love That Goes Beyond Feelings: Hosea's love was not based on feelings but on a deep commitment to God's command and to Gomer. Couples can learn from this that love in

marriage sometimes requires going beyond emotions and choosing to act in love, even when feelings falter.

10. Hope and Restoration in God's Timing: The story of Hosea and Gomer illustrates that God's timing can bring about restoration even in situations that seem hopeless. Couples can trust that, in God's time, wounds can heal, and love can be renewed, if they remain faithful to each other and to God.

Week 20

Faithfulness, Redemption, and New Beginnings

Weekly Readings:

Day 134- Judges 18, Judges 19; John 8:12-30; Psalm 60:5-12
Day 135- Judges 20, Judges 21; John 8:31-59; Psalm 61:1-8
Day 136- Ruth 1, Ruth 2; John 9:1-34; Proverbs 12:8-17
Day 137- Ruth 3, Ruth 4; John 9:35-41, John 10:1-21; Psalm 62:1-12
Day 138- 1 Samuel 1, 1 Samuel 2:1-26; John 10:22-42; Psalm 63:1-11
Day 139- 1 Samuel 2:27-36, 1 Samuel 3, 1 Samuel 4; John 11:1-44; Psalm 64:1-10
Day 140- 1 Samuel 5, 1 Samuel 6, 1 Samuel 7; John 11:45-57, John 12:1-11; Proverbs 12:18-27

Weekly Reflection:

This week's readings introduce us to the deep loyalty and love found in the story of Ruth, as well as the journey of Samuel's mother, Hannah, whose prayers and trust in God's faithfulness are answered in miraculous ways. In Ruth, we see a beautiful example of devotion, sacrifice, and redemption. Ruth's loyalty to Naomi reflects the commitment and faithfulness that are essential in marriage. As a couple, this story serves as a reminder of the blessings that flow from deep loyalty, support, and shared faith.

In John 10, Jesus declares, "I am the good shepherd." This assurance of God's care over us resonates within marriage. Like sheep guided by a shepherd, couples thrive when they follow God's lead, leaning on Him for wisdom and protection. Discuss together how you can allow God to be the guide and protector of your marriage.

In 1 Samuel 1, Hannah's story of longing for a child and her eventual joy is a powerful reminder of God's faithfulness and the importance of patience in waiting. In your relationship, whether in times of waiting, loss, or new beginnings, place your trust in God's timing and purpose. God's faithfulness to Hannah shows that He truly hears our deepest desires.

Weekly Discussion Prompts:

1. Loyalty and Commitment: Ruth's commitment to Naomi is a beautiful expression of loyalty. How can you show greater commitment to each other, especially in challenging times?

2. Faith in Action: Naomi and Ruth took bold steps of faith despite their hardships. How can you encourage each other to act in faith within your marriage?

3. God as Our Shepherd: Jesus describes Himself as the "good shepherd" who cares for His sheep. Reflect on ways you can allow God to guide your decisions as a couple, bringing peace and direction.

4. The Power of Praying Together: Like Hannah, who cried out to God, prayer is a powerful tool. How can you prioritize prayer together, especially in times of need or uncertainty?

5. Trusting in God's Timing: Hannah had to wait for God's answer. Is there something you're both waiting for? Discuss how you can strengthen each other's faith as you trust in God's timing.

6. Support in Seasons of Suffering: Ruth's loyalty shows a deep commitment to love even through suffering. How can you support each other during difficult times?

7. Embracing Redemption in Marriage: Ruth's story is one of redemption and new beginnings. How can you bring a sense of renewal to your relationship, forgiving past hurts and embracing the future?

Joint Couple Activity:
"Faith and New Beginnings Journal": Set aside time to create a journal together. Write about moments where God has shown His faithfulness in your marriage. Include prayers, answered or pending, and note times of new beginnings. This journal can serve as a reminder of God's presence and a source of encouragement during challenging times.

Couple for Week 20: Abraham and Keturah

After the death of Sarah, Abraham married Keturah, who became his second wife (or concubine, according to some interpretations). Keturah bore Abraham six sons: Zimran, Jokshan, Medan, Midian, Ishbak, and Shuah. Together, Abraham and Keturah had a lineage that would eventually spread across various regions, playing significant roles in the development of different tribes and nations. Although these sons did not inherit the covenant promise that was given to Isaac, Abraham provided for them and sent them away to settle in the east, ensuring that Isaac would remain his primary heir.

Lessons for Couples:

1. Life After Loss: Abraham's marriage to Keturah after Sarah's death shows that love and companionship can continue even after the loss of a spouse. This serves as a reminder that, after grieving, it's okay to open one's heart to new relationships and companionship in God's timing.

2. Legacy and Provision for Family: Abraham made provisions for Keturah's sons while also safeguarding Isaac's inheritance. Couples can learn from this the importance of planning thoughtfully for each family member, balancing fairness with the fulfillment of specific responsibilities or promises.

3. The Importance of Family Unity: By ensuring that Keturah's sons would settle elsewhere, Abraham minimized potential conflicts within his family. This teaches couples the value of family unity and the importance of thoughtful decisions that maintain peace among family members.

4. God's Purpose in New Beginnings: Abraham's relationship with Keturah illustrates that God has a purpose for every season of life. Couples, even in later stages of life, can embrace new beginnings, trusting that God can still use them to accomplish His plans.

5. Respect and Honor in Second Marriages: Abraham treated Keturah with respect, providing for her children while honoring God's promises to Isaac. This shows the importance of honoring both present relationships and past commitments, particularly when blending families.

6. Openness to God's Blessings in Later Life: Abraham's life shows that God's blessings aren't limited by age. Couples can find encouragement in knowing that God's plans for them may continue to unfold even in later years, as long as they remain open to His guidance.

7. Trusting God with Future Generations: Abraham trusted God with the future of all his children, even as he fulfilled the covenant with Isaac. Couples can apply this by trusting God with their children's and grandchildren's futures, knowing that His plans are ultimately for their good.

8. Embracing Roles of Mentorship and Wisdom: Abraham, in his later years, became a father and leader for many. This teaches couples that as they grow older, they can take on roles of mentorship and guidance for their family and community, sharing the wisdom they've gained.

Week 21

Trusting God's Plan and Growing in Humility

Weekly Readings:

Day 141- 1 Samuel 8, 1 Samuel 9, 1 Samuel 10:1-8; John 12:12-26; Psalm 65:1-13
Day 142- 1 Samuel 10:9-27, 1 Samuel 11, 1 Samuel 12; John 12:37-50, John 13:1-17; Psalm 66:1-12
Day 143- 1 Samuel 13, 1 Samuel 14:1-23; John 13:18-38; Psalm 66:13-20
Day 144- 1 Samuel 14:24-52, 1 Samuel 15; John 14:1-31; Proverbs 12:28, Proverbs 13:1-9
Day 145- 1 Samuel 16, 1 Samuel 17:1-37; John 15, John 16:1-4; Psalm 67:1-7
Day 146- 1 Samuel 17:38-58, 1 Samuel 18; John 16:5-33, John 17:1-5; Psalm 68:1-6
Day 147- 1 Samuel 19, 1 Samuel 20; John 17:6-26; Psalm 68:7-14

Weekly Reflection:

This week centers on themes of trust, humility, and courage in the face of life's battles. In 1 Samuel, we encounter the story of Israel's first king, Saul, and the young shepherd David, chosen by God for his humility and faith. David's battle against Goliath illustrates that with God, no obstacle is insurmountable. In marriage, we often face "giants" of our own, whether they're challenges in communication, financial strain, or health issues. Reflect on how David's faith in God can inspire you to face these challenges together, trusting that God fights with and for you.

In John 13, Jesus washes His disciples' feet, a powerful act of humility and service. Jesus' example is especially meaningful for marriage. Serving each other with humility and love strengthens the bond between partners and allows for deeper unity. Discuss ways you can humbly serve each other, acknowledging that acts of kindness and selflessness are powerful expressions of love.

In John 14, Jesus tells His followers, "Do not let your hearts be troubled." Lean on each other and remember that God's peace is available to you as a couple, even during difficult seasons. This peace, rooted in His love and sovereignty, can be the foundation of your relationship.

Weekly Discussion Prompts:

1. Trust in God's Plan: Reflect on how David trusted God's guidance, even when facing a giant. How can you both rely on God when facing challenges together?

2. Serving Each Other: Jesus washed His disciples' feet as an act of humble service. What small acts of service can you do for each other to show love in your everyday life?

3. Embracing God's Peace: Jesus encouraged His followers not to be troubled. How can you invite God's peace into your relationship, especially when feeling anxious or overwhelmed?

4. Facing Giants Together: Whether they're external or internal struggles, discuss the "giants" you each face. How can you support each other in these battles, drawing strength from your faith?

5. Humility and Leadership: Saul struggled with obedience and pride, while David was humble in heart. How can you practice humility within your marriage, especially in times of conflict or decision-making?

6. God as Protector: Psalm 68 speaks of God as a defender. Reflect together on times when you have felt God's protection in your marriage. How can these experiences inspire gratitude and faith?

7. Strengthening Each Other's Faith: Discuss ways you can actively strengthen one another's faith. How can you remind each other of God's promises and pray together for specific challenges?

Joint Couple Activity:

"Serving in Love" Exercise: Plan a day to serve each other in meaningful ways. You could prepare a meal, write a heartfelt note, or do an activity the other enjoys. Let this day remind you of Jesus' example of humility and love, strengthening your bond as you express care and devotion.

A Team for Week 21: Noah and His Wife

Noah and his wife stand as one of the earliest examples of a couple united in faith. Known for their role in the story of the Great Flood, they shared the monumental task of preparing for a cataclysm that would wipe out nearly all of humanity. Chosen by God for his righteousness, Noah was given the seemingly impossible command to build an ark—a massive wooden structure capable of housing his family and a pair of every living creature on earth. Despite ridicule and isolation, Noah and his wife obeyed God's instructions, demonstrating unwavering faith and commitment to the task set before them. Together, they persevered, waiting on God's timing as the rain fell for forty days and nights, trusting that His purpose would ultimately be revealed. Their family became the foundation for the renewal of human and animal life on earth, leaving a legacy of faith and obedience that continues to inspire.

Lessons for Couples

1. Faith in God's Plan Amid Uncertainty: Noah and his wife trusted God's command even when it didn't seem logical by human standards. They likely faced scorn and skepticism from their community, yet they chose to move forward with confidence in God's wisdom. For couples, this story illustrates the importance of seeking God's direction together, trusting that even when the journey is unclear, faith can guide the way.

2. Mutual Support and Shared Sacrifice: Building an ark of such size required intense labor, dedication, and sacrifice. Noah's wife is an example of a spouse who remained steadfast in her support, even when it meant hard work and facing unknowns. Couples today can draw strength from their example, remembering the value of mutual support and shared sacrifice, especially when life presents daunting tasks. In a relationship, helping each other carry burdens fosters a sense of unity and purpose.

3. Creating a Foundation for Future Generations: Noah and his wife not only saved their own family but also ensured a future for all humankind. Their story encourages couples to consider their legacy, building a foundation rooted in faith, love, and righteousness. As partners, working together to instill values in their family or community can lead to blessings that outlast their lifetime.

4. Standing Together in Isolation and Trials: As they entered the ark, Noah's family left behind everything familiar, relying solely on God and each other. They endured the loneliness of the flood with no certainty other than their faith in God's promises. This illustrates the importance of a couple's unity in difficult times; when the world feels isolating, standing together with faith can sustain them through even the darkest seasons.

5. Trust in God's Timing: The floodwaters surrounded them for months, and Noah's family waited patiently for God's sign to leave the ark. This period of waiting teaches couples

the value of patience and trust. While they may desire quick answers or immediate solutions, true faith often involves trusting in God's timing. In marriage, knowing when to move forward or when to wait requires a shared commitment to seeking and trusting God's direction.

6. Renewal and New Beginnings: After the flood, Noah and his wife stepped out into a new world, tasked with rebuilding and renewing life on earth. Couples are reminded that even after seasons of loss or hardship, God provides new beginnings and the strength to start afresh. Like Noah and his wife, couples can find hope in God's ability to bring purpose out of trials and look forward to the future with optimism and faith.

Noah and his wife's story is a profound testament to partnership rooted in faith, resilience, and dedication. By walking in step with God and each other, they overcame extraordinary challenges. Couples today can find encouragement in their example, knowing that with mutual support and trust in God's plan, they too can withstand the floods that life may bring.

Week 22

Forgiveness, Humility, and Trusting in God's Redemption

Weekly Readings:

Day 148- 1 Samuel 21, 1 Samuel 22, 1 Samuel 23; John 18:1-24; Proverbs 13:10-19
Day 149- 1 Samuel 24, 1 Samuel 25; John 18:25-40; Psalm 68:15-20
Day 150- 1 Samuel 26, 1 Samuel 27, 1 Samuel 28; John 19:1-27; Psalm 68:21-27
Day 151- 1 Samuel 29, 1 Samuel 30, 1 Samuel 31; John 19:28-42, John 20:1-9; Psalm 68:28-35
Day 152- 2 Samuel 1, 2 Samuel 2:1-7; John 20:10-31; Proverbs 13:20-25, Proverbs 14:1-4
Day 153- 2 Samuel 2:8-32, 2 Samuel 3:1-21; John 21:1-25; Psalm 69:1-12
Day 154- 2 Samuel 3:22-39, 2 Samuel 4, 2 Samuel 5:1-5; Acts 1:1-22; Psalm 69:13-28

Weekly Reflection:

This week focuses on forgiveness, humility, and God's plan for redemption, as seen in the life of David and the resurrection of Jesus. In 1 Samuel, we see David's choice to forgive Saul, even when he has the chance to retaliate. David's mercy and humility show that true strength lies in trusting God's justice. Discuss together how forgiveness has played a role in your relationship, and reflect on how you can continue to show mercy to each other, just as God shows mercy to us.

In John's Gospel, we walk through the events of Jesus' trial, crucifixion, and resurrection. Christ's sacrifice is the ultimate act of love and forgiveness, reminding us of the grace we are called to extend to one another. When times are difficult, consider how you can offer grace and understanding to each other, following Christ's example.

In Acts 1, we see the promise of the Holy Spirit and the beginning of the early Church. As a couple, the Holy Spirit is present to guide you, offering wisdom, peace, and strength to face life's challenges. Together, ask the Holy Spirit to deepen your bond and fill your relationship with His fruit—love, joy, peace, and patience.

Weekly Discussion Prompts:

1. Forgiveness in Marriage: Reflect on how David forgave Saul repeatedly. In what ways can you practice forgiveness in your relationship? How has forgiveness helped you grow closer as a couple?

2. Humility and Grace: David responded to Saul's pursuit with humility. How can you both practice humility in times of conflict or misunderstanding?

3. Christ's Sacrifice and Love: Jesus endured suffering out of love for us. How does Christ's love inspire you in your own relationship, especially in moments of sacrifice or difficulty?

4. Experiencing God's Redemption: The resurrection brings hope of new beginnings. What areas in your relationship would benefit from a renewal of hope, love, or forgiveness?

5. Guided by the Holy Spirit: The early Church relied on the Holy Spirit for strength and unity. How can you invite the Holy Spirit to guide and strengthen your marriage?

6. The Gift of Patience: Proverbs emphasizes the importance of patience. Discuss moments when practicing patience has strengthened your relationship. How can you cultivate more patience in daily life?

7. Relying on God's Strength: Psalm 69 speaks of calling on God in times of distress. How can you support each other by praying together and seeking God's strength when challenges arise?

Joint Couple Activity:

"Practicing Forgiveness" Reflection: Set aside time to share anything that has caused hurt or misunderstanding recently, and intentionally forgive each other. Pray together, asking God for a renewed spirit of love and mercy in your relationship. Let this activity remind you of the power of grace and the importance of forgiving each other as Christ forgives us.

Couple for Week 22: Micaiah and His Wife

Micaiah is a prophet mentioned in the Bible, particularly in 1 Kings 22, where he stands as a faithful messenger of God in the face of great opposition. King Ahab of Israel and King Jehoshaphat of Judah sought the counsel of prophets regarding a military campaign against Ramoth-Gilead. While 400 prophets predicted success, Micaiah, at the risk of displeasing the kings, prophesied their defeat. His prophecy came true when Ahab was killed in battle, highlighting Micaiah's unwavering commitment to truth. However, little is mentioned about Micaiah's wife, as the Bible primarily focuses on his prophetic role and boldness in speaking God's truth.

Lessons for Couples:

1. Standing Firm in God's Truth: While Micaiah is known for his boldness in speaking God's truth, this can be a powerful example for couples. Standing firm in what God says, even when it's unpopular or uncomfortable, requires mutual strength and trust. Couples can support each other in staying true to God's word, even when society or others may pressure them to compromise.

2. Supporting Each Other in Obedience: Micaiah was steadfast in declaring God's message, despite the danger and opposition he faced. Though his wife's role is not explicitly mentioned, we can assume that her support and faith would have been vital, especially during challenging times. In marriage, it's important to support one another in obeying God's commands and staying true to His calling, even when it's difficult.

3. Courage in the Face of Opposition: Micaiah's courage in delivering an unpopular message is a reminder that couples might face situations where they have to stand alone or go against the flow. Together, they can find strength in God and in each other, remaining faithful to His calling even when others may not understand or approve.

4. God's Sovereignty and Faithfulness: Micaiah's prophecy came true, showing that God's word is always faithful and true. Couples can find comfort and confidence in God's sovereignty, knowing that He is always in control, no matter how uncertain life may seem.

5. Mutual Encouragement in Marriage: Though the Bible doesn't elaborate on Micaiah's relationship with his wife, it's likely that the challenges he faced as a prophet would have required support from his family. In marriage, it's important to encourage each other in times of struggle, offering emotional and spiritual support to help each other persevere in faith.

6. Living with Integrity and Honor: Micaiah did not back down from his convictions, even when it meant angering the king and risking his life. Couples can learn from this the

importance of living with integrity and honoring God in all aspects of life, especially in decisions that might not align with popular opinion.

7. Trusting God with Outcomes: Micaiah trusted God's word would come to pass, even when the prophecy was unpopular. Couples should remember that obedience to God's will is not always about the immediate outcome but about trusting God and remaining faithful, regardless of what others might say or do.

8. Role of a Godly Spouse: Though the Bible doesn't specifically address Micaiah's wife, her role can be inferred as supportive, especially during such a tumultuous time. This encourages couples to always be supportive and loving, trusting God's plan and encouraging one another in their roles.

Week 23

Repentance, Restoration, and the Power of the Holy Spirit

Weekly Readings:

Day 155- 2 Samuel 5:6-25, 2 Samuel 6; Acts 1:23-26, Acts 2:1-21; Psalm 69:29-36
Day 156- 2 Samuel 7, 2 Samuel 8; Acts 2:22-47; Proverbs 14:4-14
Day 157- 2 Samuel 9, 2 Samuel 10; Acts 3; Psalm 70:1-5
Day 158- 2 Samuel 11, 2 Samuel 12; Acts 4:1-22; Psalm 71:1-8
Day 159- 2 Samuel 13; Acts 4:23-37, Acts 5:1-11; Psalm 71:9-18
Day 160- 2 Samuel 14, 2 Samuel 15:1-12; Acts 5:12-42; Proverbs 14:15-24
Day 161- 2 Samuel 15:13-37, 2 Samuel 16:1-14; Acts 6, Acts 7:1-19; Psalm 71:19-24

Weekly Reflection:

This week invites you to reflect on repentance, restoration, and the transformative power of the Holy Spirit. In 2 Samuel, we observe King David's profound journey from success to sin, repentance, and eventual restoration. David's life serves as a reminder that no one is beyond God's mercy. Discuss the role of repentance in your own lives and relationship, and how extending forgiveness to each other helps strengthen your bond.

In Acts, the arrival of the Holy Spirit empowers the disciples to spread the Gospel boldly. The early Church's spirit of unity, generosity, and courage invites you to reflect on how the Holy Spirit can work powerfully within your marriage. Talk together about how you can open yourselves more to the Spirit's guidance, especially in moments of difficulty or decision-making.

As you study Proverbs and Psalms, notice how these readings emphasize wisdom, humility, and trust in God. As a couple, lean into these virtues, asking God for the wisdom to approach each day with humility and faith.

Weekly Discussion Prompts:

1. Repentance in Marriage: Reflect on David's story of repentance. How can seeking forgiveness and offering grace to each other deepen your relationship?

2. Restoration Through God's Grace: David's life was marked by God's restorative love. How have you experienced restoration or healing in your relationship? What areas might still need God's touch?

3. Living with Integrity: Acts highlights the importance of integrity in the early Church. How can you both live with integrity in your relationship, especially in your words and actions toward each other?

4. The Gift of the Holy Spirit: The disciples were empowered by the Holy Spirit to carry out God's work. How can you invite the Holy Spirit to guide your marriage and family life?

5. Generosity and Unity: The early Christians shared everything and looked out for each other's needs. What does generosity look like in your relationship? Are there ways you can support each other more fully?

6. Wisdom for Daily Decisions: Proverbs encourages wise decision-making. What decisions or challenges are you currently facing that could benefit from God's wisdom?

7. Trusting God in Adversity: Psalm 71 speaks of trusting God through trials. Share times when you've had to trust God through difficult moments together. How did your faith bring you through?

Joint Couple Activity:

"Renewing Our Vows of Love and Forgiveness": Set aside a time to affirm your commitment to one another. Reflect on the past week and share any moments when you could have been more understanding, patient, or forgiving. Then, each of you take turns expressing your commitment to continue growing in love, forgiveness, and unity. Conclude by praying together, asking God to fill your relationship with His grace, wisdom, and strength.

Couple for Week 23: Samson and His Wife

(First Marriage to a Philistine Woman)

Samson, one of the judges of Israel, is known for his incredible strength, which was a divine gift linked to his Nazirite vow. His first marriage, which is highlighted in the Book of Judges, involves a Philistine woman from Timnah. His parents were against this marriage, as it was an alliance with the enemy of Israel, but Samson insisted on marrying her. The story is filled with conflict, particularly surrounding the riddle Samson posed at his wedding feast, which led to betrayal and enmity between him and the Philistines. This marriage ended in tragedy after Samson's wife was given to his best man, and later, she and her father were killed by the Philistines.

Lessons for Couples:

1. The Importance of Godly Wisdom in Decision-Making:

   Samson's parents advised against the marriage, yet Samson pursued it out of his own desire. This decision led to pain and tragedy. For couples, this serves as a reminder to seek godly counsel and wisdom when making important decisions, particularly in marriage. It's important to evaluate whether choices align with God's will, especially when personal desires or external pressures cloud judgment.

2. Marriage Is More Than Personal Desire:

   Samson's marriage was driven by his personal desires and not necessarily by God's plan. His choice to marry outside of Israelite faith led to conflict and suffering. For couples, the lesson here is that marriage is not just about personal fulfillment or physical attraction; it is a covenant rooted in shared faith, values, and God's guidance.

3. The Dangers of Allowing External Influences to Control Relationships:

   The Philistines played a significant role in the conflict of Samson's marriage. His wife's betrayal, influenced by the pressure from her people, caused a rift that ultimately led to separation. This highlights the importance of maintaining strong boundaries with external influences and protecting the sanctity of the marital relationship from harmful outside pressures.

4. Conflict and Misunderstanding Can Erode Trust:

   Samson's riddle and the resulting betrayal highlight how easily misunderstandings and lack of communication can create distrust in a marriage. The Bible shows that conflicts, if not addressed and resolved with honesty and understanding, can lead to deeper divisions. Couples should prioritize clear, honest communication and work through their issues together.

5. Commitment to God's Will in Marriage:

Samson's life was full of moments where he failed to uphold his Nazirite vow and neglected God's will. His marriage story reminds couples of the importance of remaining committed to God's purposes for their union. A marriage centered on God and His plan is far more likely to endure hardship and flourish despite difficulties.

6. Forgiveness and Reconciliation:

Though Samson's first marriage ended tragically, his story also reflects God's ability to work through failure and human mistakes. Couples can learn that even after mistakes, there is room for reconciliation, healing, and restoration. Marriage requires forgiveness and the willingness to rebuild trust after betrayals or disappointments.

7. Protecting Marriage from Distractions and Idols:

Samson's actions, particularly his later relationships with Delilah, were deeply influenced by his personal desires, which led him away from God's plan for his life and his marriage. For couples, it is essential to avoid distractions or "idols" that can take priority over the marriage relationship and God's calling. Keeping God at the center of the relationship provides strength and direction.

8. Learning from Mistakes and Growing Together:

Samson's first marriage ended in failure, but the story is not without hope. Couples can learn from the mistakes of others, such as Samson's hasty decisions and inability to communicate effectively, to avoid similar pitfalls. Recognizing flaws and growing through them together strengthens the marriage.

Week 24

Leadership, Legacy, and the Power of God's Presence

Weekly Readings:

Day 162- 2 Samuel 16:15-23, 2 Samuel 17, 2 Samuel 18:1-18; Acts 7:20-43; Psalm 72:1-20

Day 163- 2 Samuel 18:19-33, 2 Samuel 19; Acts 7:44-60, Acts 8:1-3; Psalm 73:1-14

Day 164- 2 Samuel 20, 2 Samuel 21; Acts 8:4-40; Proverbs 14:25-35

Day 165- 2 Samuel 22, 2 Samuel 23:1-7; Acts 9:1-31; Psalm 73:15-28

Day 166- 2 Samuel 23:8-39, 2 Samuel 24:1-25; Acts 9:32-43, Acts 10:1-23; Psalms 74:1-9

Day 167- 1 Kings 1, 1 Kings 2:1-12; Acts 10:23-48, Acts 11:1-18; Psalm 74:10-17

Day 168- 1 Kings 2:13-46, 1 Kings 3:1-15; Acts 11:19-30, Acts 12:1-19; Proverbs 15:1-10

Weekly Reflection:

This week, our readings focus on leadership, legacy, and the power of God's presence in our lives and relationships. In 2 Samuel, we see the unfolding drama of leadership struggles, betrayals, and reconciliation. David's leadership, marked by personal failures and humility, teaches us that true leadership is about trusting God and seeking His guidance, even in times of crisis. The complexities of relationships—both familial and political—reflect the difficulties and opportunities that we face in marriage and family life. As a couple, reflect on how your relationship mirrors these dynamics, and how you can strengthen your leadership and mutual support within your home.

The Acts readings show the early Church's boldness in proclaiming the Gospel, even in the face of persecution. The stories of Stephen and Philip encourage us to be bold in our faith and to be willing to stand firm for what we believe, even when it's difficult. In your marriage, you are called to be a unified front, boldly witnessing to each other and those around you. How can you both support one another in your individual and shared spiritual journeys?

As we meditate on Proverbs and Psalms, the emphasis is on the righteousness of God's leadership and His provision for His people. Trusting in God's wisdom and seeking His guidance in all decisions, big and small, will bring peace and clarity to your relationship.

Weekly Discussion Prompts:

1. Leadership and Humility: Reflect on David's leadership and how he handled the challenges of betrayal and conflict. How can you both demonstrate humility and wisdom in your relationship, especially during times of difficulty?

2. Legacy of Faith: David's legacy of faith was shaped by his trust in God. What kind of legacy do you hope to leave in your family and community? How can you nurture a strong spiritual foundation together?

3. Witnessing Together: The early Church, even in persecution, boldly proclaimed the Gospel. How can you as a couple be a bold witness to your faith, both within your home and outside?

4. God's Guidance in Leadership: Both David and Solomon had moments where they sought God's wisdom for leading. How do you seek God's wisdom in your daily lives and decisions? Are there decisions in your marriage that require you to seek God's guidance together?

5. Handling Conflict: How do you handle conflict in your relationship, and what can you learn from David's experiences of reconciliation? How can you approach conflict with love, wisdom, and trust in God?

6. Persevering in Faith: Stephen and Philip faced great opposition in their missions but remained faithful. What challenges or opposition do you face in your spiritual journey, and how can you encourage one another to stay firm in faith?

7. Trusting in God's Provision: Psalm 72 speaks of God's provision for His people. How do you see God's provision in your relationship, and how can you rely on His wisdom and care as you navigate challenges?

"Building a Legacy of Faith": Together, write a prayer or vision statement for your family or relationship. Discuss what kind of legacy you want to create in the next five to ten years. Consider areas of your marriage where you want to grow, both spiritually and relationally. Pray together for guidance in these areas, asking God to help you build a foundation that reflects His love, wisdom, and strength. Share specific ways you can support each other in this journey.

Couple for Week 24: Lot and His Wife

Lot, the nephew of Abraham, was a man who lived in the prosperous city of Sodom. When God decided to destroy Sodom and its sister city Gomorrah due to their wickedness, He sent angels to warn Lot and his family. They were instructed to flee the city and not look back. Lot's wife, however, disobeyed this command and looked back at the burning city, turning into a pillar of salt. Lot, with his two daughters, escaped to a small town called Zoar, and from there, the story of his wife's disobedience became a tragic lesson.

Lessons for Couples:

1. The Dangers of Attachment to the Past:

   Lot's wife looked back at Sodom, despite being warned not to, and turned into a pillar of salt. This action symbolizes a deep attachment to the past, especially to the sinful lifestyle of Sodom. For couples, it serves as a reminder that lingering in the past can hinder progress and growth in the present and future. Holding on to old habits, regrets, or material attachments can prevent the couple from moving forward into God's plan for their lives.

2. Obedience to God's Commands:

   God gave clear instructions to Lot's family: do not look back. Lot's wife's disobedience to this command resulted in her tragic end. This highlights the importance of obeying God's instructions, even when we don't fully understand or agree with them. In marriage, obedience to God's will—whether in difficult or easy times—can help avoid unnecessary pitfalls and lead to blessings.

3. Distraction from God's Protection:

   Lot's wife's disobedience came at a critical moment when her family's safety depended on following God's directive. The act of looking back was a distraction that prevented her from focusing on God's salvation. For couples, this is a reminder that distractions—whether from past experiences, fears, or desires—can divert attention away from the greater blessings and protection God wants to give. Keeping focus on God's guidance and promises is essential for lasting peace and joy.

4. The Importance of Moving Forward Together:

   Lot and his wife were supposed to leave Sodom together, yet her action of looking back signifies a failure to move forward with her husband. For couples, it's essential to grow together, leaving behind old hurts, past mistakes, and regrets. The couple's journey is one of mutual growth, where both partners need to support each other in embracing the future, even when it's difficult to let go of the past.

5. God's Warning Should Not Be Taken Lightly:

   The destruction of Sodom and Gomorrah was a clear manifestation of God's judgment, and the command to leave was a direct warning. Lot's wife's choice to disregard God's warning leads to a tragic consequence. For couples, this illustrates that God's warnings should be heeded with seriousness and urgency. Ignoring God's guidance in relationships can lead to disastrous consequences, while trusting in His wisdom brings protection and blessings.

6. The Importance of Trusting God's Timing:

   Lot and his family were given a chance to escape and were instructed to flee without looking back. Lot's wife's hesitation to follow God's command shows a lack of trust in His timing and provision. Couples can learn from this the importance of trusting in God's plan, timing, and leading in their marriage, especially during times of uncertainty or hardship.

7. Letting Go of Sinful Habits and Attachments:

   Sodom's destruction represents God's judgment on sin, and Lot's wife's attachment to it symbolized the pull of sinful desires. For couples, this story reminds them of the importance of letting go of sin and anything that might hinder spiritual growth in their marriage. Whether it is harmful habits, addictions, or toxic relationships, couples should work together to distance themselves from anything that does not align with God's holiness.

8. God's Mercy and Protection for Those Who Follow His Word:

   Though Lot's wife turned into a pillar of salt, God showed mercy to Lot and his daughters. This reminds couples that even when one partner falters, God's protection and grace are still available to those who continue to follow His lead. Couples are called to support each other in faith, helping one another stay focused on God's will and avoid the temptations that can lead to destruction.

Week 25

Wisdom, Choices, and Divine Guidance

Weekly Readings:

Day 169- 1 Kings 3:16-28, 1 Kings 4, 1 Kings 5; Acts 12:19-25, Acts 13:1-12; Psalm 74:18-23
Day 170- 1 Kings 6, 1 Kings 7:1-22; Acts 13:13-41; Psalm 75:1-10
Day 171- 1 Kings 7:23-51, 1 Kings 8:1-21; Acts 13:42-52, Acts 14:1-7; Psalm 76:1-12
Day 172- 1 Kings 8:22-66, 1 Kings 9:1-9; Acts 14:8-28; Proverbs 15:11-20
Day 173- 1 Kings 9:10-28, 1 Kings 10, 1 Kings 11:1-13; Acts 15:1-21; Psalm 77:1-9
Day 174- 1 Kings 11:14-43, 1 Kings 12:1-24; Acts 15:22-41; Psalm 77:10-20
Day 175- 1 Kings 12:25-33, 1 Kings 13, 1 Kings 14:1-20; Acts 16:1-15; Psalm 78:1-8

Weekly Reflection:

This week's readings call us to consider the profound wisdom of God and the importance of seeking His guidance in our choices. King Solomon's wisdom is showcased in his judgment (1 Kings 3:16-28), where his understanding is not only remarkable but divinely granted. The decisions Solomon made shaped the future of Israel, and his wisdom remains a model of godly discernment. For couples, these passages prompt us to ask: How can we be wise in our decisions as a couple, both in our relationship and in our family life?

Solomon's reign, marked by prosperity and monumental achievements in the building of the temple (1 Kings 6-8), also highlights how important it is to remember God's presence and honor Him in all we do. As we make decisions in our marriages, especially as we plan for the future, it's important to consider how we can align those choices with God's will and prioritize His guidance over personal desires.

In Acts, we see the apostles and the early church forging ahead with boldness, carrying out the mission of God despite persecution. The readings invite us to ask how we can support one another in carrying out God's call in our lives, just as the early church did. Their commitment to spreading the Gospel challenges us to examine our own willingness to be faithful, no matter the cost.

Finally, the Psalms and Proverbs give us much to reflect on as they point us to God's faithfulness, justice, and the value of righteous living. As a couple, this is a time to meditate on God's promises, trusting that He will guide us and bless our choices when we honor Him.

Weekly Discussion Prompts:

1. Wisdom in Decision-Making: Solomon's wisdom was given by God to guide the people. How can you seek wisdom together in your relationship? What decisions do you face where God's wisdom should be the foundation?

2. Honoring God in Our Actions: Solomon's temple was built to honor God. How can you honor God together in your marriage and family life? Are there specific actions or choices that you feel called to take that would show God's priority in your relationship?

3. Persevering in Faith: The early church faced persecution but remained faithful. How do you support each other in remaining strong in your faith, even during challenges or doubts?

4. Building a Spiritual Foundation: Just as Solomon built a temple for God's presence, what are some ways you can build a stronger spiritual foundation in your relationship? How can you make time for prayer, worship, and Scripture together?

5. The Role of Prayer: Solomon's prayer in 1 Kings 8 demonstrates deep reliance on God's guidance. How do you incorporate prayer in your relationship? How can you make prayer a more central part of your daily life together?

6. Faithfulness in Times of Prosperity and Adversity: Solomon's reign began with great prosperity, but later in his life, his choices led him away from God. How can you stay faithful to God, regardless of life's circumstances, and encourage one another to walk in God's ways?

7. Generosity and Service: The apostles boldly served, even in the face of difficulty. How can you serve others together, and what role does generosity play in your marriage? How can you both be intentional in acts of service, both within your home and in your community?

"Building a Legacy of Wisdom": Together, read 1 Kings 3:16-28 and discuss the key elements of Solomon's wise judgment. How can you apply these elements to your own decision-making as a couple? Identify one area of your life—whether it's finances, parenting, or future planning—where you will commit to seeking wisdom from God. Create a plan for how you will go about making that decision together, keeping God at the center.

Couple for Week 25: Zechariah and Elizabeth

Zechariah and Elizabeth were a righteous couple, both from priestly families, living in the days of King Herod. Despite their faithful lives, they were childless, and Elizabeth was considered barren, which caused them much sorrow in their old age. Zechariah, a priest, was performing his duties in the temple when the angel Gabriel appeared to him, announcing that his wife would bear a son, to be named John. Zechariah, skeptical due to their old age, questioned the angel, and as a result, he was struck mute until the child was born. Elizabeth, however, believed the message, and in time, she gave birth to John, who would later become known as John the Baptist. Zechariah's speech was restored after he named his son, in obedience to the angel's instructions.

Lessons for Couples:

1. Trust in God's Timing and Promises:

    Zechariah and Elizabeth waited many years for a child, and their faith in God remained strong despite the hardship. Their story teaches couples the importance of trusting God's timing, especially when waiting for something important, whether it's children, healing, or dreams to be fulfilled. God's timing is always perfect, and even in times of doubt, we are called to trust in His plan for our lives.

2. Faith Over Doubt:

    While Elizabeth believed the angel's message immediately, Zechariah's initial reaction was one of doubt. His questioning of God's promise resulted in him being temporarily silenced. This serves as a reminder to couples that faith, rather than doubt, is essential in a relationship with God. In moments of uncertainty, it's important to trust in God's word, knowing that He will fulfill His promises in due time.

3. God Works in Unexpected Ways:

    Zechariah and Elizabeth, both advanced in age, would not have expected to have a child. Yet, God worked a miracle in their lives. This teaches couples that God often works in unexpected ways, and His plans for us can surpass our wildest expectations.

Couples should remain open to God's unexpected ways of blessing them, whether through children, opportunities, or challenges that bring growth.

4. Endurance and Patience in Faith:

Elizabeth endured years of waiting and societal disappointment, as being childless was seen as a great misfortune at the time. Yet, she continued to live a life of faithfulness. Their story encourages couples to remain patient and endure hardships in their journey together. The reward often comes after seasons of waiting, and couples should support each other in maintaining faith and hope.

5. The Power of Prayer:

Zechariah and Elizabeth were both devout, and they prayed earnestly for a child. Their story illustrates the power of persistent prayer, even when it seems like the answer may never come. Couples should pray together regularly, bringing their desires, hopes, and struggles before God, trusting that He hears and answers prayer in His way and time.

6. The Role of Obedience in Receiving God's Blessings:

When Zechariah questioned the angel, he was temporarily silenced as a sign of his unbelief. However, when he obediently named his son John, as instructed by the angel, his speech was restored. This emphasizes the importance of obedience to God's commands in receiving His blessings. For couples, following God's guidance in their relationship—whether in matters of faith, family, or finances—ensures they remain aligned with God's will and receive His blessings.

7. Celebrating God's Miracles Together:

When Elizabeth gave birth to John, both she and Zechariah rejoiced in God's miraculous gift. Couples are called to celebrate God's blessings together, no matter how big or small. This strengthens their bond, acknowledging that God's hand is at work in their lives, and it encourages gratitude in the relationship.

8. Righteousness in the Midst of Adversity:

Zechariah and Elizabeth lived righteous lives despite their personal suffering and societal pressure. They didn't let their situation define their faithfulness to God. For couples, this is a lesson in remaining steadfast in their walk with God, even during challenging times. The righteousness that comes from honoring God is what truly matters, not external circumstances.

Week 26

Courage, Faith, and God's Unwavering Presence

Weekly Readings:

Day 176- 1 Kings 14:21-31, 1 Kings 15, 1 Kings 16:1-7; Acts 16:16-40; Proverbs 15:21-30
Day 177- 1 Kings 16:8-34, 1 Kings 17, 1 Kings 18:1-15; Acts 17:1-21; Psalm 78:9-16
Day 178- 1 Kings 18:16-46, 1 Kings 19; Acts 17:22-34, Acts 18:1-8; Psalm 78:17-31
Day 179- 1 Kings 20, 1 Kings 21; Acts 18:9-28, Acts 19:1-13; Psalm 78:32-39
Day 180- 1 Kings 22:1-53; Acts 19:14-41; Proverbs 15:31-33, Proverbs 16:1-7
Day 181- 2 Kings 1, 2 Kings 2:1-25; Acts 20:1-38; Psalm 78:40-55
Day 182- 2 Kings 3, 2 Kings 4:1-37; Acts 21:1-26; Psalm 78:56-72

Weekly Reflection:

This week's passages lead us through powerful displays of God's faithfulness and call on us to be courageous in our faith, just as the prophets and early disciples were. Elijah's confrontation with the prophets of Baal (1 Kings 18) demonstrates the triumph of unwavering belief in God over fear and societal pressures. Elijah's strength came from his complete dependence on God, reminding us to rely on Him in difficult times. How can couples embody this same boldness in their relationship, especially in moments that test their faith?

In Acts, we see Paul and Silas facing imprisonment with grace, singing praises even in chains. Their joyful resilience offers a profound example of maintaining hope, no matter the situation. Together, reflect on how you can bring hope and positivity to each other, even in challenging times. This faith-based optimism can be a source of strength and unity in marriage.

The Psalms and Proverbs provide wisdom and warnings. The psalmist reflects on Israel's history, showing that God remains steadfast even when His people falter. These readings are a reminder for couples to nurture faith together, keeping God at the center of their journey. Proverbs teaches about the importance of wise speech and humility, qualities that are vital to a healthy and respectful relationship.

Weekly Discussion Prompts:

1. Courage in Faith: Elijah faced great opposition but stood firm in his beliefs. How can you both be courageous in your faith, even if it means going against the norms or facing criticism?

2. Sustaining Joy in Hardship: Paul and Silas sang hymns while imprisoned. How do you support each other to remain hopeful and find joy, even when things get difficult?

3. Reflecting on God's Faithfulness: Psalm 78 recounts God's faithfulness despite Israel's rebellion. In what ways has God been faithful in your life together? How can you honor that in your relationship?

4. Encouraging Each Other Spiritually: Elijah found support and comfort in God. How can you encourage each other's spiritual journey, ensuring both of you continue to grow in faith?

5. Practicing Humility and Patience: Proverbs advises humility and patient speech. How can you both work to speak kindly and avoid harsh words? What steps can you take to become more patient with each other?

6. Acknowledging God in Decisions: Proverbs 16:1-7 speaks of seeking God's will in our plans. How do you include God in your joint decisions, big and small, as a couple?

7. Leaving a Legacy of Faith: Elisha continued Elijah's work after his departure. What kind of spiritual legacy do you hope to build together, and how can you ensure that it will inspire others?

Joint Couple Activity:

"Prayers in the Storm": Like Paul and Silas who prayed in prison, spend some time this week praising God together through prayer and song. Choose a hymn or psalm that resonates with both of you and sing it together. Reflect on a difficult time you've faced as a couple and express gratitude for how God supported you during that period. End with a prayer, asking for the courage and joy to face future challenges with a heart of praise.

Couple for Week 26: David and Abigail

David and Abigail's story is one of wisdom, courage, and humility. Abigail was the wife of Nabal, a wealthy but foolish man who insulted David and his men when they sought hospitality from him. Nabal refused to offer any help to David and even mocked him, which greatly angered David. In response, David planned to avenge the insult by attacking Nabal and his household. However, Abigail, Nabal's intelligent and resourceful wife, intervened. She took food and supplies to David, apologizing for her husband's actions and urging David not to shed blood over a foolish man. Her wise and humble approach calmed David's anger, and he thanked God for sending her to prevent him from making a rash decision. Eventually, God struck Nabal dead, and David took Abigail as his wife.

Lessons for Couples:

1. Wisdom in Handling Conflict:

   Abigail's quick thinking and wisdom saved her household from destruction. She showed David a better way—one that did not involve vengeance or rash decisions. This teaches couples the importance of using wisdom and discernment in conflict situations. Instead of reacting impulsively, it's vital to pause, seek understanding, and find a peaceful resolution. Abigail's calm and respectful intervention turned a dangerous situation into an opportunity for reconciliation.

2. Respecting and Supporting Your Spouse:

   Although Abigail's husband, Nabal, was foolish and unkind, she chose to act with grace, protecting him from harm and diffusing the situation with David. Her actions show that a spouse's wisdom can make a huge difference in the dynamics of a relationship. Couples are called to support and protect each other, even when one person may be making unwise decisions. Abigail's loyalty to her husband, despite his faults, highlights the importance of supporting each other through difficult times.

3. Humility in the Face of Adversity:

   Abigail humbly approached David, acknowledging her husband's wrongdoing and taking responsibility for the situation. Her humility prevented further escalation and allowed for reconciliation. In relationships, humility is key to diffusing tensions and restoring peace. Instead of pride or defensiveness, responding with humility can open doors for understanding and healing.

4. Acting with Integrity and Courage:

   Abigail didn't hesitate to stand up to her husband's foolishness when it put others at risk. She took action to prevent harm, showing immense courage and integrity. Couples can learn from Abigail's willingness to do what was right, even when it was difficult or uncomfortable. Sometimes, doing what's best for the relationship may require stepping out of one's comfort zone and making tough choices for the greater good.

5. Forgiveness and Letting Go of Grudges:

David's initial desire for revenge was quelled by Abigail's intervention. In his gratitude, David let go of the anger that had motivated him to take action against Nabal. This illustrates the power of forgiveness in relationships. When we forgive, we allow peace to reign and prevent bitterness from poisoning our hearts. Couples should aim to forgive quickly and not allow resentment to build.

6. God's Providence and Timing:

The timing of Abigail's intervention was no accident. She acted when David was on the verge of making a rash decision. God's providence was evident in how Abigail was placed in the right position to intervene and prevent destruction. This teaches couples to trust in God's timing and guidance in their relationships. Even in moments of stress or tension, God is working behind the scenes to guide our steps and provide opportunities for peace and resolution.

7. Understanding the Power of a Gentle Answer:

Abigail's words to David were calm, respectful, and full of wisdom. She did not confront him with aggression or anger, but instead approached him with a humble, gentle spirit. Her example teaches couples the power of a gentle response in difficult conversations. Instead of escalating conflict, a kind and thoughtful response can defuse tension and lead to constructive dialogue.

8. God Honors Righteous Actions:

David recognized that it was God who had sent Abigail to stop him from committing an unjust act. Her righteous intervention led to a peaceful resolution, and God honored her actions. For couples, this teaches that God rewards those who act righteously, even in difficult circumstances. Righteousness, integrity, and a heart for peace are always seen and honored by God.

Week 27

Trusting God's Guidance in Uncertain Times

Weekly Readings:

Day 183- 2 Kings 4:38-44, 2 Kings 5, 2 Kings 6:1-23; Acts 21:27-40, Acts 22:1-22; Psalm 79:1-13
Day 184- 2 Kings 6:24-33, 2 Kings 7, 2 Kings 8:1-15; Acts 22:22-30, Acts 23:1-11; Proverbs 16:8-17
Day 185- 2 Kings 8:16-29, 2 Kings 9; Acts 23:12-35; Psalm 80:1-7
Day 186- 2 Kings 10, 2 Kings 11; Acts 24:1-27; Psalm 80:8-19
Day 187- 2 Kings 12, 2 Kings 13, 2 Kings 14:1-22; Acts 25:1-22; Psalm 81:1-7
Day 188- 2 Kings 14:23-29, 2 Kings 15; Acts 25:23-27, Acts 26:1-23; Proverbs 16:18-27
Day 189- 2 Kings 16, 2 Kings 17; Acts 26:24-32, Acts 27:1-12; Psalm 81:8-16

Weekly Reflection:

This week's readings draw our attention to God's care and intervention during times of hardship and uncertainty. In 2 Kings, we see miraculous moments, from Elisha's acts of healing to the provision of food during famine, reminding us that God meets our needs, even in the most desperate situations. Reflect on the ways God has provided for you as a couple, especially during times when you couldn't see a clear path forward. How has His provision strengthened your trust in Him?

Acts continues the story of Paul, who faces persecution, trials, and imprisonment with an unshaken faith. His courage under pressure and his willingness to speak the truth no matter the consequence serve as powerful examples. Together, discuss the sacrifices you have made or may need to make for your faith. Like Paul, seek to find purpose and peace, even in the storms of life.

The Psalms and Proverbs this week echo the themes of guidance and reliance on God's wisdom. Proverbs calls us to humility, while Psalms invite us to cry out to God in times of need, trusting that He will hear and restore us. As a couple, practice placing your trust in God together, especially in the choices you make for your future.

Weekly Discussion Prompts:

1. Faith Amid Uncertainty: Elisha provided food for the people in a time of famine. How do you both rely on God's provision when life seems uncertain?

2. Bearing Witness Through Hardship: Paul uses his trials as an opportunity to witness. How can you, as a couple, be a testimony to others, especially during challenging times?

3. Recognizing God's Intervention: Look back on moments when God seemed to intervene in your relationship or family. How did these experiences shape your faith as a couple?

4. Trusting God's Wisdom: Proverbs speaks of humility and guidance. In what areas of your relationship do you need to lean more on God's wisdom?

5. Unity in Prayer During Trials: The Psalmist cries out for God's help during difficult times. How can praying together deepen your trust and reliance on God?

6. Boldness in Your Faith: Like Paul, how can you both practice boldness in living out your faith, even when it's not easy?

7. Humbly Seeking Direction: Proverbs warns against pride and encourages a heart open to correction. Are there areas where you may be resisting God's guidance? How can you humbly seek His direction together?

Joint Couple Activity:

"Shared Prayers for Guidance": This week, write a joint prayer asking for God's guidance and wisdom over a specific area in your relationship or family life. Pray this prayer together each day, asking God to provide direction and clarity. End the week by discussing any insights, feelings, or signs of guidance you may have noticed, celebrating the ways God has worked through your shared prayer.

Couple for Week 27: Isaiah and the Prophetess

Isaiah, one of the great prophets of the Old Testament, married a woman referred to as "the prophetess" (Isaiah 8:3). While her name is not explicitly stated in Scripture, she played a significant role in Isaiah's prophetic ministry. Together, they had children, whose names carried symbolic meanings that reflected God's messages to the people of Israel. For example, their first son was named Shear-Jashub, meaning "A remnant shall return," symbolizing the hope of God's people being restored after exile. Their second son was named Maher-Shalal-Hash-Baz, meaning "Speed the spoil, hasten the plunder," indicating the impending judgment and destruction of Israel's enemies.

Isaiah's marriage to the prophetess was part of a larger narrative where their family was used by God to deliver prophetic messages to the nation of Judah. The naming of their children, as directed by God, served as a living testimony to the people, warning them of impending judgment and pointing to God's ultimate plan for redemption.

Lessons for Couples:

1. Purpose in Partnership:

   Isaiah and the prophetess worked together in God's service, and their marriage had a clear purpose in fulfilling God's plan. Their union was not just a personal relationship, but also a partnership in the mission of bringing God's word to His people. For couples today, this is a reminder that marriages can be deeply impactful and purposeful. Couples are called to share a common vision and work together for a higher purpose, whether in ministry, family life, or serving others.

2. Obedience to God's Calling:

   Isaiah and his wife were obedient to God's direction, even when it involved the naming of their children in a way that was symbolic of future events. Their willingness to follow God's instructions, even when it may have been difficult or misunderstood by others, shows the importance of obedience in a marriage. Couples are encouraged to seek God's will for their lives and to follow His lead, trusting that His plan for them will bring about blessings, even when it requires sacrifice or stepping out in faith.

3. Living Out God's Word Together:

   By naming their children in accordance with God's direction, Isaiah and his wife allowed their family to serve as a living testimony of God's message. For couples, this highlights the power of living out the principles of God's word in everyday life. The way a couple interacts, raises their children, and supports each other can be a powerful witness to God's love, grace, and truth.

4. Shared Spiritual Responsibilities:

   Isaiah and the prophetess shared the responsibility of being God's messengers. This partnership in spiritual matters emphasizes that marriage is not just a union of two people, but a union in which both partners are called to support and encourage each other in their walk with God. Whether it's praying together, studying the Bible, or making decisions based on faith, couples are called to nurture each other's spiritual growth and work together to fulfill God's purposes.

5. Symbolism in Family Life:

    The names of Isaiah's children were symbolic of God's judgment and mercy. In a similar way, families today can use their lives, actions, and decisions as symbols of God's presence and work in the world. Couples can reflect on how their own actions, values, and even the names they give their children, can be testimonies of God's faithfulness and message to those around them.

6. God's Timing and Providence:

    The children of Isaiah and the prophetess were born during a time of great political unrest in Israel. The prophetic acts surrounding their births showed that even in difficult times, God is sovereign and working out His plan. For couples, this teaches that God's timing is always perfect. Even during times of uncertainty or struggle, couples can trust that God is at work in their lives and in the world, bringing about His purposes in His time.

7. Living with Hope and Warning:

    Isaiah's ministry carried both a message of judgment and hope. His family, through their names, carried a dual message: while judgment was coming, there was also the promise of a remnant that would return. For couples, this teaches the balance of living with both a sense of hope and urgency. Even in challenging times, couples can remind each other of God's ultimate promise of redemption and work together to fulfill His calling.

Week 28

Finding Strength and Courage in God's Faithfulness

Weekly Readings:

Day 190- 2 Kings 18, 2 Kings 19:1-13; Acts 27:13-44; Psalm 82:1-8
Day 191- 2 Kings 19:14-37, 2 Kings 20; Acts 28:1-16; Psalm 83:1-18
Day 192- 2 Kings 21, 2 Kings 22; Acts 28:17-31; Proverbs 16:28-33, Proverbs 17:1-4
Day 193- 2 Kings 23, 2 Kings 24:1-7; Romans 1:1-17; Psalm 84:1-7
Day 194- 2 Kings 24:8-20, 2 Kings 25; Romans 1:18-32; Psalm 84:8-12
Day 195- Jonah 1, Jonah 2, Jonah 3, Jonah 4; Romans 2:1-16; Psalm 85:1-7
Day 196- Amos 1, Amos 2; Romans 2:17-29, Romans 3:1-8; Proverbs 17:5-14

Weekly Reflection:

This week's readings journey through the stories of God's protection, the importance of repentance, and the power of God's faithfulness to His people. In 2 Kings, Hezekiah faces incredible threats from a powerful enemy, yet he turns to God in complete trust, praying for deliverance. God's miraculous response is a reminder of His faithfulness in our lives, especially during moments when circumstances seem insurmountable. As a couple, reflect on any "Hezekiah moments" in your relationship, where trusting God in the face of difficulties led to unexpected provision or protection.

The Acts of the Apostles draws to a close as Paul, still in chains, continues his mission with courage and conviction. Despite storms, shipwrecks, and the uncertainty of his future, Paul never loses sight of his calling. His persistence reminds us that God's purpose in our lives isn't hindered by challenges; rather, it often grows stronger through them. How can you both lean on each other for strength and courage to pursue what God has called you to do together?

Finally, the transition to Romans and the stories of Jonah and Amos call us to a spirit of repentance and a commitment to living out the Gospel. As you both seek to serve God, ask yourselves: How can you continually align your hearts with His?

Weekly Discussion Prompts:

1. Trusting God in Battles: Hezekiah trusted God when the enemy surrounded him. How do you both find strength in God when facing struggles together?

2. Living with Purpose Despite Trials: Paul's journey was full of trials, yet he remained focused. How can you each encourage one another to keep faith and purpose strong, even during personal or shared challenges?

3. Praying for Miraculous Provision: Hezekiah prayed, and God answered. As a couple, pray together for any specific "impossible" needs you're facing. How can you create a regular time for shared prayer?

4. Listening to God's Call to Repentance: The story of Jonah emphasizes the importance of repentance. How do you both seek to continually grow in alignment with God's will?

5. Encouraging Each Other to Share God's Love: Romans reminds us that the Gospel is for everyone. How can you, as a couple, actively share God's love with those around you?

6. Finding Joy in God's Presence: Psalm 84 expresses a deep longing to be close to God. How can you both cultivate a deeper love and joy for God's presence in your daily lives?

7. Humbly Following God's Guidance: Proverbs warns against pride. Where do you need to be more open to God's correction and guidance as a couple?

Joint Couple Activity:

"Building a Prayer Fortress": Together, create a prayer journal where you list both individual and shared needs, as well as answered prayers. Over time, this will serve as a testament to God's faithfulness, especially during challenges. Take turns leading each other in prayer each day this week, asking for God's guidance and thanking Him for the ways He is working in your relationship.

Couple for Week 28: Joseph and Asenath

Joseph, the son of Jacob, became a powerful leader in Egypt after being sold into slavery by his brothers. During his time in Egypt, Joseph interpreted Pharaoh's dreams and was made the vizier, second only to Pharaoh. As part of his elevation, Joseph married Asenath, the daughter of Potiphera, a priest of On (also known as Heliopolis) in Egypt (Genesis 41:45). Asenath is one of the lesser-known women in the Bible, and little is revealed about her life before her marriage to Joseph. However, it is understood that she was an Egyptian woman, and through their marriage, she became part of the fulfillment of God's promise to Joseph and his family.

Joseph and Asenath had two sons, Manasseh and Ephraim, whose names were also significant in the biblical narrative. Manasseh's name means "God has made me forget all my trouble," reflecting Joseph's personal journey of forgiveness and healing. Ephraim's name means "God has made me fruitful in the land of my suffering," a testimony to God's blessings despite adversity.

Their story is significant because it shows God's ability to work in and through relationships that cross cultural and ethnic boundaries, showing that God's plan for His people is often broader than we can imagine.

Lessons for Couples:

1. God's Sovereignty in Relationships:

   Joseph's marriage to Asenath was part of God's plan, even though she was from a different culture and faith background. This demonstrates how God works in relationships regardless of external circumstances or backgrounds. For couples, this teaches that God is sovereign over our relationships. No matter the circumstances or challenges a couple faces, they can trust that God is working through their union for a greater purpose.

2. Forgiveness and Healing:

   Joseph's name for his first son, Manasseh, signifies the forgiveness he experienced after years of hardship. His relationship with Asenath, and the blessing of children, was part of God's healing work in Joseph's life. This is a powerful reminder that couples can be agents of healing for each other. Forgiveness, both from others and within a marriage, brings emotional restoration and peace. Couples are encouraged to forgive one another and allow God to heal any past wounds that may hinder their relationship.

3. God's Blessings in Adversity:

   Ephraim's name, which means "fruitful in the land of my suffering," reflects how Joseph recognized God's blessings even during times of difficulty. Joseph experienced personal suffering but later saw how God used those hardships to bring about good. For couples, this is a reminder that even in difficult times, God can bring blessings. Challenges can be opportunities for growth, and couples should support each other in viewing trials as a way God refines them together.

4. Embracing Cultural Differences:

   Joseph's marriage to Asenath highlights how relationships can bring together people from different cultures, backgrounds, and even faiths. While their marriage bridged two cultures, it was also one that reflected Joseph's commitment to God. Couples today can learn that embracing differences, whether cultural, personal, or even religious, can lead to richer relationships. It teaches the importance of respecting each other's backgrounds and finding common ground in shared values and love for God.

5. Trusting God's Timing:

Joseph's rise to power and his marriage to Asenath didn't happen immediately. He had to wait for God's timing after being betrayed by his brothers and enduring years of hardship. For couples, this teaches the importance of waiting on God's perfect timing. Trusting that God has a plan for your marriage and that He works in His timing can alleviate anxiety and strengthen faith in His provision.

6. A Family of Faith:

Despite Asenath's Egyptian background, she became part of God's covenant people through her marriage to Joseph. The couple raised their children in faith, which is reflected in the names of their sons. The names of Manasseh and Ephraim were testimony to Joseph's faith in God's goodness. For couples, this teaches the importance of raising children with a strong faith foundation. Regardless of background, faith can bring a family together and guide them through life's challenges.

7. Commitment to Each Other and God's Plan:

Joseph's faithfulness to God and his role as a godly leader were reflected in his marriage to Asenath. He stayed true to his faith and his relationship with God, despite the difficulties he faced in Egypt. Couples can learn from this example that marriage requires commitment not only to each other but also to God's plan for their lives. By putting God at the center of their relationship, couples can walk in unity and fulfill their divine purpose together.

Week 29

Righteousness and Restoration

Weekly Readings:

Day 197- Amos 3, Amos 4; Romans 3:9-31; Psalm 85:8-13
Day 198- Amos 5; Romans 4:1-15; Psalm 86:1-10
Day 199- Amos 6, Amos 7; Romans 4:16-25, Romans 5:1-11; Psalm 86:11-17
Day 200- Amos 8, Amos 9; Romans 5:12-21; Proverbs 17:15-24
Day 201- Hosea 1, Hosea 2; Romans 6:1-14; Psalm 87:1-7
Day 202- Hosea 3, Hosea 4, Hosea 5; Romans 6:15-23, Romans 7:1-6; Psalm 88:1-9
Day 203- Hosea 6, Hosea 7; Romans 7:7-25; Psalm 88:9-18

Weekly Reflection:

In this week's readings, we encounter themes of justice, redemption, and transformation. Amos calls out the complacency of Israel, challenging us to reflect on areas in our own lives and relationships that may need spiritual renewal. The prophet's warnings remind us that our actions should reflect God's justice and compassion. As a couple, consider how you can support each other in living with integrity and compassion toward others.

In Romans, Paul speaks of God's grace and righteousness, emphasizing that we are justified by faith, not by works. This divine grace isn't a license to continue in sin but a call to a transformed life. How can you both encourage each other to live in a way that reflects God's redeeming love, moving toward holiness in your relationship and personal lives?

Finally, Hosea introduces the powerful story of God's relentless love for His people, even when they stray. Just as Hosea remains faithful to his unfaithful spouse, God pursues us with love and calls us back to Him. Reflect on this divine love as a model for your own marriage, nurturing a bond that mirrors God's enduring faithfulness.

Weekly Discussion Prompts:

1. Identifying Complacency: Amos challenges Israel's complacency. In what ways can you work together to avoid complacency in your spiritual lives and marriage?

2. Living Out Righteousness by Faith: Romans speaks of faith as the path to righteousness. How can you strengthen each other's faith and walk together in righteousness?

3. Facing Struggles with Hope: Romans 5 discusses how suffering produces hope. Reflect on a time you faced a trial together. How did that experience help you grow stronger?

4. Understanding Grace in Relationships: Hosea's story of forgiveness and grace can inspire us. Are there areas where you need to offer or receive grace from each other?

5. Striving for Holiness: Romans encourages us to live apart from sin. How can you hold each other accountable for growing in holiness?

6. Embracing God's Pursuit: Hosea reminds us of God's love even when we falter. How can you create a relationship that reflects God's enduring love and commitment?

7. Daily Renewal through Prayer: The Psalms remind us of God's sustaining love. How can you both incorporate regular, heartfelt prayer for your relationship?

Joint Couple Activity:

"Grace-Filled Love Letters": Write each other a letter reflecting on moments when you've experienced grace and forgiveness in your relationship. Share these letters at the end of the week, allowing them to serve as a reminder of the love and understanding that binds you together, just as God's grace binds us to Him.

Couple for Week 29: Cleopas and His Wife

Cleopas is a relatively obscure figure in the Bible, mentioned only in the Gospel of Luke. He is known primarily for being one of the two disciples who encountered the resurrected Jesus on the road to Emmaus (Luke 24:13-35). Cleopas and his companion (who is unnamed in the passage but is often thought to be his wife, based on early Christian tradition) were walking from Jerusalem to Emmaus, discussing the events of Jesus' crucifixion and the reports of His resurrection. Jesus appeared to them along the way, but they were initially kept from recognizing Him. After a conversation with Jesus, which included a Bible study of sorts, they invited Him to stay with them. It was only when Jesus broke bread with them that their eyes were opened, and they recognized Him. They immediately returned to Jerusalem to share the news of Jesus' resurrection with the apostles.

Cleopas and his wife (or companion) are notable in the biblical narrative for their reaction to the revelation of Jesus' identity. After recognizing Jesus, they immediately became witnesses to His resurrection, which highlights their devotion and willingness to spread the good news. Their story is also a powerful reminder of the transformative power of encountering the risen Christ.

Lessons for Couples:

1. Openness to Jesus in Everyday Life: Cleopas and his wife were engaged in a simple, everyday activity—walking from Jerusalem to Emmaus. However, they were open to a spiritual conversation with Jesus, even when they didn't recognize Him. This teaches couples to remain open to Jesus in the everyday moments of their lives, recognizing that He can speak to them and reveal Himself in unexpected ways. They are reminded to invite Jesus into their daily conversations and experiences, trusting that He is with them even in the ordinary moments.

2. Seeking Christ Together: In their walk together, Cleopas and his companion demonstrated a shared pursuit of understanding and faith. As they discussed the events of Jesus' death and resurrection, they were open to the guidance of Jesus, even before they recognized Him. Couples can learn from this that seeking Christ together strengthens their relationship. Whether through prayer, study, or simply sharing their spiritual journeys, couples are encouraged to support one another in their walk with God.

3. Hospitality and Welcoming Jesus: Cleopas and his wife invited Jesus to stay with them when He was preparing to move on. This act of hospitality allowed them to experience the moment when Jesus revealed Himself. For couples, this is a reminder to create an environment of openness and hospitality in their homes. When couples make space for Jesus in their relationship and home, they create an opportunity for deeper intimacy and spiritual revelation. Jesus honors the invitation to stay and commune with them.

4. Recognizing Jesus in the Breaking of Bread: The moment when Cleopas and his wife recognized Jesus was when He broke bread with them. This moment of communion was significant not only for them but for all Christians, as it symbolizes the Eucharist. Couples can learn the importance of communion in their own relationships, not just physically through meals but also spiritually. Sharing in spiritual practices like prayer, worship, and communion can help couples recognize Jesus more clearly in their lives and strengthen their bond.

5. Immediate Obedience and Witnessing: After recognizing Jesus, Cleopas and his wife did not hesitate—they immediately returned to Jerusalem to share the news with the apostles. This teaches couples the importance of immediate obedience to God's call. When couples experience a revelation or blessing from God, they are called to share it

with others. Their relationship becomes a vessel for witnessing the love and resurrection of Christ, not only in their own lives but to others around them as well.

6. Hope in Times of Doubt: Before their encounter with the risen Jesus, Cleopas and his wife were confused and disheartened by the events surrounding Jesus' death. However, after recognizing Jesus, their hope was restored. Couples can learn that even in times of confusion and doubt, Jesus brings hope and clarity. Through their shared faith and the presence of Christ, couples can find comfort and reassurance in difficult times, knowing that Jesus is with them, guiding them through their trials.

7. Deepening Faith Through Shared Experience: Cleopas and his wife's shared experience on the road to Emmaus deepened their faith and understanding of Jesus' mission. Couples can learn from this that shared spiritual experiences—whether through Bible study, prayer, or serving together—can strengthen their faith and their relationship with each other. A couple's spiritual journey together is an opportunity for growth and transformation, helping them to know Jesus more intimately and reflect His love in their relationship.

Week 30

God's Unfailing Love and Transformation

Weekly Readings:

Day 204- Hosea 8, Hosea 9; Romans 8:1-17; Proverbs 17:25-28, Proverbs 18:1-6
Day 205- Hosea 10, Hosea 11; Romans 8:18-39; Psalm 89:1-8
Day 206- Hosea 11, Hosea 12, Hosea 13, Hosea 14; Romans 9:1-21; Psalm 89:9-13
Day 207- 1 Chronicles 1, 1 Chronicles 2:1-17; Romans 9:22-33, Romans 10:1-4; Psalm 89:14-18
Day 208- 1 Chronicles 2:18-55, 1 Chronicles 3, 1 Chronicles 4:1-8; Romans 10:5-21, Romans 11:1-10; Proverbs 18:7-16
Day 209- 1 Chronicles 4:9-43, 1 Chronicles 5; Romans 11:11-32; Psalm 89:19-29
Day 210- 1 Chronicles 6; Romans 11:33-36, Romans 12:1-21; Psalm 89:30-37

Weekly Reflection:

This week, we journey through the depths of God's unwavering love and the call to transformation in our lives. In Hosea, we see God's sorrow over Israel's unfaithfulness and His relentless love in calling His people back. Hosea reminds us of the depth of God's compassion—even when we stray, He draws us back, longing for relationship and renewal. As a couple, reflect on how forgiveness and restoration play a role in your relationship. Are there ways you can embrace each other with a forgiving spirit, echoing God's patience and mercy?

In Romans, Paul's words bring us to the heart of God's redemptive plan and the transformation available through the Holy Spirit. We are reminded that "there is now no condemnation for those who are in Christ Jesus" (Romans 8:1), and we are invited to live in the Spirit, shedding the burdens of sin. How can you encourage each other in walking a Spirit-filled life, embracing God's peace and joy together? Romans 12 offers a powerful guide for living in harmony with others and embracing humility, love, and forgiveness—values that strengthen your bond.

Finally, 1 Chronicles brings us back to the lineage and history of God's people, emphasizing the faithfulness that has carried from generation to generation. Just as God has been faithful through the ages, He is faithful to each of us today. Let this legacy inspire you to strengthen your commitment to one another and to nurture a love that stands as a testament to God's grace.

Weekly Discussion Prompts:

1. Reflecting God's Forgiveness: Hosea's call to return to God is filled with forgiveness. How can you actively show each other forgiveness and build a relationship that reflects God's love?

2. Living Without Condemnation: Romans 8 reminds us we are free from condemnation. How can you help each other let go of guilt and live with a fresh perspective?

3. Embracing the Holy Spirit: What does it mean to live a Spirit-led life in your relationship? How can you nurture the fruit of the Spirit—love, joy, peace, patience, etc.—in your marriage?

4. Recognizing God's Love in Trials: Romans 8:18-39 assures us that nothing can separate us from God's love. How does this truth encourage you when facing challenges as a couple?

5. Unity and Humility: Romans 12 speaks of serving others humbly. How can humility and a spirit of service strengthen your relationship and your interactions with others?

6. Building a Legacy of Faith: Chronicles reminds us of the importance of our spiritual legacy. What kind of legacy do you hope to build together, and how can you live in a way that reflects this vision?

7. Daily Renewal in Prayer: As Psalm 89 celebrates God's faithfulness, consider dedicating a special time this week to pray together, seeking God's guidance for your journey ahead.

Joint Couple Activity:

"Words of Encouragement": Take time each day this week to offer words of encouragement and affirmation to each other. Remind each other of God's promises and the qualities you see in one another that reflect His goodness. End the week by sharing how these moments of encouragement strengthened your connection.

Couple for Week 30: Nabal and Abigail

The story of Nabal and Abigail is found in 1 Samuel 25. Nabal was a wealthy but harsh and foolish man, while Abigail was his intelligent, beautiful, and wise wife. Nabal's wealth came from his extensive land, and he had many sheep and cattle. One day, while David and his men were in the wilderness near Nabal's property, David sent a message to Nabal, asking for provisions as a gesture of goodwill for having protected Nabal's shepherds. David and his men had kept the area safe from bandits, and he expected hospitality in return.

However, Nabal, whose name means "fool," responded rudely, refusing to provide any assistance and insulting David. Enraged by this, David decided to take revenge and prepare to attack Nabal's household. Upon hearing of this, Abigail, Nabal's wife, acted swiftly. She gathered provisions and went to meet David, seeking to prevent the conflict. She humbly apologized for her husband's behavior, acknowledged David's future as king, and begged for mercy. She presented the gifts as a peace offering and urged David not to take vengeance into his own hands. David, impressed by her wisdom and humility, accepted her plea and spared Nabal's life.

Later, when Abigail returned home and informed Nabal of the events, he was struck with fear and had a heart attack. Ten days later, he died. After his death, David sent for Abigail and took her as his wife.

Lessons for Couples:

1. Wisdom and Discernment in Conflict: Abigail's wisdom in handling the situation with David shows the power of a calm, wise, and discerning approach to conflict. Instead of reacting rashly like her husband, she took action to prevent harm and ensure peace. Couples can learn from Abigail's example by approaching conflicts with patience, thoughtfulness, and a willingness to listen and resolve issues peacefully. Abigail showed that, in difficult times, wisdom can avert disaster.

2. The Importance of Humility: Abigail's humility was evident in the way she acknowledged David's rightful anger and apologized for her husband's foolishness. She did not let her pride get in the way of doing what was right, even though Nabal, her husband, had acted badly. Humility in marriage is essential, and couples can learn to admit when they are wrong and seek reconciliation, as Abigail did.

3. Taking Responsibility: Though Nabal was the one who had wronged David, Abigail took responsibility for the situation and acted to right the wrong. She did not blame others or try to make excuses for her husband. In marriage, it is important to take responsibility for one's actions and decisions. Couples can learn from Abigail that sometimes it takes one partner to step up and take responsibility to bring about healing and resolution.

4. The Power of a Wise Partner: Abigail's actions not only saved her household but also gained her favor with David, who eventually took her as his wife after Nabal's death. Abigail's wisdom was an invaluable asset to her family and marriage. Couples can learn from this that having a wise and thoughtful partner can help guide the relationship

through tough situations. Both partners should value and cultivate wisdom and discernment, especially when faced with difficult decisions.

5. Forgiveness and Mercy: David showed mercy to Nabal and his household after Abigail interceded. He chose to forgive Nabal's offense and avoid vengeance. This teaches couples the power of forgiveness and the importance of letting go of anger and bitterness. Holding onto grudges can damage relationships, whereas showing mercy and choosing forgiveness can strengthen the bond between spouses.

6. Respect for One Another's Roles: Abigail's approach showed a deep respect for her husband, even though his actions were disgraceful. While she acted to protect their family, she did so in a way that honored her husband's role, understanding that she was stepping in during a time of crisis. Respect is essential in any marriage, and even during disagreements or difficult situations, couples can learn to treat one another with dignity and honor.

7. God's Providence in Difficult Times: Abigail's actions ultimately worked out for the best. God used her wisdom to save her household and, in the end, elevated her by bringing her into a new marriage with David. The story illustrates that, even when faced with challenging circumstances, God can use difficult situations for His purposes and bring about positive outcomes for those who trust Him. Couples can trust that, even in the midst of struggles, God can work through them to bring good.

8. Strength and Courage in Marriage: Abigail showed great courage in confronting a dangerous situation to protect her family. It takes strength and bravery to stand up for what is right, especially when it involves stepping into an uncomfortable or dangerous situation. Couples can learn to support one another through tough times, demonstrating courage and strength together in their marriage.

Week 31

Unity, Humility, and God's Sovereign Faithfulness

Weekly Readings:

Day 211- 1 Chronicles 7, 1 Chronicles 8; Romans 13:1-14; Psalm 89:38-45
Day 212- 1 Chronicles 9, 1 Chronicles 10:1-14; Romans 14:1-18; Proverbs 18:17-24, Proverbs 19:1-2
Day 213- 1 Chronicles 11, 1 Chronicles 12:1-22; Romans 14:19-23, Romans 15:1-13; Psalm 89:46-52
Day 214- 1 Chronicles 12:23-40, 1 Chronicles 13, 1 Chronicles 14; Romans 15:14-33; Psalm 90:1-10
Day 215- 1 Chronicles 15, 1 Chronicles 16:1-36; Romans 16; Psalm 90:11-17
Day 216- 1 Chronicles 16:37-43, 1 Chronicles 17, 1 Chronicles 18; 1 Corinthians 1:1-17; Proverbs 19:3-12
Day 217- 1 Chronicles 19, 1 Chronicles 20, 1 Chronicles 21; 1 Corinthians 1:18-31, 1 Corinthians 2:1-5; Psalm 91:1-8

Weekly Reflection:

This week's readings bring together themes of humility, unity, and the timeless sovereignty of God. 1 Chronicles presents us with stories of Israel's heritage, triumphs, and failures, while Romans and 1 Corinthians teach us about living in unity with others, humility before God, and reliance on His wisdom. Through the accounts of Israel's leaders, we see the importance of turning to God in all endeavors and honoring His will above our own desires. As a couple, consider how you might incorporate a spirit of humility and dependence on God into your shared life.

In Romans 13–16, Paul encourages Christians to live peacefully with each other, to serve others in love, and to honor authorities as we embody Christ's love and humility. Reflect on how you can support each other in daily acts of humility, from serving one another to showing grace in areas of disagreement. Romans 15 reminds us that unity is found in putting others first and fostering peace. This is crucial in marriage and is beautifully reinforced as Paul closes his letter with personal greetings that reflect his love for his fellow believers.

Moving into 1 Corinthians, we see a powerful reminder of God's wisdom, which is far beyond human understanding. In marriage, it can be tempting to rely on worldly wisdom, but God calls us to seek His guidance and truth. How can you, as a couple, rely more on God's wisdom rather than your own, trusting in His perfect plan for your lives?

Weekly Discussion Prompts:

1. Living in Peace: Romans 13 discusses honoring authorities and living in peace. How can you bring a spirit of peace into your marriage, even in times of disagreement?

2. Bearing Each Other's Burdens: Romans 14–15 emphasizes mutual support. How can you better support each other's personal journeys with God, even if you are at different places in your faith?

3. Humility in Action: Reflect on how humility plays a role in your marriage. In what ways can you demonstrate humility to one another, valuing each other's perspectives and needs?

4. Unity and Love: Paul's letters to the Romans and Corinthians are full of encouragement for unity. How do you intentionally foster unity in your marriage, and what actions can strengthen this bond?

5. Trusting in God's Wisdom: Proverbs reminds us of God's guidance. How can you lean more on God's wisdom and less on personal understanding in decisions you make together?

6. Legacy of Faith: Chronicles highlights the legacy of Israel's leaders. What kind of spiritual legacy do you hope to build in your marriage, and how can this inspire your actions today?

7. Serving God Together: Paul's life was dedicated to serving God. Consider ways you can serve God together, whether through church involvement, acts of kindness, or praying for others.

Joint Couple Activity:

"Prayer of Dedication": This week, pray together daily, dedicating each area of your marriage to God's care. Each day, choose one aspect (finances, communication, future plans, family, etc.) to bring before God, asking for His guidance and grace. Reflect on how it feels to surrender each part of your relationship to God.

Couple for Week 31: Aaron and Elisheba

Aaron, the older brother of Moses, was a significant figure in the Bible as the first high priest of Israel. His wife, Elisheba, was from the tribe of Judah and the daughter of Amminadab. Their marriage is mentioned briefly in the Bible, primarily in Exodus 6:23, Leviticus 10:1-2, and Numbers 26:59.

Aaron and Elisheba had four children: Nadab, Abihu, Eleazar, and Ithamar. These children were part of the priestly family and assisted Aaron in his religious duties. However, tragedy struck when Nadab and Abihu, two of Aaron's sons, offered "unauthorized fire" before the Lord and were consumed by fire as a result (Leviticus 10:1-2). This was a pivotal moment in Aaron's life, as he faced a personal and familial crisis, and it was a test of his faith and leadership.

Although there is little narrative about Elisheba, she must have been a woman of strength, as she supported her husband through the challenging times of leading the Israelites and witnessing the loss of their sons. Throughout their marriage, Aaron and Elisheba remained committed to God's covenant, helping to establish and maintain the priestly duties that would shape the religious life of Israel for generations.

Lessons for Couples:

1. Faith and Commitment Through Trials: Aaron and Elisheba's marriage was not without its trials, especially with the death of their sons. Despite the painful and tragic loss of Nadab and Abihu, Aaron continued to serve God faithfully, and there is no mention of Elisheba faltering in her support of her husband. This teaches couples that faith and commitment to each other and to God are crucial, even when faced with hardship and loss. Couples can learn from Aaron and Elisheba the importance of standing firm in faith, even when facing personal or familial struggles.

2. Supporting Each Other's Calling: Aaron and Elisheba were both part of God's plan for Israel, with Aaron serving as high priest and Elisheba supporting him in his role. Though Elisheba's direct involvement in the priestly duties is not highlighted, she played an integral part in supporting her husband's ministry and ensuring the continuation of God's covenant through their children. In marriage, partners should support one another's callings, whether it's a spiritual, professional, or personal mission, understanding that they are a team working toward a common goal. Elisheba exemplifies the role of a wife in supporting her husband's leadership and ministry.

3. The Role of Family in God's Plan: Aaron and Elisheba's children were central to the priestly line, highlighting the importance of family in fulfilling God's purposes. As parents, Aaron and Elisheba had a crucial role in raising their children to honor God and carry on their family's legacy. Even though tragedy struck with the loss of two of their sons, the family remained pivotal in Israel's spiritual leadership. Couples can learn that

their role as parents and spouses is integral to God's greater plan. Raising children in faith and guiding them through both triumphs and struggles is an important responsibility in marriage.

4. Leadership and Responsibility: Aaron's leadership as the high priest required both personal and public responsibility. While Aaron may have faced criticism or doubt (particularly after the incident with the golden calf in Exodus 32), he continued to lead the Israelites faithfully. Elisheba, as his wife, likely supported his leadership, even during difficult times. This partnership in leadership can inspire couples to work together, sharing the responsibilities and burdens of leadership in their families, communities, or workplaces. Couples who share leadership roles in marriage can learn to support and strengthen each other through times of difficulty, ensuring the family thrives spiritually, emotionally, and physically.

5. Grief and Healing Together: The loss of Nadab and Abihu was a traumatic event for Aaron and Elisheba. In these moments of grief, it is important for couples to lean on each other for strength and comfort. Though the Bible doesn't describe how they processed the loss together, the support of a spouse in such difficult times is invaluable. Couples can learn that in moments of grief, they should draw close to each other and to God, trusting that healing will come through mutual support and prayer.

6. Living According to God's Commands: Aaron and Elisheba's marriage was centered on following God's commands, as seen in their roles in the priesthood. Despite personal and familial hardships, their commitment to God's law and service remained unwavering. Couples can take from their example the importance of prioritizing God's will in their relationship, especially in raising children or making decisions that affect the family. Marriage and family life should be built on the foundation of God's commands, seeking to honor Him in all things.

7. Respecting Each Other's Roles: In their roles as priest and wife of the priest, Aaron and Elisheba would have respected each other's duties. Even though Elisheba did not have the same public role as Aaron, her role was no less important. She supported him and their family by ensuring the continuity of the priesthood through their sons. Couples can learn the importance of respecting each other's roles in marriage, acknowledging that each partner has unique contributions that strengthen the relationship and the family.

Week 32

Wisdom, Dedication, and God's Eternal Perspective

Weekly Readings:

Day 218- 1 Chronicles 22, 1 Chronicles 23; 1 Corinthians 2:6-16; Psalm 91:9-16
Day 219- 1 Chronicles 24, 1 Chronicles 25, 1 Chronicles 26:1-19; 1 Corinthians 3; Psalm 92:1-15
Day 220- 1 Chronicles 26:20-32, 1 Chronicles 27; 1 Corinthians 4; Proverbs 19:13-22
Day 221- 1 Chronicles 28, 1 Chronicles 29; 1 Corinthians 5; Psalm 93:1-5
Day 222- 2 Chronicles 1:1-17; 1 Corinthians 6; Psalm 94:1-11
Day 223- Ecclesiastes 1, Ecclesiastes 2, Ecclesiastes 3:1-22; 1 Corinthians 7:1-16; Psalm 94:12-23
Day 224- Ecclesiastes 4, Ecclesiastes 5, Ecclesiastes 6; 1 Corinthians 7:17-35; Proverbs 19:23-29, Proverbs 20:1-4

Weekly Reflection:

In this week's readings, we are invited to explore wisdom, the significance of dedication, and God's eternal perspective. 1 Chronicles describes King David's meticulous preparation for the temple, teaching us the value of legacy and intentionality in our faith journeys. This dedication reflects how our decisions today can lay a spiritual foundation for future generations.

Ecclesiastes reminds us that many earthly pursuits are ultimately fleeting without God, encouraging us to focus on what truly matters and to find contentment in the Lord. 1 Corinthians reminds us that godly wisdom, distinct from worldly wisdom, is rooted in the Spirit and guides us in relationships, including marriage, with purity, respect, and love.

Weekly Discussion Prompts:

1. Preparing for Legacy: In 1 Chronicles 22, David prepares his son Solomon for building the temple. How can you, as a couple, prepare and lay a legacy of faith for future generations in your family?

2. Spiritual Wisdom: Reflecting on 1 Corinthians 2, discuss how godly wisdom might shape your decisions differently from worldly wisdom. How can you prioritize spiritual values in your home?

3. Joy in God's Work: Psalm 92 celebrates the joy and flourishing that comes from living in God's presence. How do you experience God's joy and strength as a couple? What activities or practices draw you closer to this joy?

4. Honoring Boundaries: In 1 Corinthians 5 and 6, Paul discusses maintaining purity. How can you support each other in creating and upholding healthy boundaries that honor God within and outside your marriage?

5. Contentment and Perspective: Ecclesiastes reveals the futility of many pursuits. How can this perspective help you focus on lasting values together? Where might you need to let go of anxieties over temporary concerns?

6. Serving One Another: Proverbs highlights wise relationships and the value of humility. What practical ways can you show love, humility, and understanding toward each other, even when facing daily challenges?

7. Celebrating Small Blessings: Reflecting on Ecclesiastes' encouragement to enjoy life's simple blessings, share with each other some small things that bring you joy. How can you intentionally bring these moments into your life more often?

Joint Couple Activity:

"A Temple of Priorities": Just as David gathered resources for the temple, sit together and list your top priorities as a couple. Consider areas like faith, family, personal goals, community service, and quality time together. With each priority, outline one specific action you can take to nurture it in the coming weeks.

Couple for Week 32: Tamar and Judah

The story of Tamar and Judah is found in Genesis 38 and is a remarkable and complex narrative that highlights themes of justice, loyalty, and God's providence. Judah, one of the twelve sons of Jacob, was married to a woman named Shua, and together they had three sons: Er, Onan, and Shelah. Tamar was given to Er, the firstborn, as his wife. However, Er was wicked in the sight of the Lord, and God struck him dead. According to the levirate marriage custom, it was then the responsibility of Onan, Er's brother, to marry Tamar and produce an heir for his brother. But Onan, unwilling to fulfill this duty, also displeased God and was killed.

After the deaths of both of her husbands, Tamar was left a widow with no children. Judah promised to give his youngest son, Shelah, to her when he was old enough, but Judah failed to fulfill his promise. Tamar, seeing that she was not being given the opportunity to have children, took matters into her own hands. She disguised herself as a prostitute and positioned herself where Judah would encounter her. Judah, not recognizing her, solicited her services and, as a pledge for payment, gave her his seal, cord, and staff. Tamar became pregnant and, upon discovering she was with child, Judah ordered her to be burned for her perceived immorality.

However, Tamar revealed that the father of her child was the man who owned the seal, cord, and staff. Judah acknowledged his wrongdoing, admitting that he had not fulfilled his promise to her. Tamar gave birth to twin sons, Perez and Zerah, and through her actions, she ensured the continuation of Judah's family line, which eventually led to the birth of King David and, ultimately, Jesus Christ.

Lessons for Couples:

1. Faithfulness and Trust: One of the most important lessons from the story of Tamar and Judah is the importance of faithfulness and trust in a relationship. Judah failed to uphold his promise to Tamar by withholding his son Shelah, thus leaving her without an heir and in a vulnerable position. Tamar's actions, though unconventional, ultimately led to her securing the promise of a child. Couples can learn from this story the value of being true to their word and ensuring that commitments made in marriage and family life are honored, both in small promises and major responsibilities.

2. God's Sovereign Plan: The story of Tamar and Judah may seem like an isolated incident of deception and human failure, but God's sovereign plan was at work throughout the entire situation. Despite Judah's failure to fulfill his obligations, God used Tamar's courage and ingenuity to continue His promise to Abraham. Tamar's actions led to the birth of Perez, an ancestor of David and, ultimately, Jesus Christ. Couples can learn that even when things seem difficult or when they encounter failure, God's purpose will ultimately prevail, and He is always at work in their lives, even in the midst of brokenness.

3. Righteousness in Difficult Circumstances: Tamar's story also shows that sometimes, when faced with injustice or difficult circumstances, individuals must take action to ensure justice is served. Tamar acted out of desperation to secure her rightful place in Judah's family, even when it meant confronting him with his failure. Couples can learn that it is important to take action when necessary to rectify wrongs, but also to do so with wisdom and integrity, ensuring that their actions are motivated by righteousness rather than self-interest.

4. The Importance of Parenthood: The levirate marriage system was established to ensure the continuation of family lines and protect widows. Tamar's desire to have children was not just for her own sake but for the preservation of her husband's family and inheritance. When Judah failed to provide for her, Tamar took matters into her own hands to ensure that the family line continued. Couples can learn from this the deep value of parenthood and family legacy, understanding that children are a blessing and part of God's purpose for future generations.

5. Humility and Accountability: Judah's response to the revelation of Tamar's actions is an important lesson in humility and accountability. When Tamar presented Judah with the seal, cord, and staff, he could not deny his failure to fulfill his promise. He acknowledged his wrongs and declared that Tamar was more righteous than he. In marriage and relationships, it is important for couples to hold each other accountable, be willing to admit when they are wrong, and seek reconciliation and restoration. Judah's admission of guilt and willingness to make things right is an example of humility that couples can apply in their own lives.

6. The Power of Integrity: Despite the circumstances, Tamar's integrity stands out. She did not seek vengeance or resort to sinful behavior, but she acted to preserve her dignity and ensure justice. By taking matters into her own hands, she made sure that her rights were respected. Tamar's character reveals that integrity is crucial, even in difficult situations. Couples can learn that maintaining integrity and ensuring that their actions align with God's moral standards is more important than seeking temporary solutions or shortcuts.

7. God Can Redeem Broken Situations: Perhaps the most striking aspect of the story is how God took a broken, messy situation and used it for His redemptive purposes. Tamar's actions were controversial, and the circumstances were far from ideal, but God used her to bring about the continuation of Judah's family line, leading to the birth of David and eventually to the birth of Jesus. This teaches couples that no matter how broken their circumstances might seem, God can redeem any situation and use it for His glory and the good of His kingdom.

Week 33

Embracing Wisdom, Love, and Worship

Weekly Readings:

Day 225- Ecclesiastes 7, Ecclesiastes 8, Ecclesiastes 9:1-12; 1 Corinthians 7:36-40, 1 Corinthians 8:1-13; Psalm 95:1-11

Day 226- Ecclesiastes 9:13-18, Ecclesiastes 10, Ecclesiastes 11, Ecclesiastes 12; 1 Corinthians 9:1-18; Psalm 96:1-13

Day 227- 2 Chronicles 2, 2 Chronicles 3, 2 Chronicles 4, 2 Chronicles 5:1; 1 Corinthians 9:19-27, 1 Corinthians 10:1-13; Psalm 97:1-12

Day 228- 2 Chronicles 5:2-14, 2 Chronicles 6, 2 Chronicles 7:1-10; 1 Corinthians 10:14-33, 1 Corinthians 11:1; Proverbs 20:5-14

Day 229- 2 Chronicles 7:11-22, 2 Chronicles 8, 2 Chronicles 9; 1 Corinthians 11:2-34; Psalm 98:1-9

Day 230- Song of Solomon 1, Song of Solomon 2, Song of Solomon 3, Song of Solomon 4; 1 Corinthians 12:1-26; Psalm 99:1-9

Day 231- Song of Solomon 5, Song of Solomon 6, Song of Solomon 7, Song of Solomon 8; 1 Corinthians 12:27-31, 1 Corinthians 13:1-13; Psalm 100:1-5

Weekly Reflection:

This week's readings span a beautiful array of wisdom, worship, and love, touching upon deep truths for life, faith, and relationships. In Ecclesiastes, we encounter a poetic search for meaning amidst the fleeting nature of life. Solomon, revered for his wisdom, confronts life's transience, sharing insights that resonate across generations. His reflections are not about despair but about seeking contentment beyond worldly pursuits, which can feel empty and ephemeral. He invites us to live with purpose by seeing each day as a gift, encouraging us to find joy in the simple blessings God provides. Reflecting on this with your spouse, consider how you might shift your focus from temporal concerns to eternal truths. What in your life has lasting meaning? This can be an invitation to value time together, expressing gratitude for each other, and for the moments you share.

2 Chronicles transports us to a time of national and personal worship as Solomon's temple is dedicated to God. This monumental event reflects the Israelites' longing for a place where God would dwell with them. Solomon's dedication of the temple was not just about the building itself; it was an offering of the people's hearts to God. The temple was adorned with beauty, symbolizing the people's love and reverence for God. In our own lives, we are called to make our homes, hearts, and relationships places where God's presence is cherished and honored. Together as a couple, you might explore how you can make your home a "temple" that reflects God's love and peace—a sanctuary where you can pray, discuss your faith, and encourage each other's spiritual growth. Solomon's dedication inspires us to commit ourselves to a life centered around worship and reverence, especially in our closest relationships.

As we delve into 1 Corinthians, Paul's counsel to the early Christian community in Corinth highlights the essence of love, unity, and spiritual gifts. In Chapter 13, Paul describes love as patient, kind, and enduring. This passage often graces wedding ceremonies, but its wisdom extends far beyond romance, offering a blueprint for every relationship, particularly in marriage. Paul's words remind us that love is an ongoing commitment—a series of selfless actions and attitudes that build the foundation of a strong partnership. Consider together which aspects of love in this passage you might each want to deepen in your relationship. Whether it's patience, kindness, humility, or forgiveness, there's always room to grow. As you work to embody these characteristics, remember that true love mirrors God's love for us—a love that is unwavering, compassionate, and nurturing.

The Song of Solomon takes us on a journey through the poetic and intimate love between a bride and groom, reminding us of the beauty of companionship, mutual respect, and desire. This book is often interpreted as an allegory for the relationship between God and His people. In marriage, it serves as a reminder to nurture affection and appreciation, viewing your spouse not just as a partner in life but as a gift. The verses describe a couple who delights in one another and takes joy in each other's presence. Together, reflect on the qualities you admire in each other, celebrating the friendship and love that has grown over time. Reaffirming these aspects of your relationship helps build a bond rooted in joy and appreciation, a reminder that love grows deeper when it is cherished.

Finally, this week's Psalms offer songs of praise and gratitude, inviting us to acknowledge God's goodness and majesty. In Psalm 95, we are encouraged to worship with joy, acknowledging the Lord as our Maker and Shepherd. This is followed by Psalms 96 through 100, which continue this theme of exalting God. These psalms remind us of the power of collective praise and are a beautiful prompt to incorporate gratitude into your life together. Whether through prayer, song, or simply expressing thanks, finding ways to celebrate God's presence in your relationship can strengthen your bond. In moments of both joy and challenge, turning to worship helps us recognize the steadfast love of God, who walks alongside us through every season.

This week, as you explore the wisdom of Ecclesiastes, the dedication in Chronicles, the love in Song of Solomon, and the praises in the Psalms, you are invited to consider how these truths can shape and deepen your own relationship. Embrace each day with an eternal perspective, dedicating your life and love to God, embodying patience and kindness, and celebrating each other as precious gifts. Let this week be a time of reflection, gratitude, and renewed commitment to live a life of love and worship together.

Weekly Discussion Prompts:

1. Living with Contentment: Ecclesiastes teaches us to embrace life with an eternal perspective. How can you support each other in finding contentment beyond earthly achievements? What practical steps can you take to shift your focus from temporary to eternal values?

2. Strengthening Faith Through Worship: In 2 Chronicles, Solomon dedicates the temple to God. How can you make worship a priority in your relationship? Discuss ways to create an atmosphere of worship and reverence in your home.

3. Pursuing Godly Wisdom: Ecclesiastes urges us to seek wisdom and humility. Share an area where you both seek to grow in godly wisdom. How can you hold each other accountable and encourage one another on this journey?

4. Building Each Other Up in Love: 1 Corinthians 13 speaks of love's characteristics—patience, kindness, and selflessness. Choose one characteristic of love you'd like to strengthen in your relationship. What actions can you take to embody this trait?

5. Rejoicing in God's Creation: The Song of Solomon celebrates the beauty of marital love and companionship. Reflect on how God's gift of love and partnership has blessed your life. What qualities do you appreciate most in each other?

6. Serving Together with Purpose: In 1 Corinthians 12, Paul describes the church as one body with many parts, each having a unique purpose. How can you support one another's unique gifts in service to God and others?

7. Cultivating Joy and Thankfulness: This week's psalms are filled with praise and worship for God's mighty deeds. Share a moment from this past week for which you are particularly thankful. How can you incorporate more moments of gratitude into your daily life?

"A Temple of Love": Create a "Temple of Love" activity by choosing three ways to honor God in your relationship over the next month. It could be a commitment to a regular prayer time together, serving in a ministry, or supporting each other's gifts in a specific way. Write down each commitment and display it where you can both see it, reminding you to nurture this "temple" with acts of love and worship.

Couple for Week 33: Phinehas and His Wife

Phinehas was a priest and the son of Eleazar, who was the son of Aaron, the brother of Moses. His story is briefly mentioned in the Old Testament, particularly in the book of Numbers and the book of Joshua. Phinehas became a prominent figure during a time of moral and spiritual decline among the Israelites, particularly when they were involved in sinful practices with the Moabites at Baal-Peor.

In Numbers 25, the Israelites began to engage in idolatry and sexual immorality with Moabite women. As a result, God's anger was kindled, and a plague began to ravage the Israelites. Phinehas, seeing a blatant act of sin where an Israelite man brought a Midianite woman into his tent in defiance of God's laws, took action. He grabbed a spear and went into the tent, where he killed both the Israelite man and the Midianite woman, stopping the plague. His act of zeal and obedience to God's commands was highly regarded, and as a result, God made a covenant of peace with Phinehas and promised him and his descendants the priesthood forever.

While Phinehas is most known for his zeal for the Lord, the Bible does not specifically mention details about his wife or her role in his life. However, there is a significant event in 1 Samuel 4, where we encounter Phinehas' wife, who is briefly named. This is a tragic part of the story in which Phinehas, as a priest, is present during the battle between the Israelites and the Philistines. The ark of the covenant is captured, and both Phinehas and his father, Eli, die as a result of the defeat. Phinehas' wife, who was pregnant at the time, hears the news of her husband's death and the loss of the ark, causing her to go into labor prematurely. She dies during childbirth, and her child, a son, is born. Before she dies, she names the child "Ichabod," meaning "The glory has departed," reflecting the deep sorrow and tragedy of the moment.

Lessons for Couples:

1. Zeal for God's Honor: Phinehas and his actions illustrate the importance of zeal for God and His holiness. Phinehas' act of judgment against sin may seem harsh, but it demonstrates his commitment to protecting the integrity of God's people and honoring the Lord's commandments. For couples, this can serve as a reminder to maintain a zeal

for righteousness in their relationship, ensuring they are living in a way that honors God, upholding His standards in their marriage and family life.

2. Obedience in Difficult Times: Phinehas' actions in Numbers 25 were in response to a moment of great moral decline, yet he obeyed God's command despite the consequences. Couples can learn from Phinehas' commitment to doing what is right even when it is difficult. Obedience to God should be the foundation of any marriage, and it will help couples to navigate the challenges they face, even when it means making hard or unpopular decisions.

3. Faithfulness in Adversity: The tragic death of Phinehas and his wife during the Philistine battle in 1 Samuel 4 underscores the realities of life and the inevitability of loss. For couples, this event serves as a reminder that faithfulness to each other is important, especially in times of difficulty or suffering. Phinehas' wife, despite her sorrow, stayed faithful to her role as a mother, even in the face of tragedy. Couples are reminded to be steadfast in their commitment to one another, even during moments of pain or hardship.

4. The Importance of Legacy: Phinehas' legacy, in part, is seen through the priesthood passed on to his descendants. His role in the covenant of peace with God demonstrates the importance of establishing a godly legacy. Couples can learn from Phinehas' example by building a legacy of faithfulness that can be passed down to future generations. This includes teaching children to live according to God's Word, demonstrating the values of marriage, and instilling a deep sense of the importance of holiness and service to God.

5. The Impact of Tragedy on Family Life: Phinehas' wife's death during childbirth and the naming of her son, Ichabod, highlight the grief and sorrow that can sometimes accompany life. However, the story also shows how a family can respond to grief. The naming of Ichabod was a symbol of the loss of God's presence in Israel at that moment, but even in such a tragic time, the family unit had the potential for resilience. For couples, this can be a reminder of the importance of being present for one another during times of loss and grief, ensuring that they support each other through the challenging seasons of life.

6. The Weight of Responsibility: As a priest, Phinehas bore a heavy responsibility to lead his people in righteousness. His role in executing God's judgment was a reminder of the seriousness of his responsibility. Couples can learn that marriage is a sacred responsibility, requiring ongoing commitment to faith, righteousness, and sacrificial love. Just as Phinehas had to act decisively for the good of the people, couples are called to lead their family with wisdom and integrity, providing a strong spiritual foundation for their marriage.

7. Trusting God in the Face of Tragedy: The loss of Phinehas, his wife, and the ark of the covenant shows the real, painful consequences of living in a fallen world. However, it also serves as a reminder of the need to trust God through every season of life, including times of loss and hardship. While this event may have been a low point for Israel, God's plan for redemption and restoration was still in motion. Couples can learn that, even in the midst of loss, they can trust God to bring healing, restoration, and new beginnings.

Week 34

Strength in Faith, Wisdom in Leadership, and Hope in Resurrection

Weekly Readings:

Day 232- 2 Chronicles 10, 2 Chronicles 11, 2 Chronicles 12; 1 Corinthians 14:1-19; Proverbs 20:15-24
Day 233- 2 Chronicles 13, 2 Chronicles 14, 2 Chronicles 15; 1 Corinthians 14:20-40; Psalm 101:1-8
Day 234- 2 Chronicles 16, 2 Chronicles 17, 2 Chronicles 18:1-27; 1 Corinthians 15:1-34; Psalm 102:1-11
Day 235- 2 Chronicles 18:28-34, 2 Chronicles 19, 2 Chronicles 20; 1 Corinthians 15:35-49; Psalm 102:12-17
Day 236- 2 Chronicles 21, 2 Chronicles 22, 2 Chronicles 23; 1 Corinthians 15:50-58, 1 Corinthians 16:1-4; Proverbs 20:25-30, Proverbs 21:1-4
Day 237- 2 Chronicles 24, 2 Chronicles 25; 1 Corinthians 16:5-24; Psalm 102:18-28
Day 238- 2 Chronicles 26, 2 Chronicles 27, 2 Chronicles 28; 2 Corinthians 1:1-11; Psalm 103:1-12

Weekly Reflection:

This week's readings weave a tapestry of faith, leadership, resurrection hope, and enduring wisdom. From the chronicles of Israel's kings to Paul's teachings on spiritual gifts and resurrection, we explore what it means to lead with faith, grow in wisdom, and live in the hope of eternal life.

2 Chronicles highlights the reigns of several kings, some faithful and some disobedient, illustrating how their leadership directly impacted their people. King Rehoboam's poor decision to ignore wise counsel (2 Chronicles 10) and King Asa's faithfulness in calling upon God in times of trouble (2 Chronicles 14) provide stark contrasts in leadership styles. The difference between these kings serves as a reminder that our decisions—whether in leadership, marriage, or family

life—have lasting effects. Reflecting on your own decisions as a couple, think about how you can lead each other with wisdom and humility. How can you make decisions together that honor God and foster unity in your relationship?

The spiritual gifts discussed in 1 Corinthians 14 give us insight into the body of Christ and the importance of love, order, and understanding in the use of those gifts. Paul teaches that everything should be done decently and in order, and that love should be at the heart of all our actions, even in the exercise of spiritual gifts. For couples, this is a reminder that your shared purpose is to serve God and each other with love, respect, and kindness. How can you use your gifts—whether they are in prayer, hospitality, service, or encouragement—to strengthen your marriage and ministry?

Paul's reflections on the resurrection in 1 Corinthians 15 encourage us to remember that death is not the end for those who belong to Christ. Our bodies will be transformed, and we will be raised imperishable. This is a profound hope for believers, a hope that impacts how we live today. Together, you might consider how the hope of the resurrection changes the way you approach difficulties, challenges, and even daily routines. In moments of struggle, remember that you are not living for today alone, but for the eternal joy promised in Christ's resurrection.

As you reflect on Psalm 101, we are invited to commit ourselves to living a life of integrity, especially in our homes. The psalmist expresses a desire to walk in the ways of righteousness and to protect his heart from evil. Similarly, we are called to protect our relationships and our families from influences that could harm our faith and unity. Consider how you can build a stronger foundation of trust and integrity in your relationship. What steps can you take together to ensure that you walk in righteousness and honor in all areas of your life?

In the 2 Chronicles passages, the story of King Jehoshaphat's victory over a vast enemy army (2 Chronicles 20) reveals the power of prayer, unity, and trust in God. Jehoshaphat's response to a crisis was not to panic, but to call the people together to pray and seek God's guidance. This is a powerful lesson for couples, reminding us that when faced with challenges, our first response should be prayer. Together, consider the times when you have faced challenges as a couple and how you can more intentionally bring those struggles to God in prayer.

This week's Proverbs (20:25-30, 21:1-4) offer insights into how we should conduct ourselves in both personal and communal life. Proverbs speaks of the wisdom of understanding our own limitations, the importance of honesty, and the necessity of seeking God's guidance in all matters. As a couple, how can you apply these truths to your relationship? Consider the importance of clear communication, mutual respect, and a commitment to walking in integrity together.

Lastly, Psalm 103 invites us to bless the Lord for His many benefits, from forgiveness to healing and redemption. As you read through this psalm, take time to reflect on the countless ways God has blessed you both. Offer thanks together for His grace, mercy, and love in your lives.

This psalm serves as a reminder to cultivate a heart of gratitude, recognizing that God's love is constant, no matter what circumstances we face.

Weekly Discussion Prompts:

1. Leading with Wisdom: In 2 Chronicles, we see the impact of wise and foolish leadership. As a couple, how can you ensure that your decisions—big and small—are made with wisdom and prayerful consideration? How can you lead each other toward God's purposes?

2. Spiritual Gifts in Marriage: Paul encourages us to use our spiritual gifts to serve others in love. How can you use the gifts God has given you to bless and encourage each other in your marriage? Share specific ways you can serve together as a couple.

3. The Hope of Resurrection: Reflecting on 1 Corinthians 15, how does the resurrection of the dead shape your outlook on life's struggles and challenges? How can this eternal perspective affect your marriage and daily living?

4. Living with Integrity: Psalm 101 calls us to walk in integrity. How can you create an environment of trust and honesty in your relationship? Are there any areas where you feel challenged to live with more integrity together?

5. Prayer in Times of Crisis: In 2 Chronicles 20, Jehoshaphat leads the people in prayer during a crisis. How do you respond when faced with difficulties as a couple? Are there areas in your life that could benefit from a deeper commitment to prayer and seeking God's guidance?

6. Cultivating Gratitude: Psalm 103 encourages us to bless the Lord for His many blessings. What are you most thankful for in your relationship? How can you express your gratitude to God for each other and for His presence in your lives?

Joint Couple Activity:

"A Resurrection of Hope": Reflecting on the hope of the resurrection, take time this week to share your hopes and dreams for the future. Whether it's about your family, your ministry, or your personal goals, talk about how the hope of eternal life shapes your plans. Write down one goal or dream you have for your relationship, and commit to praying for it together each day this week.

Couple for Week 34: The Levite and His Wife

The story of the Levite and his concubine is one of the most tragic and complex narratives in the Bible, illustrating the destructive impact of family disharmony, moral decay and social injustice. This account, found in Judges 19–21, depicts how a horrific act of violence led to broader consequences for the Israelite tribes and serves as a cautionary story about societal responsibility, respect, and justice.

The Story of the Levite and His Concubine:

- A Troubled Relationship: The story begins with a Levite living in the hill country of Ephraim, whose concubine leaves him and returns to her father's house in Bethlehem. After four months, the Levite decides to reconcile with her and travels to bring her back. This reconciliation attempt highlights the strain in their relationship and the lack of mutual commitment and respect. The Levite's journey to retrieve her foreshadows the complex and painful events that follow.

- The Events in Gibeah: On their journey back, the Levite and his concubine stop in the town of Gibeah in the territory of Benjamin. An elderly man offers them hospitality for the night, but men from the town surround the house and demand that the Levite be brought out to them so they can abuse him. In a tragic turn of events, the Levite sends his concubine outside instead, and she is brutally assaulted by the men throughout the night. In the morning, she collapses at the door, and when the Levite finds her, he coldly tells her to get up, only to discover that she has died.

- The Outcry and Call for Justice: The Levite responds by taking a shocking action: he cuts his concubine's body into twelve pieces and sends them to each of the tribes of Israel as a call for justice. This gruesome act shocks the Israelites, who gather together to address the atrocity. The tribes demand that the Benjaminites surrender the men of Gibeah who committed the crime, but the Benjaminites refuse, resulting in a civil war.

- The War with Benjamin: The Israelites go to war against the tribe of Benjamin. After a devastating battle that nearly wipes out the tribe, the Israelites realize the severity of their actions and mourn for the tribe they nearly destroyed. To prevent the tribe of Benjamin from disappearing, they devise a plan to provide wives for the remaining Benjaminites, attempting to restore the tribe but through further morally questionable means.

Lessons for Couples:

1. The Consequences of a Broken Relationship: The Levite and his concubine's relationship appears strained, lacking trust, mutual respect, and commitment. The initial separation and the Levite's indifferent treatment of her reflect a dysfunctional relationship where each partner's needs are neglected. For couples, this story underscores the importance of respect, mutual care, and commitment. Healthy relationships are built on compassion

and understanding, while disregard for each other's well-being can lead to further discord.

2. The Dangers of Moral Decay in Society: The violence that unfolds in Gibeah reflects a broader societal breakdown in Israel, where people did "what was right in their own eyes" (Judges 21:25). This story highlights the consequences of a society lacking a moral compass, where unchecked wickedness leads to destructive behavior. Couples can see the importance of maintaining shared values and fostering an environment of respect, not only in their relationship but also within their communities.

3. Standing Against Injustice: The Levite's reaction to the concubine's death—demanding justice—was necessary, but his initial failure to protect her is notable. Couples can learn from this story about the importance of standing against injustice at all times, both in their relationship and society. True compassion includes defending and protecting one another, not merely seeking justice after harm has been done.

4. The Cost of Unforgiveness and Vengeance: The resulting civil war and near destruction of the tribe of Benjamin illustrate how vengeance and a lack of forgiveness can lead to greater harm. Couples can learn that anger and vengeance often have lasting, unintended consequences that can destroy relationships and communities. Instead of seeking retaliation, resolving conflicts through communication, forgiveness, and understanding is a healthier and more sustainable approach.

5. The Role of Leadership and Responsibility: The failure of Israel's leaders to guide and protect their people contributes to the tragic events in this story. Couples can take this as a reminder of the importance of responsible leadership, both in relationships and in society. Good leadership fosters safety, accountability, and justice, whereas neglect or abuse of authority can lead to ruin. In marriage, both partners share responsibility for creating an environment of care and respect.

6. The Impact of Indifference and Objectification: The Levite's treatment of his concubine as a disposable object rather than a valued partner leads to tragic consequences. His actions highlight the dangers of indifference and objectification. For couples, this serves as a reminder that relationships should be rooted in love, empathy, and respect for one another's dignity. A lack of respect for each other can lead to harm and a breakdown of trust.

Week 35

Restoration, Renewal, and the Call to Reconciliation

Weekly Readings:

Day 239- 2 Chronicles 29, 2 Chronicles 30, 2 Chronicles 31:1; 2 Corinthians 1:12-22; Psalm 103:13-22
Day 240- 2 Chronicles 31:2-21, 2 Chronicles 32, 2 Chronicles 33:1-20; 2 Corinthians 1:23, 2 Corinthians 2:1-11; Proverbs 21:5-16
Day 241- 2 Chronicles 33:21-24, 2 Chronicles 34, 2 Chronicles 35:1-19; 2 Corinthians 2:12-17, 2 Corinthians 3:1-6; Psalm 104:1-18
Day 242- 2 Chronicles 35:20-27, 2 Chronicles 36; 2 Corinthians 3:7-18; Psalm 104:19-30
Day 243- Micah 1, Micah 2, Micah 3, Micah 4; 2 Corinthians 4; Psalm 104:31-35
Day 244- Micah 5, Micah 6, Micah 7; 2 Corinthians 5:1-10; Proverbs 21:17-26
Day 245- Isaiah 1, Isaiah 2; 2 Corinthians 5:11-21, 2 Corinthians 6:1-2; Psalm 105:1-11

Weekly Reflection:

This week's readings present themes of restoration, renewal, and reconciliation. From the healing and reforms under King Hezekiah's reign to Paul's call for the ministry of reconciliation, we are reminded of God's ongoing work in restoring His people, and how we, as believers, are called to be agents of that same restoration in the world.

In 2 Chronicles, we see a powerful narrative of renewal as King Hezekiah leads the people of Judah back to God. His reforms, which include the cleansing of the temple and the reinstitution of the Passover (2 Chronicles 29-30), symbolize God's willingness to forgive and restore those who turn back to Him. This calls to mind the importance of repentance and the joy of experiencing God's forgiveness. For couples, this may be a time to reflect on the areas in your relationship that need restoration. Have there been moments where you've turned away from God or from each other? How can you bring those areas of your relationship to God for healing and renewal?

Psalm 103 emphasizes God's compassion and readiness to forgive. The psalmist marvels at God's mercy, recognizing that He does not treat us as our sins deserve but instead shows love and forgiveness. As you reflect on this, consider how you can extend the same grace to one another. Just as God forgives us, we are called to forgive each other, building a relationship based on mercy and understanding.

The apostle Paul's writings in 2 Corinthians expand on the theme of reconciliation. In 2 Corinthians 1, he speaks of God's faithfulness and the comfort we receive in our troubles, which we can then offer to others. This emphasizes the importance of empathy and mutual support within marriage. In times of difficulty, how can you comfort one another with the same comfort you have received from God? Think of a specific way you can be a source of comfort to your spouse during challenging times.

Paul continues in 2 Corinthians 3, describing the transformative power of the gospel, a message of hope that brings lasting change. Just as the Israelites were transformed by the covenant, we are made new in Christ. This renewal is not just for our spirits but also for our relationships. Consider how the gospel has impacted your marriage. Are there areas where you both need to experience the transformative power of Christ more fully?

The book of Micah speaks of judgment and hope. Micah prophesies both the consequences of Israel's sin and the promise of restoration. In Micah 4, we see a vision of a time when God will bring peace and healing to His people. For couples, this can be a reminder that even in times of difficulty or hardship, God has a plan for healing and restoration. If there are challenges you're facing, remember that God's plan is always to bring you back to wholeness.

In Isaiah 1 and 2, the prophet calls God's people to return to Him and live righteously. There is a strong message of judgment for those who turn away from God, but also a call to restoration for those who repent. This can encourage couples to turn back to God, trusting in His ability to heal and restore. Reflect together on areas where you might need to return to God, asking for His guidance in bringing renewal to your marriage.

Weekly Discussion Prompts:

1. Repentance and Renewal: Reflecting on Hezekiah's reforms in 2 Chronicles, what areas of your relationship could use renewal? Are there specific habits, misunderstandings, or tensions that need to be addressed? How can you both bring those to God for healing?

2. Forgiveness: Psalm 103 speaks of God's forgiveness. How does God's mercy challenge the way you forgive each other? Are there areas where you need to extend more grace to one another?

3. Comforting Each Other: In 2 Corinthians 1, Paul speaks of the comfort we receive in times of trouble. How can you offer comfort to your spouse in times of difficulty? How can you create a deeper atmosphere of support in your marriage?

4. Transformation in Christ: Paul teaches in 2 Corinthians 3 that the gospel transforms us. What areas of your relationship have been transformed by the gospel? How has your understanding of Christ's love for you affected the way you love and serve each other?

5. Restoring Peace: Micah 4 paints a picture of peace and healing. In what ways can you create peace in your home and marriage? How can you be agents of reconciliation in your relationship, and what role does prayer play in this?

6. Righteous Living: Isaiah calls us to return to God and live righteously. What does righteous living look like in your marriage? Are there areas where you need to grow in living according to God's word together?

Joint Couple Activity:
"Restoration and Renewal in Prayer": Take time this week to pray together for the areas of your marriage that need renewal. Ask God to bring healing where there is hurt and restoration where there is brokenness. Consider setting aside a time each day to pray together, inviting God to transform and restore your relationship. At the end of the week, write down one specific area where you have seen God bring renewal in your marriage.

Couple for Week 35: Esau and Judith

Esau, the older twin brother of Jacob, is a well-known figure in the Bible. His story is primarily found in the Book of Genesis. Esau is often remembered for selling his birthright to his brother Jacob for a bowl of stew (Genesis 25:29-34), and for losing his father Isaac's blessing to Jacob through deception (Genesis 27). Despite these challenges, Esau later reconciled with his brother, Jacob, and became the father of the Edomites.

Judith, Esau's wife, is mentioned in the Bible in Genesis 26:34-35. She was the daughter of Beeri the Hittite and the sister of Basemath, Esau's other wife. Judith's marriage to Esau is often depicted in a negative light, as she was one of the foreign wives whom Esau took from the surrounding nations, which caused great displeasure to his parents, Isaac and Rebekah. The Bible mentions that the marriage of Esau to Judith and Basemath was a source of bitterness for his parents because these marriages were outside of the covenant family and their faith.

Judith's role in the Bible is rather limited, but she plays a significant part in the broader context of Esau's decisions and their impact on his family. The marriages of Esau to Judith and Basemath are described as "a grief of mind" to Isaac and Rebekah (Genesis 26:35), as these unions were seen as violations of the spiritual heritage and covenant promises made to Abraham.

Lessons for Couples:

1. Respect for Family Values and Traditions: Esau's marriages to Judith and Basemath, foreign women who did not share the faith of his family, caused significant pain and disappointment to his parents. For modern couples, this serves as a reminder of the importance of respecting family values and the significance of shared faith and beliefs in marriage. A strong foundation of mutual respect for each other's family traditions can contribute to a more harmonious relationship.

2. Choosing a Life Partner Wisely: Esau's decision to marry women from outside the covenant family led to a lack of harmony within his own family. This teaches the value of choosing a partner who shares the same values, beliefs, and life goals. A couple's faith and worldview can shape their marriage, and being aligned on these matters can help avoid future discord.

3. The Impact of Marriage Choices on Family: The choice of a spouse affects not only the couple but also the extended family. Esau's marriages caused his parents to experience deep grief. This reminds couples that their choices, especially regarding whom they marry, have ripple effects on the lives of those around them, particularly their families.

4. Seeking Parental Blessing and Guidance: Esau's parents, Isaac and Rebekah, were deeply distressed by his choice of wives, and this highlights the importance of seeking the guidance and blessing of parents, especially in cultures and faith traditions that value parental wisdom. While the Bible doesn't always provide a clear endorsement of arranged marriages, it does emphasize the importance of seeking counsel and considering the opinions of those who have a deep interest in the well-being of the individuals involved.

5. God's Sovereignty Over Marriage and Family: Despite Esau's poor choices in marriage, God continued to fulfill His promises to Abraham and his descendants, and Esau's lineage eventually became the nation of Edom. This demonstrates that while human decisions can lead to complications and conflicts, God's plan and purpose can still be carried out. For couples, this teaches that God is sovereign over all circumstances, even when things don't go as planned.

6. Avoiding Bitterness and Resentment: Esau's marriages created a root of bitterness within his family, causing his parents grief and tension. For couples, it's important to avoid allowing negative emotions like bitterness or resentment to fester, especially when family relationships are impacted. Open communication and addressing problems in a healthy manner can prevent long-term hurt and division.

7. Reconciliation is Possible: Despite the pain Esau caused his family, he eventually reconciled with Jacob, his brother, years after the conflict over the birthright and blessing. This story teaches couples that no matter how challenging things may be in the relationship, reconciliation is possible through forgiveness, humility, and effort.

Week 36

God's Judgment and Mercy

Weekly Readings:

Day 246- Isaiah 3, Isaiah 4, Isaiah 5:1-7; 2 Corinthians 6:3-18, 2 Corinthians 7:1; Psalm 105:12-22
Day 247- Isaiah 5:8-30, Isaiah 6, Isaiah 7, Isaiah 8:1-10; 2 Corinthians 7:2-16; Psalm 105:23-36
Day 248- Isaia]h 8:11-22, Isaiah 9, Isaiah 10:1-19; 2 Corinthians 8:1-15; Proverbs 21:27-31, Proverbs 22:1-6
Day 249- Isaiah 10:20-34, Isaiah 11, Isaiah 12, Isaiah 13; 2 Corinthians 8:16-24, 2 Corinthians 9:1-5; Psalm 105:37-45
Day 250- Isaiah 14, Isaiah 15, Isaiah 16; 2 Corinthians 9:6-15; Psalm 106:1-15
Day 251- Isaiah 17, Isaiah 18, Isaiah 19; 2 Corinthians 10; Psalm 106:16-31
Day 252- Isaiah 20, Isaiah 21, Isaiah 22, Isaiah 23; 2 Corinthians 11:1-15; Proverbs 22:7-16

Weekly Reflection:

This week's readings draw us into the tension between God's judgment and His mercy, two themes that run deeply through Scripture and offer powerful insights into both our personal lives and our marriages. The messages of Isaiah highlight the consequences of sin, but they also carry hope and the promise of God's eventual restoration. Similarly, Paul's letters in 2 Corinthians offer insight into the importance of perseverance, faith, and reconciliation within relationships.

In Isaiah, we witness a strong prophetic message against the moral and spiritual decay of Judah and Israel. In Isaiah 5, the "song of the vineyard" vividly portrays God's disappointment with His people, who failed to live up to their calling. The imagery of a vineyard—intended to produce good fruit but yielding only wild grapes—serves as a powerful metaphor for relationships that fail to honor God's purposes. For couples, this is a moment to reflect on the fruit of your relationship: Is your marriage bearing fruit for God's kingdom? Are you cultivating love, peace, and righteousness, or are there areas where sin, selfishness, or neglect are hindering growth?

Isaiah 6 reveals the prophet's calling and the holiness of God. When Isaiah sees the Lord, he is confronted with his own unworthiness and that of his people. This vision of God's holiness challenges us to consider our own actions and attitudes toward God in our marriages. Do we honor God's presence in our relationship? Are we allowing His holiness to shape how we love, serve, and forgive one another?

Paul's letter to the Corinthians addresses issues of faith, perseverance, and holiness, echoing the themes found in Isaiah. In 2 Corinthians 6:3-18, Paul speaks of the need to remain pure and separated from worldly influences, a message that calls for both individual and relational sanctification. For couples, this may be a reminder to evaluate whether external influences are negatively impacting your marriage. Are there distractions, temptations, or unhealthy habits that are threatening the purity of your relationship? How can you both commit to living in a way that honors God together?

In 2 Corinthians 7:1, Paul encourages the Corinthians to "cleanse ourselves from every defilement of body and spirit, bringing holiness to completion in the fear of God." This call to purity can be a powerful prompt for couples to reflect on their spiritual health. How can you grow in holiness together as a couple? What practices—such as prayer, Bible study, or service— can you incorporate into your daily life to deepen your relationship with God and one another?

The challenge of living in the world but not being of it, which Paul writes about, is particularly poignant for marriages today. There are so many distractions and pressures that can lead couples to focus on anything but their relationship with God and each other. Reflecting on Isaiah's call to righteousness, ask yourselves: How can you grow closer to God, purifying your relationship from external pressures and selfish desires?

Isaiah 9 presents the beautiful promise of the coming Messiah, the one who will bring peace and justice. This prophetic message is a powerful reminder for couples that despite the difficulties and challenges in life, God's ultimate plan for us is one of peace and restoration. The coming of Christ is not only a future hope but a present reality in our marriages. When Christ is at the center of a relationship, His peace reigns, and His justice restores what is broken.

In Isaiah 10 and Isaiah 11, we see the promise of God's judgment on the wicked but also the hope of restoration through the Messiah. For married couples, these chapters invite reflection on how to live justly with one another, following God's principles of justice and mercy. How can you uphold righteousness in your relationship, seeking to act justly with one another, even when it's difficult?

Paul's teachings in 2 Corinthians 9 on generosity also provide an opportunity to reflect on the importance of generosity in relationships. Just as we are called to be generous with our resources, we are also called to be generous in our love, forgiveness, and support for one another. Marriage, like all relationships, requires constant self-sacrifice and the willingness to give of ourselves for the good of the other.

Weekly Discussion Prompts:

1. God's Judgment and Mercy: Isaiah's messages often highlight the consequences of turning away from God. Are there areas in your marriage where you have strayed from God's will? What steps can you take to turn back to Him and restore what has been broken?

2. Holiness in Marriage: Isaiah 6 portrays the holiness of God, and Paul calls us to holiness in 2 Corinthians 7. What does holiness look like in your relationship? Are there areas where you need to grow in purity and holiness together?

3. Overcoming External Pressures: How do external influences (e.g., social media, work stress, unhealthy friendships) impact your marriage? How can you protect your relationship from these pressures and focus more fully on God's purposes for you as a couple?

4. Generosity in Marriage: In 2 Corinthians 9, Paul speaks about generosity in giving. How can you both be more generous with your time, love, and attention in your marriage? Are there ways you can serve and bless one another more freely?

5. Living Out Justice and Mercy: Isaiah 10 and 11 highlight God's justice and mercy. How can you live justly and mercifully with your spouse? Are there areas in your relationship that need reconciliation, and how can you work towards that this week?

6. Hope in Christ: Reflecting on Isaiah 9's promise of the Messiah, how does Christ's coming bring hope and peace to your marriage? How can you build a stronger foundation in Him this week?

Joint Couple Activity:

"Purifying Your Relationship Together": This week, set aside time to pray and reflect on areas where your marriage could use purification or renewal. Take turns praying aloud for specific areas of your relationship, asking God to cleanse your hearts, minds, and actions. At the end of the week, write down one way you've seen God purify or restore your marriage.

Couple for Week 36: Jacob and Leah

Jacob and Leah's story is primarily found in Genesis 29-35. Jacob, the son of Isaac and Rebekah, had a complicated relationship with Leah, the older daughter of Laban. Jacob initially fell in love with Rachel, Leah's younger sister, and agreed to work for Laban for seven years in exchange for Rachel's hand in marriage. However, Laban deceived Jacob on the wedding night by giving him Leah instead of Rachel, as Leah was the older sister. Jacob only realized the deception the following morning, and Laban justified the trickery by stating that it was customary for the older daughter to marry first.

Jacob agreed to work another seven years to marry Rachel, the woman he truly loved. Though Jacob's heart was set on Rachel, he was married to Leah, and this created a complex dynamic in their relationship. Leah, feeling unloved and overlooked by Jacob, began to bear him children, while Rachel remained barren for a time. This led to competition between the sisters, with Leah's increasing fertility and Rachel's desperate desire for children. Over time, both Leah and Rachel used their maidservants as surrogates to bear children for Jacob, further complicating the family dynamics.

Leah bore Jacob six sons—Reuben, Simeon, Levi, Judah, Issachar, and Zebulun—as well as a daughter, Dinah. After years of rivalry and tension, Jacob finally left Laban's household and returned to Canaan with his wives and children. Despite the complexities of their relationship, Leah remained a key figure in the lineage of Israel. Her son Judah became the ancestor of King David and, ultimately, the line through which Jesus Christ was born.

Lessons for Couples:

1. The Pain of Feeling Unloved: Leah's story highlights the emotional pain of feeling unloved or overlooked. She was given to Jacob in a marriage that lacked mutual affection. For couples, it is important to understand the deep impact of emotional neglect and work to foster love, affection, and appreciation for one another. Feeling loved and valued is crucial for a thriving relationship.

2. God's Grace in Times of Disappointment: Though Jacob did not love Leah as he loved Rachel, God saw Leah's suffering and opened her womb, blessing her with many children. This teaches that even in difficult or painful circumstances, God can provide blessings and use us in ways that bring about His greater purposes. For couples, this is a reminder that God is present even in the most difficult times, and He can bring good out of situations that may seem bleak.

3. Competing for Attention and Affection: Leah and Rachel's rivalry over Jacob's affection and children caused significant tension in their family. This shows the destructive effects of competition and comparison in a relationship. Couples should aim to build a

partnership based on mutual respect and love rather than competition, and they should recognize the harm that comparison can cause.

4. Building Unity Despite Rivalry: Although there was conflict and rivalry between Leah and Rachel, both women played crucial roles in the formation of the twelve tribes of Israel. This demonstrates that, despite personal differences or challenges, working together toward a common purpose—especially when that purpose aligns with God's will—can bring about great results. Couples can learn from this the importance of working as a team, even when facing challenges.

5. The Importance of Communication: Jacob's lack of emotional connection with Leah was not only hurtful to her but also contributed to the tension in their relationship. Clear communication in marriage is essential to maintaining understanding and emotional intimacy. Couples should prioritize honest conversations and ensure that their emotional needs are met, avoiding misunderstandings that lead to feelings of neglect.

6. God's Use of Imperfect Situations: Leah's marriage to Jacob was not ideal, but God used the situation to further His purposes. Leah's son, Judah, played a pivotal role in the genealogy of Israel, which eventually led to the birth of Jesus. This teaches that even when a relationship is not perfect or circumstances are difficult, God can still use those situations to fulfill His plans. Couples should remember that God can bring purpose and meaning to even the most challenging times in their lives.

7. Patience and Trust in God's Timing: Leah's journey involved waiting and trusting in God's timing. Despite the rivalry and her feeling unloved, she chose to keep having children, trusting that God had a purpose for her life. This teaches couples the importance of patience, both with each other and in the process of trusting God's plan for their relationship.

8. Unconditional Love and Commitment: Leah's love for Jacob remained steadfast even when Jacob showed preference for Rachel. While Jacob did not return Leah's affection in the same way, Leah's commitment to her family and her faith was unwavering. Couples can learn the value of unconditional love and commitment, even when the feelings or circumstances are challenging.

Week 37

Trust in God's Deliverance and Strength

Weekly Readings:

Day 253- Isaiah 24, Isaiah 25, Isaiah 26; 2 Corinthians 11:16-33; Psalm 106:32-39
Day 254- Isaiah 27, Isaiah 28; 2 Corinthians 12:1-10; Psalm 106:40-48
Day 255- Isaiah 29, Isaiah 30:1-18; 2 Corinthians 12:11-21; Psalm 107:1-9
Day 256- Isaiah 30:19-33, Isaiah 31, Isaiah 32; 2 Corinthians 13; Proverbs 22:17-27
Day 257- Isaiah 33, Isaiah 34, Isaiah 35; Galatians 1; Psalm 107:10-22
Day 258- Isaiah 36, Isaiah 37; Galatians 2:1-10; Psalm 107:23-32
Day 259- Isaiah 38, Isaiah 39, Isaiah 40; Galatians 2:11-21, Galatians 3:1-9; Psalm 107:33-43

Weekly Reflection:

This week's readings invite us to reflect on trusting in God's deliverance in times of trouble, as well as finding strength in Him even when life feels overwhelming. The themes of divine judgment, comfort, and hope interweave throughout the passages, showing us how to persevere through life's challenges by looking to God as our source of strength and refuge.

Isaiah presents powerful imagery of God's ultimate triumph over evil and His promise to deliver His people. In Isaiah 24, the judgment of God is portrayed as a time of reckoning for the earth and its inhabitants. Yet, in the midst of this judgment, Isaiah 25 offers a vision of hope—a banquet of rich food for all peoples, where God will wipe away every tear. This juxtaposition between judgment and mercy is central to understanding God's character: He is just, but He is also a refuge for the oppressed. Couples can reflect on this dynamic in their own marriages—acknowledging the challenges or struggles they face but also recognizing the promises of God's comfort and deliverance.

As you read through Isaiah 26, the people of God declare their trust in the Lord as their eternal rock. The chapter reminds us that God's peace is available to those who keep their minds stayed on Him, a promise that can strengthen us in moments of uncertainty. For couples, this is an invitation to build your marriage on the solid foundation of God's peace, knowing that even in the midst of struggles, His peace can guard your hearts.

In 2 Corinthians, Paul's letter to the Corinthians provides a practical model of perseverance through trials. In 2 Corinthians 11:16-33, Paul recounts the hardships he endured for the sake of the gospel: imprisonments, beatings, and the constant threat of death. Despite these challenges, Paul continues to boast not in his own strength but in God's power to sustain him. This passage invites couples to reflect on how they face difficulties together. When struggles arise, are you leaning on your own strength or trusting in God's grace to carry you through?

2 Corinthians 12:1-10 offers a profound lesson about strength in weakness. Paul speaks of his "thorn in the flesh," a persistent struggle that God did not remove. Yet, God's response to Paul was: "My grace is sufficient for you, for my power is made perfect in weakness." This passage reminds us that sometimes God allows us to face challenges, not to break us, but to refine our faith and reveal His strength. In marriage, couples often experience seasons of weakness—be it emotional, spiritual, or physical. But it is in these moments that God's grace shines brightest. Reflecting on this, how can you both embrace your weaknesses as opportunities for God's power to be made known in your marriage?

In Isaiah 30, the people of Israel are urged to trust in God rather than relying on alliances with foreign nations. Despite their rebelliousness, God promises that He will fight for them and deliver them from their enemies. This passage invites reflection on where you place your trust. In your marriage, do you turn to God for deliverance in times of trouble, or do you seek solutions elsewhere? Trusting God is essential for couples as they face life's challenges, knowing that He is always ready to act on their behalf.

As we turn to Isaiah 33-35, we see the contrast between the fate of the wicked and the restoration of God's people. Isaiah 33 speaks of God's justice, while Isaiah 34 pronounces judgment on the nations. But in Isaiah 35, we find a beautiful promise of restoration: the desert will rejoice and blossom, and the eyes of the blind will be opened. For couples, this speaks to the hope of renewal and transformation. Are there areas of your marriage that feel like a barren desert? Trust in God's promise of restoration—He can bring new life and beauty where there was once dryness.

In Galatians, Paul continues to speak of the freedom we have in Christ, reminding us that we are no longer bound by the law but are heirs of the promise through faith. This message of freedom can be life-changing for couples who are struggling with past hurts or brokenness in their marriage. The gospel offers freedom from guilt, shame, and sin, and it is in Christ that true healing and reconciliation occur. How can you both embrace the freedom Christ offers and extend that freedom to one another in your relationship?

Weekly Discussion Prompts:

1. God as Our Refuge: Reflect on the imagery of God as a refuge and deliverer in Isaiah 25. When difficulties arise in your marriage, how can you more fully turn to God as your refuge? In what ways can you support one another in trusting God for deliverance?

2. Peace in the Midst of Trials: Isaiah 26 speaks of perfect peace for those whose minds are stayed on God. How can you cultivate more of God's peace in your marriage, especially during stressful or uncertain times?

3. Strength in Weakness: In 2 Corinthians 12, Paul embraces his weakness as an opportunity for God's power to shine. Are there areas of weakness in your marriage where you can invite God's strength and grace to transform your relationship?

4. Building Trust in God: In Isaiah 30, God urges His people to trust in Him rather than in worldly solutions. In your marriage, how can you both grow in your trust in God rather than relying on your own understanding or resources?

5. Restoration and Renewal: Reflecting on Isaiah 35, how can you both allow God to restore and renew areas of your marriage that may feel dry or broken? How can you trust in His ability to transform your relationship?

6. Embracing Freedom in Christ: In Galatians, Paul speaks of the freedom we have in Christ. How can you both embrace this freedom in your marriage, letting go of past hurts, and living in the grace of God's forgiveness?

Joint Couple Activity:

"Restoring Peace in Your Marriage": This week, take time to reflect on any areas of your relationship that need healing or restoration. Together, pray for God's peace to flood those areas. Ask God to restore any brokenness and to guide you both in His ways. Afterward, discuss practical steps you can take to build trust and intimacy in your relationship, and share what you feel God is calling you to do next.

Couple for Week 37: Ahab and Jezebel

Ahab and Jezebel's story is primarily found in the 1 Kings 16-21 and 2 Kings 9. Ahab was the king of Israel, the son of Omri, and reigned in the northern kingdom during a time of significant moral decline. He married Jezebel, the daughter of King Ethbaal of Sidon, a powerful and ambitious woman who worshipped Baal, a pagan god. This marriage was politically strategic, but it also led to spiritual disaster for Israel.

Jezebel, a zealous supporter of Baal, sought to establish the worship of Baal in Israel and eradicate the worship of Yahweh. She persuaded Ahab to build an altar to Baal in Samaria and promoted idol worship, leading many Israelites astray. She also ruthlessly persecuted and killed the prophets of God, particularly targeting the prophet Elijah, who opposed her idolatry and sin.

Ahab, though initially passive in his leadership, became complicit in Jezebel's actions, showing a weakness for her influence. One of the most notorious events in their story occurred when Jezebel orchestrated the death of Naboth, a vineyard owner, so that Ahab could take possession of Naboth's vineyard. Ahab was disheartened when Naboth refused to sell him the vineyard, and Jezebel took matters into her own hands. She falsely accused Naboth of blasphemy, leading to his execution. When Ahab took possession of the vineyard, the prophet Elijah confronted him, prophesying God's judgment upon him and his household for their wickedness.

The couple's downfall culminated in their eventual deaths. Jezebel was thrown from a window by her servants at the command of Jehu, who was anointed king by the prophet Elisha. She was trampled by horses, and her body was eaten by dogs, fulfilling the prophecy of Elijah. Ahab's death came in battle, and the judgment against his house continued after his death, as his sons were killed, and his dynasty was destroyed.

Lessons for Couples:

1. The Danger of Negative Influence: Jezebel's influence on Ahab was one of the most destructive aspects of their marriage. While Ahab was king, he allowed Jezebel's sinful desires and priorities to lead him astray, resulting in spiritual decline and judgment for Israel. This teaches couples that one partner's negative influence can lead the other down a path of destruction. It is important to be mindful of the influences we allow into our relationships and to encourage one another toward righteousness.

2. The Importance of Spiritual Leadership: Ahab's passivity in spiritual matters, particularly in his marriage to Jezebel, allowed evil to flourish. He followed Jezebel's lead, even when it led him into sin, instead of leading his household in the ways of the Lord. Couples should encourage each other in their spiritual lives, with both partners taking

an active role in cultivating faith and worship in the home. Spiritual leadership is crucial for a marriage to thrive in the Lord.

3. The Consequences of Sinful Actions: Ahab and Jezebel's sinful decisions—especially the murder of Naboth for personal gain—led to God's judgment upon them and their family. Their actions not only caused personal harm but also had long-lasting consequences for Israel. This story serves as a warning that sin has consequences, not only for those who commit it but also for others. Couples should be vigilant against making sinful decisions and remember that their choices can affect their family, community, and future generations.

4. The Power of Repentance: While Ahab's actions were deeply sinful, there is a moment in the story when he humbles himself before God in repentance after hearing Elijah's prophecy of judgment. God shows mercy by delaying the judgment during Ahab's lifetime, though it eventually came to pass. This teaches couples that repentance and humility can open the door to God's mercy, even when facing the consequences of sin. In relationships, it is essential to remain humble and open to repentance when mistakes are made.

5. The Dangers of Idolatry and Compromise: Jezebel's promotion of idol worship and her manipulation of Ahab to abandon the worship of God is a stark reminder of the dangers of idolatry. In modern relationships, idolatry can take many forms—be it materialism, power, status, or even unhealthy relationships. Couples must guard against allowing anything to take the place of God in their lives and prioritize Him above all else.

6. Standing Against Unrighteousness: Elijah, the prophet of God, stood courageously against the evil practices of Ahab and Jezebel, even though it meant facing great opposition. He did not allow the power of Ahab and Jezebel to intimidate him into silence. Couples can learn from Elijah the importance of standing up for what is right and holding each other accountable in love, even in the face of societal pressures or personal challenges. Standing firm in righteousness strengthens both individuals and the marriage as a whole.

7. The Dangers of an Ungodly Marriage: Ahab and Jezebel's marriage was founded on selfishness, manipulation, and a desire for power, rather than mutual love, respect, and faithfulness to God. This dynamic caused their marriage to spiral into corruption and destruction. Couples can learn that building a marriage on godly principles—love, faithfulness, mutual respect, and shared values—is essential for lasting success. Marriages rooted in selfish ambition and ungodly influences will ultimately face difficulties that are difficult to overcome.

8. God's Justice Will Prevail: Despite the power and influence of Ahab and Jezebel, God's justice eventually prevailed. Their sins were exposed, and they faced the consequences. This reminds couples that no evil or injustice goes unnoticed by God. Even when

wrongdoers appear to thrive, God's justice will ultimately prevail, and His plans will not be thwarted. Couples should trust that God will bring justice in His timing and remain committed to living rightly before Him.

Week 38

God's Faithfulness in Restoration and Salvation

Weekly Readings:

Day 260- Isaiah 41, Isaiah 42; Galatians 3:10-25; Proverbs 22:28-29, Proverbs 23:1-9

Day 261- Isaiah 43, Isaiah 44:1-23; Galatians 3:26-29, Galatians 4:1-20; Psalm 108:1-5

Day 262- Isaiah 44:24-28, Isaiah 45, Isaiah 46; Galatians 4:21-31, Galatians 5:1-6; Psalm 108:6-13

Day 263- Isaiah 47, Isaiah 48, Isaiah 49:1-7; Galatians 5:7-26; Psalm 109:1-20

Day 264- Isaiah 49:8-26, Isaiah 50, Isaiah 51:1-16; Galatians 6; Proverbs 23:10-18

Day 265- Isaiah 51:17-23, Isaiah 52, Isaiah 53, Isaiah 54; Ephesians 1; Psalm 109:21-31

Day 266- Isaiah 55, Isaiah 56, Isaiah 57:1-13; Ephesians 2; Psalm 110:1-7

Weekly Reflection:

This week, we are invited to reflect on God's faithfulness in restoration and salvation, as well as how He offers His grace to all who seek Him. Isaiah continues to proclaim messages of judgment and hope, emphasizing God's power to restore His people and deliver them from oppression. Through His mercy, God promises salvation, renewal, and victory over all enemies.

In Isaiah 41, we hear God's reassurance to His people. Amidst fear and exile, God promises to strengthen and help them. This is the foundation for trusting God, knowing that He has already promised His presence and provision. Isaiah 42 further emphasizes God's salvation through His chosen servant, the Messiah, who will bring justice and deliverance to the nations. The imagery in these chapters invites us to reflect on God's strength and His desire to bring justice to the world. For couples, this may inspire reflection on how God is calling you to stand for justice and peace in your own lives, especially in difficult times.

Galatians 3:10-25 underscores the futility of relying on the law for salvation, showing that it is only through faith in Jesus Christ that we are made right with God. Galatians 3:26-29 highlights that in Christ, there is no division between Jew and Gentile, slave and free, male and female— all are one in Christ. This speaks to the inclusive nature of God's grace and invites couples to reflect on how they, too, can be a witness to that unity in their relationships and communities.

In marriage, mutual respect, equality, and understanding are crucial in reflecting the unity Christ desires for His body.

In Isaiah 43, God declares His eternal love for His people and promises to bring them out of exile. This powerful declaration, "Fear not, for I have redeemed you; I have called you by your name, you are mine," is a reminder that no matter how far we may stray, God is always calling us back. For couples, this is a comforting reminder that God's love and redemption are always available. Just as He never abandons us, we are called to support and love one another through all circumstances, forgiving and restoring each other when necessary.

Galatians 4:21-31 presents the allegory of Hagar and Sarah, which contrasts the law and grace, showing that those who are of faith are children of the free woman. This analogy reveals that living in freedom under God's grace is what He desires for His people, rather than being burdened by the law. Galatians 5:1-6 builds on this theme, urging believers to stand firm in the freedom Christ offers. For married couples, the message of grace in this passage encourages you to offer grace to one another, rather than holding onto expectations or laws that may create barriers to true love and unity.

In Isaiah 49:8-26, God speaks of His promise of restoration, redemption, and the return of His people to their land. This chapter is filled with hope for those who have suffered, reminding them that God has not forgotten them. Isaiah 50-54 contains prophetic words that point to the suffering servant (Jesus Christ) who will bear the sins of the world. As we reflect on these chapters, we can find comfort in the fact that God's salvation is accomplished through Jesus' sacrifice, and His love and care for us are unwavering.

The reading in Ephesians 1 reminds us that we are chosen and blessed by God, with a purpose in Christ. Through Him, we have received redemption, forgiveness, and an eternal inheritance. This echoes the theme of God's faithfulness, and for couples, it is a reminder of the powerful role you play in each other's lives—chosen to walk together in His grace.

Weekly Discussion Prompts:

1. God's Assurance: Reflect on Isaiah 41:10, where God promises to strengthen and uphold His people. How can you encourage one another in your marriage when fear or doubt creeps in? How can you remind each other of God's promises?

2. Living in Unity: In Galatians 3:28, Paul speaks of the unity we have in Christ. How can you work together as a couple to reflect this unity in your marriage, setting aside any divisions and focusing on the love and grace that unite you?

3. Grace Over Law: In Galatians 4:21-31, we see the contrast between the law and grace. How can you both let go of legalistic expectations in your marriage and embrace the freedom and grace that Christ offers in your relationship?

4. God's Redemptive Love: Isaiah 43:1 reminds us that God has called us by name and we are His. In your marriage, how can you extend God's redemptive love to one another, offering forgiveness and healing when needed?

5. Standing Firm in Freedom: Reflect on Galatians 5:1-6 and how freedom in Christ changes our relationships. How can you, as a couple, ensure that you stand firm in the freedom Christ offers, rather than being trapped by unhealthy expectations or pressures?

6. Sharing in Christ's Sacrifice: As you read Isaiah 53, meditate on the suffering servant who bore our sins. How does the sacrifice of Christ shape the way you love and serve one another in your marriage?

7. Purpose in Christ: In Ephesians 1, we are reminded of our purpose in Christ. How can you both remind each other of the eternal purpose you share as a couple? How can you align your goals and dreams with God's greater plan for your lives?

Joint Couple Activity:
"Celebrating God's Faithfulness Together": Take time this week to reflect on the areas where God has been faithful in your marriage. Share with each other specific instances where you've seen His hand at work in your relationship. Afterward, write down or create a visual representation (such as a scrapbook or memory jar) of the ways God has shown His love and faithfulness to you both. This can serve as a reminder of His continual presence in your lives and strengthen your bond as a couple.

Couple for Week 38: Rehoboam and Naamah

Rehoboam and Naamah's story is primarily found in 1 Kings 14:21-31 and 2 Chronicles 12:13-16. Rehoboam was the son of King Solomon and succeeded him as king of Judah after Solomon's death. Naamah was the Ammonite wife of Rehoboam, and together they had a son named Abijah, who would later become king of Judah.

Rehoboam's reign began with challenges, as the northern tribes of Israel, led by Jeroboam, rebelled against him after Solomon's death. Jeroboam's rebellion split the kingdom of Israel into two parts: the northern kingdom of Israel and the southern kingdom of Judah, where Rehoboam reigned. The division of the kingdom was a consequence of Solomon's actions, including his heavy taxation and forced labor policies, which led to widespread dissatisfaction among the people.

Despite his father Solomon's wisdom, Rehoboam initially failed to consult God when facing the rebellion. Instead, he sought advice from his peers, following the counsel of young men who advised him to be harsher with the people than his father had been. This decision led to the further alienation of the northern tribes, and Israel was permanently divided.

Rehoboam's reign also saw a decline in spiritual and national stability. His marriage to Naamah, who was an Ammonite, likely had an influence on his policies and decisions. The Ammonites were often hostile toward Israel, and their idolatrous practices may have contributed to the spiritual decline in Judah during Rehoboam's rule. Rehoboam's failure to turn the hearts of the people back to God, combined with his reliance on his own wisdom and the influence of foreign idols, resulted in Judah's eventual decline and vulnerability to external threats.

In the latter part of his reign, Rehoboam faced the invasion of Egypt under Pharaoh Shishak, who attacked Jerusalem and took many of the treasures from Solomon's temple. This was a consequence of Rehoboam's failure to remain faithful to God, and although he repented, the damage was done. Rehoboam's reign is marked by instability, rebellion, and failure to restore unity in Israel.

Lessons for Couples:

1. The Importance of Wise Counsel: Rehoboam's greatest mistake was rejecting the wise counsel of the older, more experienced advisors in favor of the advice of his peers. This led to the division of the kingdom and strife within his reign. For couples, this story serves as a reminder to seek and value wise counsel, particularly in times of decision-making. Surrounding oneself with godly, experienced advisors who can offer wisdom and perspective is crucial for making sound decisions in marriage and family life.

2. The Influence of Spiritual Direction in Marriage: Rehoboam's marriage to Naamah, an Ammonite, may have influenced his spiritual decisions. The Ammonites were often associated with idolatry and enemy opposition to Israel. This can serve as a lesson for couples to carefully consider how their relationships—especially marriages—can influence their spiritual walk. Marrying someone with differing beliefs or values can create tension in a marriage, especially when it comes to shared spiritual practices and priorities. Couples should ensure that their faith is central to their marriage and that they encourage one another in their spiritual growth.

3. The Consequences of Rejecting God's Will: Rehoboam's failure to seek God's direction, particularly when faced with the rebellion of the northern tribes, shows the dangers of relying on one's own judgment instead of seeking God's will. Couples can learn from Rehoboam's mistakes by understanding that their decisions—whether in marriage, family, or finances—should be made in prayer and in alignment with God's will. Ignoring God's guidance can lead to conflict, division, and missed opportunities for peace and prosperity.

4. The Danger of Idolatry and Foreign Influence: Naamah, as an Ammonite, likely brought with her the influence of idol worship and foreign customs. This may have led to the

spiritual decline in Judah during Rehoboam's reign. For couples, this story underscores the danger of allowing external influences, particularly worldly or idolatrous practices, to invade the marriage and the home. Couples should guard against allowing influences that may lead them away from their faith and lead to spiritual compromise.

5. The Impact of Leadership in Marriage: Rehoboam was the king, and his decisions affected the entire kingdom. Similarly, the decisions one spouse makes in a marriage can greatly affect the relationship. Couples are called to lead their families with wisdom, integrity, and in alignment with God's will. In Rehoboam's case, his failure to lead with wisdom and humility led to the downfall of the kingdom. For couples, this highlights the importance of good leadership in marriage, with both spouses being involved in making decisions that honor God and bring peace and unity to the home.

6. Repentance and Restoration: Even though Rehoboam faced judgment for his disobedience, there is a moment when he humbled himself and sought the Lord. While his repentance did not stop the consequences of his actions, it did result in some temporary relief from judgment. For couples, this teaches the importance of repentance and seeking God's forgiveness when mistakes are made. When there is genuine repentance, God's mercy can bring healing and restoration to relationships, even after serious failure.

7. The Dangers of Pride and Self-Reliance: Rehoboam's pride and self-reliance, particularly in his decision to ignore the wisdom of the older advisors and follow the advice of his peers, led to disastrous consequences. For couples, it's important to recognize that pride and self-reliance can undermine relationships. Humility, openness to others' perspectives, and a reliance on God are essential for maintaining healthy, strong relationships.

8. Legacy of Faithfulness: Rehoboam's reign was marked by instability and failure to secure the future of the kingdom. In contrast, when a couple prioritizes faithfulness to God, they can establish a legacy of righteousness that impacts future generations. Couples should be intentional about leaving a godly legacy, one that is founded on faith, prayer, and obedience to God's Word.

Week 39

Living in the Light of God's Glory and Calling

Weekly Readings:

Day 267- Isaiah 57:14-21, Isaiah 58, Isaiah 59; Ephesians 3; Psalm 111:1-10
Day 268- Isaiah 60, Isaiah 61, Isaiah 62; Ephesians 4:1-16; Proverbs 23:19-28
Day 269- Isaiah 63, Isaiah 64, Isaiah 65:1-16; Ephesians 4:17-32, Ephesians 5:1-7; Psalm 112:1-10
Day 270- Isaiah 65:17-25, Isaiah 66; Ephesians 5:8-33; Psalm 113:1-9
Day 271- Nahum 1, Nahum 2, Nahum 3; Ephesians 6; Psalm 114:1-8
Day 272- Zephaniah 1, Zephaniah 2, Zephaniah 3; Philippians 1:1-26; Proverbs 23:29-35, Proverbs 24:1-4
Day 273- Jeremiah 1, Jeremiah 2:1-30; Philippians 1:27-30, Philippians 2:1-11; Psalm 115:1-11

Weekly Reflection:

This week, we delve into the theme of living in the light of God's glory and calling. The passages from Isaiah are filled with warnings and promises, contrasting the judgment of sin with the hope of restoration. God's desire for His people is for them to turn from evil and to live in righteousness. These prophetic books also point to a future in which God's reign will bring peace and justice to the earth. In the New Testament, Paul further encourages believers to live worthy of the calling they have received, to walk in the light of Christ, and to reflect God's holiness in their lives.

In Isaiah 57, God speaks against those who live in idolatry and sin, but He also promises peace and healing for those who repent and return to Him. In Isaiah 58, the prophet calls out the empty rituals of fasting and religious observance that do not reflect a true heart for justice and mercy. Instead, God desires His people to practice true righteousness—feeding the hungry, clothing the naked, and bringing justice. Isaiah 59 reveals the deep separation between God and His people due to their sin, but it also promises redemption through the coming of a Savior.

Ephesians 3 is a powerful reminder of the vastness of God's love and His eternal purpose in Christ. Paul speaks about the mystery of the gospel, which has been revealed to the Gentiles—that they too are partakers in the promise of salvation. The reading challenges us to reflect on how we, as a couple or family, are living out this mystery in our daily lives, loving others as Christ has loved us, and showing the world the power of God's grace.

In Ephesians 4:1-16, Paul urges believers to live in a manner worthy of their calling. He speaks of the unity of the body of Christ, encouraging everyone to live in humility, gentleness, and patience, bearing with one another in love. For married couples, this passage offers practical advice on maintaining unity in your relationship, even when there are differences. It reminds you that, as partners in Christ, you are both part of the same body and are called to serve and support each other, working together for God's purposes.

The call to holiness continues in Ephesians 4:17-32 and Ephesians 5:1-7, where Paul instructs believers to put off their old sinful nature and put on the new self, created to be like God in true righteousness and holiness. For married couples, this call challenges you to actively pursue personal holiness and mutual sanctification. Ephesians 5:8-33 brings the practical application to marriage, encouraging couples to live in mutual submission, with husbands loving their wives as Christ loved the church and wives respecting their husbands. This passage calls for deep, sacrificial love in marriage—a love that reflects Christ's love for the church.

Psalm 111 praises God for His greatness, faithfulness, and righteousness. It is a call to reflect on God's wondrous works and to live in awe of His glory. This ties into the message of Isaiah 60—where the glory of the Lord shines forth, drawing the nations to Himself. Couples can reflect on how they can make God's glory visible in their homes and communities by living according to His Word and seeking His righteousness.

Nahum and Zephaniah offer prophecies of God's judgment on the nations, but also highlight His justice and sovereignty. Nahum 1-3 emphasizes God's power over the enemies of Israel, while Zephaniah 1-3 calls the people to repentance, warning of the coming Day of the Lord, when all will be judged according to their deeds. In these chapters, we see God's desire for justice, but also His hope for His people to return to Him with pure hearts.

Philippians 1-2 gives us a clear picture of the Christian calling: to live as citizens of heaven, to live with joy, humility, and service, and to consider others more important than ourselves. For married couples, this is a reminder that your relationship is not just about personal fulfillment but about serving one another in humility and love. In Philippians 2:1-11, we are reminded to have the mind of Christ, who humbled Himself for the sake of others.

Weekly Discussion Prompts:

1. God's Calling to Righteousness: Reflect on Isaiah 58:6-7—God desires justice, mercy, and humility, not empty rituals. How can you as a couple embody these values in your everyday life? Are there areas where you can practice greater compassion or fairness to others?

2. Unity in Christ: In Ephesians 4:1-6, Paul speaks of maintaining unity. How can you support each other in maintaining unity in your marriage, even when differences arise? How can you cultivate humility and patience as you work together in God's calling for your relationship?

3. Living as New Creations: Ephesians 4:17-24 talks about putting off the old self and putting on the new self. What old habits or patterns do you need to let go of to live more fully in the new life Christ offers? How can you help each other in this process?

4. Sacrificial Love in Marriage: Ephesians 5:25-33 speaks to husbands loving their wives sacrificially as Christ loved the church. What does this look like in practical terms for your relationship? How can you both reflect Christ's love in your daily interactions?

5. Serving with Humility: Reflect on Philippians 2:1-4 and how Christ's humility is the model for Christian living. In your marriage, how can you both serve each other in humility, putting each other's needs above your own?

6. Living in the Light of God's Glory: In Isaiah 60:1-3, God's glory is revealed and draws others to Him. How can your marriage reflect God's glory to those around you? What practical steps can you take to live in a way that draws others to Christ?

7. The Day of the Lord: In Zephaniah 3:9-20, God promises to gather and restore His people. How can you and your spouse prepare for the coming of the Lord, living with a sense of expectation and readiness for His return?

Joint Couple Activity:

"Reflecting God's Glory Together": Take time this week to set aside an evening to reflect on ways you can live out God's glory together as a couple. Spend time in prayer, asking God to reveal areas where you can shine His light in your marriage and in your community. You may also want to plan an act of service or charity that you can do together, reflecting the love and justice God calls us to in Isaiah 58.

Couple for Week 39: Ananias and Sapphira

The story of Ananias and Sapphira is found in Acts 5:1-11. Ananias and Sapphira were a married couple in the early Christian church. They sold a piece of property and, like many others in the Christian community, brought part of the proceeds to the apostles, claiming that it was the full amount. However, they secretly kept back a portion of the money for themselves while pretending to donate everything.

Ananias was the first to present the money to the apostles, and Peter, through the Holy Spirit, immediately discerned that Ananias was lying. Peter confronted him, asking why he had lied to the Holy Spirit. Peter pointed out that Ananias was not lying to men but to God. At that moment, Ananias fell dead, and his body was carried out for burial.

Three hours later, Sapphira came in, unaware of what had happened to her husband. Peter asked her if the amount she and Ananias had given was the full price they received for the property. She also lied, confirming the false amount. Peter confronted her as well, and she too fell dead, carried out by the same men who had buried her husband. The event struck fear into the entire church and the people in Jerusalem, and the story serves as a sobering reminder of the seriousness of dishonesty and deceit.

Lessons for Couples:

1. The Dangers of Deception in Marriage: Ananias and Sapphira's story highlights the destructive nature of dishonesty. The couple's joint decision to deceive the apostles and, more importantly, to lie to God, brought severe consequences. For couples, it is a reminder that dishonesty, even in seemingly small matters, can have serious repercussions. Trust is foundational in marriage, and deception undermines that trust, causing harm to the relationship.

2. The Importance of Integrity: Ananias and Sapphira's failure to be truthful about the amount they gave reveals the importance of integrity. In marriage, it's essential to maintain honesty in all areas, whether it concerns finances, decisions, or personal feelings. Integrity builds a relationship where both spouses feel safe and respected, fostering trust and unity.

3. Accountability Before God: While Ananias and Sapphira were lying to the apostles, Peter reminded them that they were ultimately lying to God. This highlights that couples are accountable to God for their actions, both individually and as a partnership. Marriage is not just an earthly covenant but one that involves accountability before God. Couples should strive to honor God in their decisions, knowing that their actions are seen by Him.

4. The Harmful Impact of Hidden Sin: Ananias and Sapphira's hidden sin had devastating effects, not only on them but also on the early church, which was shaken by the event.

For couples, this serves as a reminder that hidden sin—whether in the form of secretive behaviors, unconfessed issues, or unresolved conflicts—can negatively affect the relationship and others around them. Couples should avoid harboring hidden sins and instead focus on transparency and mutual accountability.

5. The Need for Mutual Trust: Both Ananias and Sapphira participated in the lie together, which shows how one partner's dishonesty can involve the other. In marriage, mutual trust is vital for the health of the relationship. When one spouse deceives or hides the truth from the other, it affects the entire relationship. Trust is built on openness, honesty, and a willingness to share even the difficult things.

6. The Power of the Holy Spirit in Marriage: The Holy Spirit played a significant role in revealing the deceit of Ananias and Sapphira. For couples today, this reminds them that the Holy Spirit is present in their lives, helping them discern truth and guiding them in their relationship. Couples should be attuned to the Holy Spirit's guidance, allowing Him to lead them in honesty, transparency, and truthfulness within their marriage.

7. The Consequences of Greed: Ananias and Sapphira's sin was rooted in their desire to keep part of the money for themselves while appearing generous. Their actions were driven by greed and a desire for recognition rather than genuine generosity. In marriage, couples should guard against greed, materialism, and selfishness. True generosity comes from a heart of love and selflessness, not from seeking approval or recognition from others.

8. Respecting the Covenant of Marriage: The couple's joint deceit in this story is a reminder that marriage is a partnership, and both partners are responsible for the actions and choices they make together. Couples should work together in mutual respect and trust, honoring their commitment to each other and to God. This story also underscores that both spouses should hold one another accountable and encourage integrity in their marriage.

9. The Importance of Open Communication: The couple's deceit stemmed from a lack of honest communication with each other and with the apostles. Couples should prioritize open, honest communication in their relationship. This helps prevent misunderstandings, builds stronger connections, and fosters a healthy relationship grounded in trust.

Week 40

Responding to God's Call in Times of Struggle and Faithfulness

Weekly Readings:

Day 274- Jeremiah 2:31-47, Jeremiah 3, Jeremiah 4:1-9; Philippians 2:12-30; Psalm 115:12-18
Day 275- Jeremiah 4:10-31, Jeremiah 5; Philippians 3, Philippians 4:1; Psalm 116:1-11
Day 276- Jeremiah 6, Jeremiah 7:1-29; Philippians 4:2-23; Proverbs 24:5-14
Day 277- Jeremiah 7:30-34, Jeremiah 8, Jeremiah 9:1-16; Colossians 1:1-23; Psalm 116:12-19
Day 278- Jeremiah 9:17-26, Jeremiah 10, Jeremiah 11:1-17; Colossians 1:24-29, Colossians 2:1-5; Psalm 117:1-2
Day 279- Jeremiah 11:18-23, Jeremiah 12, Jeremiah 13; Colossians 2:6-23; Psalm 118:1-16
Day 280- Jeremiah 14, Jeremiah 15; Colossians 3, Colossians 4:1; Proverbs 24:15-22

Weekly Reflection:

This week's readings focus on God's call to His people in times of hardship, as well as the need for faithfulness and perseverance in the face of challenges. Through the prophetic words of Jeremiah and the exhortations of Paul in his letters to the Philippians and Colossians, we are encouraged to remain steadfast in our commitment to God even when times are tough.

In Jeremiah, God speaks to the people of Israel, calling them to return to Him with a whole heart. Their failure to remain faithful has led to the breaking of the covenant, and now they face the consequences. But even in judgment, God's mercy is evident, as He continues to call them back, offering hope for restoration and renewal. In Jeremiah 3, God invites Israel to return, likening their waywardness to an unfaithful spouse. His desire is for reconciliation, but it requires a response—a turning back to Him with sincerity.

Philippians offers a picture of joy and humility amidst suffering. Paul encourages believers to work out their salvation with fear and trembling, knowing that it is God who works in them. This message is particularly poignant for couples, as it speaks to the necessity of perseverance in love—continuing to work through difficulties and challenges together, with an openness to God's transforming work in both partners. Philippians 2:12-30 reminds us to shine as lights in a dark world, living lives that reflect Christ's humility and sacrifice. Paul encourages us to consider others above ourselves, and this lesson is especially applicable in marriage, where mutual selflessness is key to a healthy, thriving relationship.

In Jeremiah 6 and 7, we see the consequences of turning away from God's commands. Jeremiah laments the hardness of the people's hearts, their refusal to listen to God's call. This highlights the importance of heeding God's voice in times of trial. Similarly, Philippians 3:12-21 reminds us that our citizenship is in heaven, and we are to live with eternity in view, not being distracted by earthly desires. For couples, this is an opportunity to reflect on how your relationship can be an eternal partnership—centered on Christ and directed toward His kingdom.

As we reflect on Jeremiah 7:30-34 and Jeremiah 8, we see that sin leads to destruction, but God promises hope through repentance. Paul, in Colossians 1:24-29, urges believers to continue in the faith, being rooted and built up in Christ. He emphasizes the mystery of the gospel, which has now been revealed to the Gentiles, urging all believers to live in a way that honors this great revelation.

In Colossians 2:6-23, Paul warns against being taken captive by empty philosophy and legalistic rituals, urging the believers to hold fast to Christ as the source of all wisdom. For married couples, this passage calls for an anchor in Christ, especially when external pressures—whether cultural or relational—tempt us to focus on the wrong things. Stay grounded in your identity in Christ and the grace He offers.

Psalm 115 calls us to trust in the Lord alone, not in idols or earthly things. It is a reminder that our hope is in God's faithfulness, not in the fleeting comforts of this world. This is a message that resonates deeply in marriage—trusting in God's faithfulness to guide and sustain your relationship through every season.

Weekly Discussion Prompts:

1. God's Call to Return: In Jeremiah 3, God calls Israel to return to Him. In what areas of your life or marriage do you need to return to God with a whole heart? How can you, as a couple, ensure that God remains at the center of your relationship?

2. Working Out Salvation Together: Philippians 2:12-13 urges us to work out our salvation with fear and trembling. How can you support each other in your spiritual growth? What practical steps can you take together to grow closer to God and to one another?

3. Overcoming Hardness of Heart: In Jeremiah 6:10, the people's hearts are described as being hardened. Are there any areas in your relationship where hardness of heart may have developed? How can you soften your hearts toward one another and God?

4. Living with Eternity in Mind: Philippians 3:20-21 reminds us that our citizenship is in heaven. How does living with eternity in view impact the way you live as a couple? How can you both prioritize eternal values over temporary ones?

5. Fighting Against Empty Philosophies: In Colossians 2:8, Paul warns against being deceived by empty philosophies. Are there worldly influences that threaten your commitment to Christ in your marriage? How can you guard against these distractions and keep Christ as your central focus?

6. Hope in the Midst of Struggle: Reflecting on Jeremiah 8:18-22, we see a deep longing for healing and restoration. What struggles are you facing as a couple that need God's healing touch? How can you actively invite God's healing and restoration into those areas?

7. Mutual Encouragement in Trials: Colossians 1:24-29 speaks of the need for endurance and perseverance in the faith. How can you encourage each other to persevere through the difficulties in your relationship, knowing that your endurance leads to spiritual maturity?

Joint Couple Activity:

"Returning to God Together": Set aside time to pray together this week, focusing on areas where you need to return to God with a whole heart. Confess any struggles you've had with selfishness or disobedience, and ask for God's help in restoring both your personal and marital relationship with Him. Reflect on ways to grow together spiritually, whether it's through regular Bible study, prayer, or serving together.

Couple for Week 40: Herod and Herodias

The story of Herod and Herodias is found in Mark 6:17-29, Matthew 14:3-12, and Luke 3:19-20. Herod Antipas, the ruler of Galilee, married Herodias, who was the wife of his brother, Philip. Herodias had initially been married to Philip, but she divorced him to marry Herod, which caused a great scandal, as it was considered unlawful by Jewish law (Leviticus 18:16). John the Baptist, who had been calling for repentance and moral righteousness, publicly rebuked Herod for his marriage to Herodias, calling it an adulterous union.

Herodias, angered by John's condemnation, harbored a grudge against him and wanted him killed. However, Herod, though troubled by John's message, protected him and feared the prophet's influence on the people. A decisive moment came when Herodias' daughter, Salome, danced before Herod during a feast and pleased him so much that he promised to give her anything she asked for, up to half of his kingdom. At her mother's instigation, Salome asked for the head of John the Baptist on a platter. Though distressed, Herod reluctantly ordered John's execution to honor his oath in front of his guests. John was beheaded in prison, and his head was delivered to Salome, who gave it to her mother, Herodias.

Lessons for Couples:

1. **The Danger of Unlawful Relationships:** Herod's relationship with Herodias was rooted in unlawful actions and deceit. Their marriage was condemned by John the Baptist as immoral and against God's law. For couples, this highlights the importance of aligning relationships with God's commands. Relationships based on sinful actions or disobedience to God's word can lead to severe consequences. Couples should strive to build marriages based on respect for divine law and moral integrity.

2. **The Consequences of Disregarding God's Word:** Herod was confronted by John the Baptist and had the opportunity to repent and turn from his sinful relationship. Instead, he ignored God's word and allowed his relationship with Herodias to flourish, even though it was clearly wrong. This choice led to the tragic and unnecessary execution of John. For couples, this serves as a warning about the dangers of ignoring God's guidance. Disregarding the moral principles that God lays out for marriage can lead to harm, not only to the individuals involved but to others around them as well.

3. **The Power of Influence:** Herodias, driven by hatred and jealousy, influenced her daughter to request the beheading of John the Baptist. This highlights the power of influence within a marriage or family, especially when it is used for evil purposes. Couples should be aware of the influence they wield over each other and be cautious of fostering negative or sinful attitudes within their relationship. A marriage built on love and respect for each other and for God will lead to positive influence and encouragement.

4. **The Importance of Protecting One Another:** Although Herodias sought to destroy John the Baptist, Herod protected him as much as he could because he feared him and believed John to be a righteous man. This reflects that even in a marriage where there is division or sinful actions, protection and care for each other should still exist. Couples are meant to be protectors for one another—spiritually, emotionally, and physically— and to help guide each other in the right direction.

5. **The Dangers of Pride and Ego:** Herod's decision to execute John the Baptist was influenced by his pride and his desire to save face before his guests. He had made an impulsive oath and, to maintain his honor in front of his court, chose to murder a righteous man rather than do what was right. Couples should be mindful of their egos and pride, which can lead to sinful decisions. Marriage should be characterized by

humility and a willingness to put one's spouse's best interests first, even if it means sacrificing personal pride.

6. The Impact of External Influences: Herod's actions were also influenced by external pressures—he did not want to go back on his oath in front of his guests, and Herodias pushed her daughter to ask for John's death. This situation shows how external pressures, such as public opinion or the desires of others, can negatively impact a marriage or decision-making process. Couples should strive to make decisions based on their shared values and God's guidance, rather than yielding to external pressure.

7. The Importance of Repentance and Correction: Herod's life could have turned out differently had he heeded John the Baptist's calls for repentance. The refusal to repent and make things right led to tragic consequences. For couples, this teaches that repentance and correction are vital in any relationship. When wrong is done, couples should be willing to recognize it, ask for forgiveness, and work toward healing the relationship.

8. The Cost of Revenge and Hatred: Herodias' hatred for John the Baptist led her to orchestrate his death. Her bitterness and desire for revenge resulted in not only the loss of an innocent life but also in a deepening of the division in her relationship with Herod. Couples should guard against harboring unforgiveness, bitterness, or a desire for revenge, as it can destroy relationships. Forgiveness and letting go of grudges are essential for maintaining peace and unity.

Week 41

Staying Faithful in the Midst of Trials and Hope in God's Promise

Weekly Readings:

Day 281: Jeremiah 16, Jeremiah 17; Colossians 4:2-18; Psalm 118:17-29

Day 282: Jeremiah 18, Jeremiah 19, Jeremiah 20; 1 Thessalonians 1, 1 Thessalonians 2:1-16; Psalm 119:1-8

Day 283: Jeremiah 21, Jeremiah 22, Jeremiah 23:1-8; 1 Thessalonians 2:17-19, 1 Thessalonians 3; Psalm 119:9-16

Day 284: Jeremiah 23:9-40, Jeremiah 24, Jeremiah 25:1-14; 1 Thessalonians 4; Proverbs 24:23-34

Day 285: Jeremiah 25:15-38, Jeremiah 26; 1 Thessalonians 5; Psalm 119:17-24

Day 286: Jeremiah 27, Jeremiah 28, Jeremiah 29:1-23; 2 Thessalonians 1; Psalm 119:25-32

Day 287: Jeremiah 29:24-32, Jeremiah 30, Jeremiah 31:1-14; 2 Thessalonians 2; Psalm 119:33-40

Weekly Reflection:

This week's readings focus on God's call to remain faithful and hopeful in the midst of uncertainty, trials, and struggles. The prophet Jeremiah speaks to the people of Israel, calling them to repentance and faithfulness as they face the consequences of their sin. Yet, even amidst judgment, there is always a message of hope and restoration—a theme echoed throughout this week's passages.

In Jeremiah, the people are facing God's judgment due to their unfaithfulness, yet God promises restoration (Jeremiah 30:1-14). This is a reminder that even in the darkest times, God has a plan for redemption. For couples, this can be a powerful message—no matter what trials you face, whether personal or relational, God's grace offers hope and the possibility of renewal.

The letters of Paul to the Thessalonians bring an encouragement to remain steadfast in faith, especially in the face of suffering. Paul reassures the believers that their work and faith are not in vain, and that they will be rewarded for their endurance (1 Thessalonians 2:19-20). This is a vital message for couples in marriage: even when facing challenges, your commitment to each other and to God is not unnoticed, and your perseverance will bear fruit. Paul also speaks about holiness in relationships (1 Thessalonians 4:1-8), encouraging believers to live in a way that is pleasing to God.

The psalms this week—especially Psalm 119—remind us of the importance of God's Word in times of difficulty. Psalm 119 speaks of how God's Word is a guide in life, a source of comfort, and a way to remain steadfast through challenges. For married couples, this is a reminder to make God's Word central in your relationship. It is the light that guides your path, the truth that holds you steady, and the love that deepens your connection.

In Colossians, Paul calls the believers to prayer and perseverance (Colossians 4:2-18). He encourages them to continue in prayer, to be watchful and thankful, and to act with wisdom. This mirrors the need for intentionality in marriage, where couples should actively pray for one another, and look for ways to serve and encourage one another in all seasons of life.

Weekly Discussion Prompts:

1. God's Call for Faithfulness: In Jeremiah 17:7-8, we see that those who trust in the Lord will be like trees planted by the water, bearing fruit even in times of drought. How can you, as a couple, plant your trust firmly in God's promises, especially when facing difficult circumstances?

2. Endurance in the Face of Suffering: 1 Thessalonians 2:17-20 speaks about the joy that comes from seeing others remain faithful. How can you encourage each other to persevere in your relationship with God, even in times of suffering or trials?

3. Holiness in Your Relationship: 1 Thessalonians 4:3-8 calls us to live holy lives, especially in our relationships. What practical steps can you take to ensure that your marriage is lived out in holiness, reflecting Christ's love and purity?

4. Living with Hope: In Jeremiah 30:18-22, God promises to restore Israel, even after they have been punished for their sin. What areas of your marriage need restoration? How can you hold onto God's promise of healing and renewal?

5. The Power of Prayer in Marriage: Colossians 4:2-4 calls us to be devoted to prayer, asking God to open doors for ministry and to work in our lives. How can you incorporate prayer into your marriage in a more intentional way? How can you pray for each other's spiritual growth?

6. Trusting in God's Word: Psalm 119:11 says, "I have hidden your word in my heart that I might not sin against you." How can you prioritize God's Word in your marriage? What steps can you take to read and reflect on Scripture together as a couple?

7. Perseverance and Reward: Reflecting on 1 Thessalonians 3:12-13, where Paul prays that the Thessalonians' hearts be strengthened, how can you support one another in your spiritual walk? How can you cultivate a marriage that grows in love and holiness?

Joint Couple Activity:

"Hope and Renewal": This week, create a prayer journal as a couple. Spend time each day praying for one another and for your marriage, asking God to restore any areas that need healing. Take turns reading Jeremiah 30:1-14 together, reflecting on the promise of restoration and hope in the Lord. After reading, write down your prayer requests and specific areas where you need God's help, both individually and as a couple. Close each prayer time by thanking God for His faithfulness and asking for the strength to endure.

Couple for Week 41: Naaman and His Wife

The story of Naaman and his wife is found in 2 Kings 5, and while their relationship is not heavily detailed, the events surrounding Naaman's healing provide important insights and lessons for couples.

Naaman was a respected commander in the Syrian army, known for his bravery and success in battle. However, he had a great personal challenge: he suffered from leprosy, a serious and debilitating disease. Despite his high status and accomplishments, his condition left him vulnerable and desperate for a cure. Naaman's wife, who was likely deeply concerned for her husband, plays a role in the story when she hears about a young Israelite servant girl who had been captured during a raid. The girl, who served Naaman's wife, told her that there was a prophet in Israel, Elisha, who could heal Naaman.

Moved by compassion and faith in the girl's words, Naaman's wife encouraged him to seek out the prophet in Israel for healing. After much persuasion, Naaman eventually visited Elisha, who instructed him to dip seven times in the Jordan River. At first, Naaman was offended by the simplicity of the cure, but after some advice from his servants, he humbled himself and obeyed Elisha's instructions. Upon following the prophet's command, Naaman was miraculously healed of his leprosy.

Lessons for Couples:

1. Support and Encouragement in Difficult Times: Naaman's wife demonstrated great care and support for her husband, encouraging him to seek healing when he was desperate. In marriage, it's essential to be a source of emotional support for one another during challenging times. This support can make all the difference in motivating a spouse to take action, especially when they are discouraged or reluctant.

2. Faith and Trust in God's Ways: Naaman's wife likely shared in her husband's journey of faith, trusting that God could bring healing. For couples, trusting in God's ways and His timing, even when the solution may seem unconventional or unclear, is crucial. In Naaman's case, the healing required him to act in humility and obedience. Similarly, couples may need to trust God's direction in their lives, even when it challenges their understanding or comfort zones.

3. Humility and Obedience: Naaman's initial reluctance to follow Elisha's simple instructions highlights the importance of humility in relationships. It was only when he humbled himself and followed the advice of his servants that he received healing. In marriage, humility is a key ingredient for growth and reconciliation. Couples must be willing to set aside pride and listen to each other, making decisions together with openness and obedience to what is best for the relationship.

4. The Power of Compassionate Guidance: Naaman's wife didn't have a direct role in the healing process, but her compassion and the advice of the young servant girl played a pivotal role in leading Naaman to seek the help he needed. In a marriage, even small gestures of kindness, guidance, or encouragement can have a huge impact on each other's lives. A spouse may not always have the answer, but offering support and pointing the other toward wise counsel can lead to healing or breakthroughs.

5. Listening to Wise Counsel: Naaman's wife also encouraged him to listen to the counsel of others, such as the young servant girl and his servants. Often, in marriage, it's easy to become caught up in our own opinions, but listening to others—whether friends, family, or professional counselors—can offer valuable perspectives. Couples who are open to advice from trusted sources are more likely to make wise decisions and experience healing.

6. Healing and Restoration: The physical healing that Naaman experienced was a profound moment of restoration, but there is a deeper lesson for couples about emotional and spiritual healing in a relationship. Just as Naaman was healed from his leprosy, couples can experience healing in their relationships, whether through forgiveness, communication, or working through difficult challenges together. Healing often requires a step of faith, humility, and obedience to God's plan.

7. A Journey of Transformation: Naaman's healing was not only physical but also spiritual. After his healing, he acknowledged the God of Israel and vowed to serve Him. Couples can learn from this transformation—sometimes the trials in marriage, such as conflict or adversity, can lead to deeper spiritual growth and a stronger bond between partners when they turn to God for help. Their relationship may experience transformation, just as Naaman's life was transformed through his obedience.

Week 42

Living Out Faith in the Midst of Adversity

Weekly Readings:

Day 288: Jeremiah 31:15-40, Jeremiah 32:1-25; 2 Thessalonians 3; Proverbs 25:1-10
Day 289: Jeremiah 32:26-44, Jeremiah 33, Jeremiah 34; 1 Timothy 1; Psalm 119:41-48
Day 290: Jeremiah 35, Jeremiah 36, Jeremiah 37; 1 Timothy 2; Psalm 119:49-56
Day 291: Jeremiah 38, Jeremiah 39, Jeremiah 40:1-6; 1 Timothy 3; Psalm 119:57-64
Day 292: Jeremiah 40:7-16, Jeremiah 41, Jeremiah 42; 1 Timothy 4; Proverbs 25:11-20
Day 293: Jeremiah 43, Jeremiah 44, Jeremiah 45; 1 Timothy 5, 1 Timothy 6:1-2; Psalm 119:65-72
Day 294: Jeremiah 46, Jeremiah 47; 1 Timothy 6:3-21; Psalm 119:73-80

Weekly Reflection:

This week's readings center on staying faithful and trusting God in the midst of both personal and collective challenges. In Jeremiah, we witness the ongoing struggle of the Israelites, facing destruction and exile as a consequence of their disobedience. Yet, God's promises of restoration and redemption remain steadfast. Through Jeremiah's messages, the Israelites are reminded that God's covenant promises will endure, even in the face of adversity.

In Paul's letters to the Thessalonians and Timothy, the call to live out our faith with integrity and perseverance rings clear. 2 Thessalonians 3 encourages believers to remain steadfast in good works and prayer, even when facing persecution or hardship. For married couples, this can be a powerful reminder: even in tough times, faithfulness to God and to each other strengthens the relationship.

The Psalms this week, particularly Psalm 119, offer rich encouragement on how to rely on God's Word in times of trouble. Psalm 119:49-56 reminds us that God's promises are a source of comfort when we are facing challenges. Psalm 119:73-80 speaks of God's faithfulness and the joy that comes from meditating on His Word. Couples are reminded to hold fast to the truth of Scripture—it is the anchor that can hold steady in the storms of life.

Weekly Discussion Prompts:

1. Faithfulness Amidst Difficulty: Reflecting on Jeremiah 32:1-25, where God promises to restore Israel, what is a promise from God that you cling to in your own marriage when facing challenges? How can this promise shape your approach to adversity together?

2. Perseverance in Marriage: In 2 Thessalonians 3:13, Paul encourages believers to never tire of doing good. How can you both maintain perseverance in your marriage, even when it seems difficult? What are practical ways to keep investing in each other through tough times?

3. God's Word as a Source of Comfort: Psalm 119:49-56 speaks of finding comfort in God's Word during times of affliction. How can you as a couple use Scripture to encourage one another in moments of distress? What Bible verses have spoken to you personally in the past?

4. Integrity in Action: 1 Timothy 3:9-10 encourages leaders to live with integrity and a clear conscience. How can you practice integrity in your marriage? What steps can you take to build trust and honesty in your relationship?

5. Handling Conflict: Jeremiah 38:1-6 shows how Jeremiah was met with rejection and conflict. How do you handle conflict in your marriage? What steps can you take to resolve differences and work towards reconciliation?

6. Holiness in Relationships: 1 Timothy 4:12 encourages believers to set an example in speech, conduct, love, faith, and purity. How can you both strive to be examples of holiness in your marriage? What are some habits you can build to foster purity in your relationship?

7. Living with Hope: In Jeremiah 31:16-17, God promises that those who mourn will one day return to their land. How can you cultivate hope and trust in God's restoration when facing trials together?

Joint Couple Activity:

"Rooted in Hope": This week, take time each day to share one Scripture verse from Psalm 119 that has been a source of encouragement or challenge to you. Write it down and reflect on how that verse can influence your relationship. After sharing, spend a few minutes praying for each other's spiritual growth and perseverance. Commit to praying together daily for a week, asking God to deepen your connection and strengthen your marriage through His Word.

Couple for Week 42: Lamech and His Wives

Lamech is a figure from the Book of Genesis, mentioned in Genesis 4:19-24. He was a descendant of Cain and the great-great-great-grandson of Adam. He is known for being the first person in the Bible to have two wives (a practice that would later become a source of tension in biblical narratives, as polygamy was often seen as a deviation from God's original plan for marriage, which was intended to be between one man and one woman).

Lamech's story is relatively brief in the Bible, but it is significant for a few key reasons.

1. Marriage to Two Wives: Lamech took two wives, Adah and Zillah. Adah bore him two sons, Jabal and Jubal, who became notable in their own rights as the ancestors of those who lived in tents and raised livestock and the ancestors of those who played the harp and flute, respectively. Zillah bore Lamech a son named Tubal-Cain, who was the ancestor of those who forged tools from bronze and iron, and a daughter, Naamah. This family was instrumental in the early development of human civilization in the areas of agriculture, music, and metallurgy.

2. Lamech's Violent Declaration: In Genesis 4:23-24, Lamech makes a striking and violent declaration to his wives. He says: *"Hear my voice, you wives of Lamech; listen to what I say: I have killed a man for wounding me, a young man for striking me. If Cain's revenge is sevenfold, then Lamech's is seventy-sevenfold."*

This statement is cryptic, but it suggests that Lamech had killed a man in retaliation for being wounded, possibly exaggerating his actions and emphasizing the vengeance he sought. Lamech's words also reference Cain, his ancestor, who had been marked by God for protection after killing his brother Abel. Lamech seems to be boasting that his vengeance is greater than Cain's, as if to assert his dominance and power.

Lessons for Couples:

1. The Dangers of Polygamy: The story of Lamech and his two wives illustrates the potential consequences of polygamy. The Bible generally presents polygamy in a negative light, and Lamech's family life may have been complicated by the existence of multiple wives. While we don't have explicit details about the emotional dynamics of Lamech's marriages, the Bible's overall stance suggests that God's ideal for marriage is monogamy (one man and one woman), as seen in the creation story of Adam and Eve. Polygamy often led to tension and rivalry between wives, as seen in later biblical stories (such as those of Abraham, Jacob, and David).

2. The Impact of Violence and Vengeance: Lamech's violent declaration about avenging an injury teaches couples the destructive effects of harboring a spirit of vengeance. In relationships, bitterness, retaliation, and the desire to "get even" can lead to escalating conflicts that destroy trust and peace. Lamech's attitude, characterized by a desire for

excessive revenge, stands in stark contrast to biblical teachings on forgiveness and reconciliation. Couples are called to forgive one another, following Christ's example of grace, rather than allowing anger and vengeance to poison their relationships.

3. The Role of Leadership: As a man with multiple wives and children, Lamech's actions set an example for his family, though not a positive one. His declaration about vengeance shows a distorted view of leadership—one rooted in self-preservation and pride. In contrast, couples are called to lead their families with love, humility, and selflessness, putting the needs of their spouses and children above their own desires for power or revenge.

4. The Importance of Communication: Lamech's declaration to his wives is made in a public, almost boastful manner. This can be a cautionary tale for couples about how they communicate, especially in times of conflict. Healthy relationships thrive on open, honest, and respectful communication. Instead of boasting or exaggerating one's actions, couples are encouraged to express their feelings in ways that foster understanding, rather than division or arrogance.

5. The Legacy of Family: The children of Lamech, through his wives Adah and Zillah, became founders of important areas of human culture. This shows the lasting impact that families can have on society. However, Lamech's own legacy is one tainted by violence and vengeance. Couples are reminded that their legacy will be shaped not only by what they achieve together but also by the values they pass down to future generations. A legacy of love, peace, and faith is far more desirable than one marked by bitterness or strife.

Week 43

God's Justice and Faithfulness in Troubling Times

Weekly Readings:

Day 295: Jeremiah 48, Jeremiah 49:1-6; 2 Timothy 1; Psalm 119:81-88

Day 296: Jeremiah 49:7-39, Jeremiah 50:1-10; 2 Timothy 2; Proverbs 25:21-28, Proverbs 26:1-2

Day 297: Jeremiah 50:11-46, Jeremiah 51:1-14; 2 Timothy 3; Psalm 119:89-96

Day 298: Jeremiah 51:15-64; 2 Timothy 4; Psalm 119:97-104

Day 299: Jeremiah 52; Titus 1; Psalm 119:105-112

Day 300: Habakkuk 1, Habakkuk 2, Habakkuk 3:1-19; Titus 2; Proverbs 26:3-12

Day 301: Lamentations 1, Lamentations 2:1-6; Titus 3; Psalm 119:113-120

Weekly Reflection:

This week, the readings explore the justice of God in the face of oppression, violence, and betrayal. In the Book of Jeremiah, the prophecies of judgment against Israel's enemies such as Moab, Ammon, and Babylon serve as a reminder of God's sovereignty over all nations. Yet, as seen in Jeremiah's lamentations, God's justice is balanced with His mercy—He does not abandon His people forever but promises restoration.

In 2 Timothy, Paul urges Timothy (and us) to remain steadfast in faith, even amidst hardship, persecution, and suffering. Paul's call to endurance speaks to the trials of life, urging believers to guard the good deposit of faith and remain faithful to the gospel, no matter the opposition. These messages resonate deeply for couples facing adversity, as they encourage perseverance and reliance on God's Word through the storms of life.

Meanwhile, Psalm 119 continues to highlight the importance of God's Word as a lamp to guide us, especially in times of trouble. The psalmist's commitment to following God's laws reminds couples that in moments of doubt or challenge, it is the Word of God that provides clarity, direction, and strength to stay faithful to the promises we have made to each other and to God.

Weekly Discussion Prompts:

1. Trusting in God's Justice: In Jeremiah 49:7-39, God speaks judgment over nations. How can couples trust in God's justice in difficult situations, especially when faced with injustice or brokenness in their relationship?

2. Guarding the Faith: In 2 Timothy 1:13-14, Paul encourages Timothy to guard the faith he has received. How can you as a couple guard the faith in your marriage, ensuring that both of you continue to grow spiritually and uphold your values together?

3. Facing Difficult Times Together: Habakkuk 2:2-4 reminds us that the righteous shall live by faith. How can you strengthen your faith when it feels like your circumstances are overwhelming? How do you lean on God's promises together when facing challenges in your relationship?

4. God's Mercy Amidst Judgment: Lamentations 2:5-6 reflects on the sorrow and desolation of Jerusalem. In times of difficulty or personal failures, how can you as a couple experience God's mercy and comfort? How can forgiveness and restoration become central in your relationship?

5. Living According to God's Word: Psalm 119:81-88 expresses a longing for God's Word amidst trials. As a couple, how can you both cultivate a deep love for the Word of God that guides your decisions and actions together? What steps can you take to make Scripture a central part of your daily life?

6. Faithfulness in Adversity: In 2 Timothy 2:3, Paul says to endure hardship like a good soldier of Christ. What does it mean to endure together in your marriage during hard times? How can you support each other to remain steadfast in love and faith when faced with difficulties?

7. Hope in God's Plan: Jeremiah 50:4-5 speaks of the return of the Israelites from exile, offering a vision of hope. In what ways can you both hold on to hope for the future, especially during tough seasons? How do you remind each other of God's faithfulness and ultimate plans for your life together?

"Praying Through Trials": This week, set aside a specific time each day for prayer together, focusing on one of the Psalms from the week's readings. Choose a passage from Psalm 119 that resonates with you, and pray it over each other, asking God to guide, protect, and strengthen your marriage. Each night, take turns expressing gratitude for God's faithfulness and pray for areas in your marriage that need healing, restoration, or guidance. Reflect on how prayer together brings you closer to God and to each other.

Couple for Week 43: Elimelech and Naomi

Elimelech and Naomi are central characters in the Book of Ruth, which tells the story of God's providence and faithfulness. Their story is one of hardship, loss, and restoration, demonstrating the importance of faith and loyalty within family and marriage.

Story Summary:

1. The Family's Tragedy: Elimelech and Naomi were Israelites who lived in Bethlehem during a time of famine. To survive, they moved with their two sons, Mahlon and Chilion, to the country of Moab. Unfortunately, Elimelech soon died, leaving Naomi a widow in a foreign land. After a decade in Moab, both of Naomi's sons also died, leaving her bereft of her husband and children.

2. Naomi's Return to Bethlehem: In her grief and despair, Naomi decided to return to Bethlehem when she heard that the famine had ended. She urged her daughters-in-law, Orpah and Ruth, to stay in Moab and remarry. Orpah reluctantly agreed, but Ruth clung to Naomi and declared her loyalty to her mother-in-law, choosing to accompany her to Bethlehem. Ruth's famous vow of loyalty is captured in Ruth 1:16-17: *"Where you go, I will go; where you stay, I will stay. Your people will be my people and your God my God. Where you die, I will die, and there I will be buried."*

3. Ruth's Loyalty and God's Provision: Upon returning to Bethlehem, Naomi and Ruth faced difficult circumstances. Ruth, being a widow, went to glean in the fields to provide for herself and Naomi. She ended up in the field of Boaz, a relative of Elimelech. Boaz showed kindness to Ruth, allowing her to gather grain and ensuring her safety. Naomi, recognizing the opportunity, encouraged Ruth to approach Boaz as a potential "kinsman-redeemer" (a relative who could marry a widow to preserve the family line). Boaz, impressed by Ruth's loyalty to Naomi, agreed to marry her, but there was a closer relative who had the first right of redemption. After this man declined to marry Ruth, Boaz married her, and they had a son, Obed, who would become the grandfather of King David.

4. Restoration and Blessing: Naomi, once grieving and empty, was now filled with joy and hope as she held her grandson. Ruth's faithfulness and Boaz's generosity led to the restoration of Naomi's family line. God had used the tragedy of Naomi's life to bring about a redemptive plan through Ruth, a Moabite woman, making her part of the lineage of David—and ultimately, the lineage of Jesus Christ.

Lessons for Couples:

1. Faithfulness and Loyalty in Marriage: The relationship between Elimelech and Naomi, while brief in the narrative, illustrates the deep commitment that can exist in marriage. Despite the difficult circumstances, Elimelech and Naomi faced the challenges of their lives together. Their partnership, built on faith and shared values, is a reminder of the importance of loyalty and support, especially in times of hardship.

Similarly, Ruth's unwavering loyalty to Naomi after Elimelech's death shows the profound impact of marital commitment and the value of support beyond death. Ruth's devotion is also a picture of the loyalty that should exist in marriages, where each partner is willing to stand by the other, no matter the challenges.

2. Embracing God's Provision: The story of Naomi and Ruth highlights how God provides for His people, even in difficult times. After the loss of her husband and sons, Naomi felt abandoned by God. However, through Ruth's perseverance, and through Boaz's kindness, God's hand of provision was evident. Couples should remember that even in times of loss and difficulty, God can work through circumstances to provide for them and restore their situation.

3. Grief and Restoration: Naomi's grief at the loss of her husband and sons is palpable, and her feelings of emptiness are evident. However, through the loyalty of Ruth and the intervention of Boaz, Naomi's life is ultimately restored. The lesson for couples is that even after deep loss or tragedy, there can be hope for restoration. God often works through others and unexpected circumstances to bring healing and renewal. Couples are reminded that God's plans are often beyond what we can immediately see, and His restoration can be deeper and more beautiful than we imagine.

4. The Importance of Family Bonds: Elimelech and Naomi's story shows that family bonds can be a source of strength, even when biological ties are severed by death. Ruth's choice to stay with Naomi, despite having the opportunity to return to her family, is a testament to the power of chosen family and the importance of caring for those we love. Couples are encouraged to nurture deep relationships not just with each other, but with extended family and those who may need support.

5. Loyalty and Love Beyond Marriage: Ruth's devotion to Naomi goes beyond the typical expectation of a daughter-in-law. She chooses to stick with Naomi even after both of her husbands have passed, showing that love and loyalty don't have to end with a

marriage. Ruth's commitment is an example of selfless love, which is not bound by blood but by shared experiences and mutual care. Couples are reminded that love and loyalty should not be contingent upon receiving something in return but should be freely given, even in the most difficult of circumstances.

6. God's Redemptive Plan: The story of Elimelech, Naomi, and Ruth culminates in God's redemptive plan, seen through the birth of Obed, the grandfather of King David. This lineage ultimately leads to Jesus Christ. Couples are encouraged to see their lives, their marriages, and their families as part of a larger redemptive story that God is unfolding. Even the most challenging seasons can be part of God's greater plan, leading to unexpected blessings and a legacy of faith.

Week 44

Hope in God's Mercy and Strength

Weekly Readings:

Day 302: Lamentations 2:7-27, Lamentations 3:1-39; Philemon 1; Psalm 119:121-128
Day 303: Lamentations 3:40-66, Lamentations 4, Lamentations 5; Hebrews 1; Psalm 119:129-136
Day 304: Obadiah 1; Hebrews 2; Proverbs 26:13-22
Day 305: Joel 1, Joel 2:1-17; Hebrews 3; Psalm 119:137-144
Day 306: Joel 2:18-32, Joel 3; Hebrews 4:1-13; Psalm 119:145-152
Day 307: Ezekiel 1, Ezekiel 2, Ezekiel 3; Hebrews 4:14-16, Hebrews 5:1-10; Psalm 119:153-160
Day 308: Ezekiel 4, Ezekiel 5, Ezekiel 6; Hebrews 5:11-14, Hebrews 6:1-12; Proverbs 26:23-28, Proverbs 27:1-4

Weekly Reflection:

This week, the readings offer a profound exploration of hope and redemption amidst the weight of suffering and exile. From the Book of Lamentations, we see the anguish of God's people in the face of judgment and destruction, but even in the midst of their sorrow, there is a call to turn to God in repentance and to hope in His mercy (Lamentations 3:22-23). Lamentations serves as a powerful reminder that even in our darkest moments, God's faithfulness remains steadfast.

In Philemon, we see the reconciliation of a broken relationship through forgiveness and restoration—a call to love one another as Christ has loved us. This connects beautifully with the themes in the Psalms, particularly Psalm 119, which emphasizes the importance of obedience to God's Word in our lives, as well as the desire to stay close to God even in the midst of hardship.

The readings from Hebrews highlight the superiority of Christ and His role as our High Priest, able to sympathize with our weaknesses. He is the ultimate source of hope and strength. For couples, this is a reminder that Christ is not distant but is near to help us in our time of need, and through Him, we find strength to endure and grow together.

Weekly Discussion Prompts:

1. **God's Mercy in Times of Suffering:** In Lamentations 3:22-23, it says, "The steadfast love of the Lord never ceases; His mercies never come to an end; they are new every morning." As a couple, how can you remind each other of God's mercy during times of hardship? What are practical ways to support one another spiritually when facing challenges?

2. **The Power of Forgiveness:** In Philemon 1, Paul appeals for reconciliation between Philemon and Onesimus. How can forgiveness and restoration play a role in your relationship? Are there areas in your marriage where you need to offer or receive forgiveness to move forward together in love?

3. **Strengthening Your Faith:** In Hebrews 4:14-16, it reminds us that we can confidently approach God's throne of grace. What does it mean to have confidence in God's grace when facing difficulties in your relationship? How can you as a couple grow in your faith and trust in God's promises?

4. **Hope Amidst Trials:** Joel 2:12-13 calls the people to repentance, saying that God is gracious and compassionate. As a couple, how can you lean on God's grace during times of trial? How do you stay hopeful even when you don't see immediate changes in difficult circumstances?

5. **Living According to God's Word:** Psalm 119:121-128 expresses the psalmist's commitment to following God's commands. What does it look like for you both to be obedient to God's Word in your marriage, especially when it's hard or when your emotions are stirred? How can you encourage one another to stay faithful to God's principles in your relationship?

6. **Standing Together in Christ:** Hebrews 2:14-18 speaks about Christ's victory over sin and death, making us partakers of His divine nature. How does the sacrifice of Christ empower your relationship? How can you both stand firm in your shared identity in Christ, especially in difficult seasons?

7. **Persevering Together:** In Ezekiel 3:16-21, God tells Ezekiel that he must speak His message to the people, even though they may not listen. As a couple, how can you persevere together in your mission to live out your faith? What are some ways to stay united in purpose when the journey feels hard?

Couple for Week 44: Jehoiada and Jehosheba

Jehoiada and Jehosheba are central figures in a critical story of survival and restoration in the history of Judah, found in the Book of 2 Kings and 2 Chronicles. Their partnership played a key role in preserving the Davidic line during a time of crisis and political instability.

Story Summary:

- Jehoiada: The High Priest Jehoiada was a high priest during the reign of King Athaliah, who had seized the throne of Judah after the death of her son, Ahaziah. Athaliah sought to exterminate the entire royal family to secure her hold on power. However, Jehoiada, as a priest, played a crucial role in protecting the rightful heir to the throne.

- Jehosheba: The Heroine Jehosheba, Jehoiada's wife, was the daughter of King Jehoram of Judah and the sister of Ahaziah. When Athaliah ordered the massacre of the royal family, Jehosheba rescued Joash, the infant son of Ahaziah, from the massacre. She hid him and his nurse in a bedroom in the Temple of the Lord, thus saving his life. For six years, Joash remained hidden, while Athaliah continued her reign.

- Jehoiada's Plan to Restore the Throne: After six years, Jehoiada, with the help of the military and the priests, orchestrated a coup to restore the throne to Joash. Jehoiada gathered the commanders of the army, the Levites, and the leaders of Israel to secretly anoint Joash as king. When the time was right, they presented the young Joash to the people, declaring him the rightful king. Athaliah, upon hearing the news, came to the Temple and was confronted with the truth. She was captured and executed, and Joash was enthroned as the king of Judah.

- Jehoiada's Role in Joash's Reign: Jehoiada continued to play a significant role in Joash's reign as his advisor. He guided Joash in his early years, helping him restore proper worship in Judah, repair the Temple of the Lord, and institute reforms. Under Jehoiada's leadership, Judah experienced a period of peace and religious renewal.

- **Jehoiada's Death and the Aftermath:** When Jehoiada died, Joash, who had been faithful to God under Jehoiada's counsel, began to listen to the wrong advisors. He turned away from the reforms Jehoiada had instituted, which led to the downfall of his reign. After Jehoiada's death, Joash's faithfulness began to falter, and he even allowed the murder of Zechariah, the son of Jehoiada, who had rebuked him for his disobedience. This tragic turning point marked the end of Joash's success and the decline of Judah's fortunes.

Lessons for Couples:

1. **The Power of Partnership in Protecting God's Plan:** Jehoiada and Jehosheba's story demonstrates how a husband and wife can work together in a shared mission to fulfill God's will. Jehosheba's courage in saving Joash and Jehoiada's wisdom in securing his reign highlight the strength that comes from a couple united in purpose. Their teamwork not only preserved the Davidic line but also ensured that God's covenant with David would continue. For couples, this is a reminder of the power of partnership in achieving great things for God's kingdom, especially when united in faith and purpose.

2. **Courage and Faithfulness in the Face of Danger:** Both Jehoiada and Jehosheba exhibited tremendous courage and faithfulness in the face of danger. Jehosheba risked her life to protect Joash from Athaliah, while Jehoiada took bold steps to confront the tyranny of Athaliah and restore the rightful king to the throne. Their actions remind couples of the importance of standing firm in the face of adversity, especially when it comes to protecting what is dear to God. Faithfulness to God and to each other can guide couples through perilous times.

3. **Guarding the Next Generation:** Jehosheba's decision to protect Joash represents a key theme in the Bible: the preservation of the next generation for God's purposes. Even when it seemed like the royal line was being destroyed, she chose to safeguard Joash's life, ensuring that God's covenant would continue. Couples can learn from this the importance of protecting and nurturing the spiritual and physical well-being of their children and those they are responsible for, as the legacy of faith is passed down through generations.

4. **The Influence of Wise Counsel:** Jehoiada's influence over Joash demonstrates the critical role of wise and godly counsel in a leader's life. As a couple, seeking godly counsel and relying on one another's wisdom can strengthen the direction and decisions made in a relationship. Jehoiada's guidance helped Joash to reign righteously for a time, and it's a reminder that couples should support each other spiritually, seeking wisdom from God and trusted advisors to navigate challenges.

5. **The Importance of Faithfulness and Integrity:** Jehoiada's long-lasting influence on Joash shows that faithfulness and integrity in relationships—whether in marriage or leadership—are essential to success. As long as Joash followed Jehoiada's guidance, he

was faithful to God, and Judah prospered. However, once Jehoiada died, Joash strayed from his spiritual roots. This warns couples about the dangers of neglecting spiritual foundations and the influence of ungodly counsel. Staying grounded in faith and supporting each other in that faith helps maintain stability in both marriage and life.

6. Restoration and God's Providence: The restoration of the throne to Joash serves as a reminder that God can bring about restoration and deliverance, even in the most seemingly hopeless situations. Jehoiada and Jehosheba's actions demonstrate that God's providence is at work, even behind the scenes. For couples, this is a reminder that God's plan for restoration and hope can unfold through their lives, even in challenging circumstances.

Week 45

God's Righteousness and the New Covenant

Weekly Readings:

Day 309: Ezekiel 7, Ezekiel 8, Ezekiel 9; Hebrews 6:13-20, Hebrews 7:1-10; Psalm 119:161-168
Day 310: Ezekiel 10, Ezekiel 11, Ezekiel 12; Hebrews 7:11-28; Psalm 119:169-176
Day 311: Ezekiel 13, Ezekiel 14, Ezekiel 15; Hebrews 8; Psalm 120:1-7
Day 312: Ezekiel 16; Hebrews 9:1-15; Proverbs 27:5-14
Day 313: Ezekiel 17, Ezekiel 18; Hebrews 9:16-28; Psalm 121:1-8
Day 314: Ezekiel 19, Ezekiel 20:1-44; Hebrews 10:1-18; Psalm 122:1-9
Day 315: Ezekiel 20:45-49, Ezekiel 21, Ezekiel 22:1-22; Hebrews 10:19-39; Psalm 123:1-4

Weekly Reflection:

This week's readings focus on the themes of judgment, repentance, and redemption. Ezekiel delivers God's messages of judgment on Israel and the nations for their unfaithfulness, yet in the midst of these stark warnings, there is a profound call to repentance and restoration. Even in the face of God's righteous anger, His grace shines through in His promise of a new covenant, a theme explored in the Book of Hebrews, where we are reminded of the superiority of Christ's priesthood and His perfect sacrifice.

In Ezekiel 9, we see the mark of the faithful placed upon the foreheads of those who lament the abominations in Jerusalem. This can be a powerful symbol of how God marks His people, calling them to stand firm in righteousness even when the world around them is in rebellion. Similarly, Psalm 119 speaks of the importance of meditating on God's Word, which is essential for navigating the spiritual challenges we face.

For couples, this week's scriptures are a reminder that God's justice is tempered with His mercy, and we must stay close to Him in obedience and faith, trusting in His promises to keep us strong through difficulties.

Weekly Discussion Prompts:

1. God's Righteous Judgment: In Ezekiel 7:3, God declares, "The end is upon you." As a couple, how do you view God's judgment on sin, both in the world and in your own lives? What does it mean to live faithfully, even when surrounded by challenges or worldly temptations?

2. Repentance and Restoration: Ezekiel 9 describes the faithful being marked for salvation while the wicked are judged. What does repentance look like in your marriage? How can you as a couple help each other turn away from sin and grow in righteousness?

3. Christ as Our High Priest: In Hebrews 7:24-25, it says that Jesus holds His priesthood permanently because He lives forever to intercede for us. How does Christ's role as High Priest encourage you in your marriage? How can you lean on His intercession when facing difficulties in your relationship?

4. New Covenant of Grace: Hebrews 8:10 speaks of the new covenant, where God's law is written on our hearts. As a couple, how can you live out God's law in your relationship? In what ways can you support each other in keeping God's commands and growing together in grace?

5. Meditating on God's Word: Psalm 119:162 says, "I rejoice at Your word as one who finds great spoil." How does the Word of God bring joy and guidance to your life as a couple? How can you prioritize the Bible in your relationship, especially when life gets busy?

6. Living with a New Identity: The Ezekiel 20 passage speaks of God's covenant with His people and their need for obedience. How can you both live in obedience to God's covenant as a married couple? What areas of your relationship could benefit from a renewed commitment to follow God's direction?

7. Strength in the New Covenant: Reflect on Hebrews 10:23, which says, "Let us hold fast the confession of our hope without wavering, for He who promised is faithful." As a couple, how can you strengthen your commitment to one another and to God's promises, especially in challenging seasons? What does hope in Christ look like in your marriage?

"Reaffirming Your Covenant Together": This week, take time to pray together and reflect on God's faithfulness in your relationship. Consider writing down God's promises in His Word that have spoken to you both and pray them over your marriage. Discuss practical ways you can apply these promises and live them out in your everyday lives. Additionally, commit to studying Scripture together this week—whether it's reading a chapter a day or meditating on a key passage, like Hebrews 10:19-23, to remind yourselves of the hope you share in Christ.

Couple for Week 45: Jehoram and Athaliah

Jehoram and Athaliah are a tragic couple in the Bible whose story illustrates the destructive power of evil alliances, disobedience to God, and the devastating consequences of allowing worldly influences to dominate one's actions and decisions. Their relationship and the events that followed their reigns serve as important lessons for couples today, especially concerning the dangers of ungodly influence and the need for personal integrity in marriage.

The Story of Jehoram and Athaliah:

- Jehoram's Ascension to the Throne: Jehoram, also called Joram, was the son of King Jehoshaphat of Judah, a generally righteous king. However, Jehoram's reign, which began after his father's death, marked a departure from the righteousness of his father. Jehoram married Athaliah, the daughter of King Ahab and Queen Jezebel of Israel, known for their wickedness and idolatry. This marriage itself was politically motivated but spiritually disastrous.

- The Influence of Athaliah: Athaliah was a powerful and evil woman who had a strong influence on her husband. Jehoram followed her example and led Judah into wickedness, embracing idolatry and abandoning the ways of the Lord. In 2 Chronicles 21:6, it's noted that Jehoram "walked in the ways of the kings of Israel, as the house of Ahab had done, for the daughter of Ahab was his wife." This marriage and Athaliah's influence caused Jehoram to commit many sins, leading him to kill his own brothers to secure the throne and follow the idolatrous practices of Israel.

- Jehoram's Reign and Consequences: During Jehoram's reign, Judah fell into moral and spiritual decay. God was angered by the evil ways of Jehoram and the influence of Athaliah, and as a result, Judah faced divine judgment. Jehoram's reign was marked by wars and defeats, and he suffered a painful illness that led to his death (2 Chronicles 21:18-20). Jehoram's failure as a king and his choice to follow his wife's wicked example had dire consequences, not only for him but also for his family and the nation of Judah.

- Athaliah's Reign After Jehoram's Death: After Jehoram's death, Athaliah's ambition to rule became evident. In a shocking act of cruelty, Athaliah ordered the slaughter of all of

Jehoram's sons, except for the infant Joash, whom she failed to kill. Athaliah then seized the throne of Judah and reigned for six years, promoting idolatry and continuing the wickedness she had helped instigate during her marriage to Jehoram. She ruled with the same evil spirit as her mother, Jezebel, and sought to completely eliminate the Davidic line.

- **The Fall of Athaliah:** Athaliah's reign came to a dramatic end when Joash, the rightful king, was rescued by Jehosheba (his aunt) and hidden in the temple for six years. After this time, a coup led by the high priest Jehoiada restored Joash to the throne. Athaliah was captured and executed (2 Kings 11:13-16). Her death marked the end of a dark chapter in Judah's history.

Lessons for Couples from Jehoram and Athaliah's Story:

1. **The Danger of Ungodly Alliances:** Jehoram's marriage to Athaliah was a disastrous alliance that led both him and Judah down a path of idolatry and wickedness. For couples, this story serves as a warning about the danger of marrying or forming alliances with those who do not share a strong commitment to faith in God. Spiritual compatibility is essential in marriage, and a partnership with someone who does not prioritize God can lead to disastrous consequences for both the individual and their family.

2. **The Influence of Spouses:** Athaliah's influence over Jehoram was profound, leading him to abandon the ways of the Lord and follow the evil practices of her family. The story illustrates the power of a spouse's influence, whether for good or ill. In marriage, couples should be mindful of how their actions and values influence one another. A godly marriage is one where spouses encourage each other to grow in faith and live according to God's will.

3. **The Dangers of Pride and Ambition:** Athaliah's ambition to rule and her ruthless actions to secure the throne reveal how destructive unchecked pride and ambition can be. Both Jehoram and Athaliah's lives were marked by selfish ambition that disregarded God's commands and the welfare of others. Couples should recognize the dangers of selfish ambition in a marriage, as it can lead to devastating consequences when personal desires take precedence over God's purposes.

4. **The Consequences of Wickedness:** The wickedness of Jehoram and Athaliah had far-reaching consequences for their children and the nation of Judah. The death of Jehoram and the near destruction of the Davidic line, coupled with the evil reign of Athaliah, serve as stark reminders that disobedience to God brings judgment. Couples should strive to live righteous lives, as their choices not only affect their relationship but also impact their family and community.

5. **The Importance of Righteous Leadership:** Jehoram's failure as a king and Athaliah's cruelty in ruling demonstrate the importance of godly leadership in marriage and

family. Both in positions of authority, they misused their power, leading their people astray. This is a reminder that, as spouses, couples should lead their families with integrity, wisdom, and a strong commitment to God's principles.

6. God's Faithfulness Despite Human Failure: Despite the wickedness of Jehoram and Athaliah, God's plan for Judah was not thwarted. He preserved the Davidic line through Joash, showing that even in the midst of evil leadership, God's purposes will prevail. This reminds couples that even when things seem to go wrong, God is sovereign, and His plan will ultimately triumph, bringing restoration where there is brokenness.

Week 46

Walking by Faith and Living in God's Promises

Weekly Readings:

Day 316: Ezekiel 22:23-31, Ezekiel 23; Hebrews 11:1-16; Proverbs 27:15-22
Day 317: Ezekiel 24, Ezekiel 25; Hebrews 11:17-40; Psalm 124:1-8
Day 318: Ezekiel 26, Ezekiel 27; Hebrews 12:1-13; Psalm 125:1-5
Day 319: Ezekiel 28, Ezekiel 29; Hebrews 12:14-29; Psalm 126:1-6
Day 320: Ezekiel 30, Ezekiel 31; Hebrews 13; Proverbs 27:23-27, Proverbs 28:1-6
Day 321: Ezekiel 32, Ezekiel 33:1-32; James 1; Psalm 127:1-5
Day 322: Ezekiel 33:21-33, Ezekiel 34, Ezekiel 35; James 2; Psalm 128:1-6

Weekly Reflection:

This week's readings encourage us to live by faith and trust in God's promises, even when we face hardship or uncertainty. Ezekiel's prophecies continue to reveal the consequences of Israel's disobedience and the coming judgment on the nations, but they also emphasize God's justice and His promise of restoration. Hebrews underscores the importance of faith, citing examples of those who lived by faith and persevered despite challenges. It reminds us that faith in God's promises strengthens us to press forward even in the face of adversity.

As couples, we are called to walk by faith, trusting in God's word and in His faithfulness to fulfill His promises. Just as the heroes of faith in Hebrews 11 endured trials with the hope of the future promise, we too must hold fast to our hope in God's plan for our lives and marriages, knowing that He is always faithful.

Psalm 125 encourages us to trust in God as our protector, while Proverbs provides wisdom on handling conflict and remaining steadfast in relationships. This week's scriptures offer both an invitation and a challenge to live in unwavering faith, to remain focused on God's promises, and to trust that He is working in us and through us for His glory.

Weekly Discussion Prompts:

1. Walking by Faith: Hebrews 11:1 defines faith as "the assurance of things hoped for, the conviction of things not seen." As a couple, how can you strengthen your faith in God's promises in your daily life? In what ways can you encourage each other when doubts or challenges arise?

2. The Heroes of Faith: In Hebrews 11:32-40, we read about men and women who endured great suffering because of their faith. What can you learn from their examples of perseverance? How does their unwavering trust in God inspire you in your marriage?

3. Perseverance in Trials: Hebrews 12:1-2 urges us to "run with endurance the race that is set before us." How can you support each other in staying faithful through difficult seasons? What are some practical ways you can strengthen your relationship when facing external pressures?

4. Peace in God's Presence: Psalm 125:1 says, "Those who trust in the Lord are like Mount Zion, which cannot be moved." How does trusting in God bring stability to your marriage? In what areas of your relationship can you cultivate greater trust in God's ability to keep you steady through life's challenges?

5. Living with Integrity: Proverbs 27:15-16 speaks of the need for a righteous person to be steadfast and unshaken. How can you uphold integrity in your marriage, especially in moments of conflict or when faced with temptation? What does it mean for you to "hold fast" to righteousness in your relationship?

6. Responding to Correction: James 1:19-21 encourages us to be "quick to listen, slow to speak, and slow to anger." How can you as a couple practice this in your daily interactions? How does humility and openness to correction strengthen your marriage?

7. Living in Harmony: In James 2:1-9, we are reminded to avoid showing favoritism and to love all people equally. How can you live out this teaching in your marriage? How can you show impartial love and respect to one another, especially when disagreements arise?

Joint Couple Activity:

"Faithful Together: Trusting God in Our Marriage": This week, take time to reflect on the promises of God that have been meaningful to you as a couple. Write them down and discuss how you can apply these promises in your daily life together. Make it a goal to pray together daily, especially in moments when you are facing challenges. Spend time this week talking about how you can support each other in walking by faith, trusting God's will, and persevering through trials. Consider reading Hebrews 11:1-16 together and discussing how these examples of faith can inspire and strengthen your relationship.

Couple for Week 46: David and Michal

David and Michal represent a complex and tragic marriage in the Bible. Their story is marked by deep love, jealousy, misunderstandings, and a breakdown of the marital relationship due to differing priorities and responses to God. Despite the initial promise of a joyful union, their marriage ultimately faces great struggles, teaching valuable lessons for couples in navigating relationships, faith, and personal integrity.

The Story of David and Michal:

- The Beginning of Their Marriage: Michal, the daughter of King Saul, was initially deeply in love with David when he was a young shepherd. She was moved by David's courage and faith in God, and when Saul learned of David's popularity, he used Michal as a pawn to trap David. Saul offered Michal's hand in marriage as a means of bringing David into his family and putting him in danger (1 Samuel 18:17-29). David accepted, fulfilling the king's demands, and married Michal.

- Separation Due to Saul's Jealousy: After their marriage, King Saul's jealousy and fear of David's growing popularity caused him to turn against David. Saul sought to kill David, leading to David's flight from the court and separation from Michal. Saul gave Michal to another man, Paltiel, and she was taken away from David. This separation lasted for years, and David, during this time, became king of Judah while Saul continued to reign over Israel.

- David's Return to Michal: After Saul's death, David became king of Israel. In his pursuit of unity among the tribes of Israel, David requested Michal be returned to him (2 Samuel 3:13-16). Michal, however, had been remarried to Paltiel, and her emotional attachment to him created a source of tension. She was taken from Paltiel and returned to David, but the transfer of Michal from one husband to another was a traumatic and difficult situation for all involved.

- Tension and Discontent in Their Marriage: When Michal saw David dancing and celebrating before the Lord as the Ark of the Covenant was brought into Jerusalem, her reaction was one of disdain. She criticized David for his uninhibited dancing, which she saw as an undignified act for the king (2 Samuel 6:16-23). David, in turn, responded sharply, defending his actions as an expression of joy and humility before God, not for public approval. Michal's criticism revealed a deep divide in their relationship: while David's heart was set on honoring God, Michal's focus seemed to be on appearances and status.

- Michal's Childlessness: The marriage between David and Michal grew increasingly strained. Following this episode of criticism, the Bible notes that Michal never bore children to David (2 Samuel 6:23). This could be seen as a consequence of their strained relationship and also reflects the broader biblical theme of the consequences of a lack of harmony and unity in marriage. The relationship between Michal and David, marked by misunderstandings and bitterness, resulted in an unfruitful marriage, both spiritually and physically.

Lessons for Couples from David and Michal's Story:

1. The Danger of Jealousy and Competition: One of the key issues in David and Michal's marriage was Saul's jealousy of David, which transferred to Michal. The root of the problem lies in the comparison and competition that can arise in relationships, especially when one partner feels insecure or threatened by the other's success. For couples today, it's crucial to focus on supporting each other's dreams and achievements rather than letting jealousy or competition cause division.

2. The Importance of Communication and Understanding: Much of the tension between David and Michal arose from a lack of understanding and communication. Michal didn't understand David's exuberance in worship, and David didn't seem to appreciate the emotional impact of being taken from her first husband. This failure to communicate and understand one another's perspectives can lead to deep hurt and unresolved conflict in relationships. Couples should make an effort to communicate openly and empathetically, especially when disagreements arise.

3. The Need for Shared Priorities in Marriage: David and Michal's relationship suffered because they didn't share the same priorities. David's primary focus was on honoring God, while Michal was concerned with appearances and the royal dignity of being the king's wife. A successful marriage requires shared values, especially regarding faith, goals, and personal conduct. Couples should ensure they are united in their spiritual walk, their vision for life, and their commitment to one another.

4. The Importance of Grace in Marriage: Michal's harsh criticism of David's dance in celebration of the Ark's return demonstrates a lack of grace, while David's response shows that grace, humility, and understanding are necessary in marriage. David didn't retaliate but responded with his own sense of joy and devotion to God. Couples can learn from this to extend grace to one another, even in moments of frustration or misunderstanding. Marriage requires both partners to be patient, kind, and forgiving.

5. The Consequences of Unresolved Conflict: The bitterness and tension between David and Michal seemed to linger throughout their marriage. Michal's inability to support David in a moment of great joy, coupled with David's rejection of her criticism, created a toxic environment in their relationship. For couples, unresolved conflicts can lead to long-term damage and dissatisfaction in the relationship. It's important to address issues and work toward reconciliation rather than allowing bitterness to fester.

6. Spiritual Unity in Marriage: David's passion for God and his unashamed worship were central to his life. Michal, however, did not share this passion, and her inability to understand David's heart for God revealed a spiritual divide between them. This division

contributed to their lack of harmony. Couples should ensure that their spiritual lives are aligned and that they are both committed to growing together in faith. Spiritual unity is foundational for a strong, thriving marriage.

Week 47

God's Restoration and Living in Holiness

Weekly Readings:

Day 323: Ezekiel 36, Ezekiel 37; James 3; Psalm 129:1-8
Day 324: Ezekiel 38, Ezekiel 39; James 4; Proverbs 28:7-17
Day 325: Ezekiel 40; James 5; Psalm 130:1-8
Day 326: Ezekiel 41, Ezekiel 42; 1 Peter 1, 1 Peter 2:1-3; Psalm 131:1-3
Day 327: Ezekiel 43, Ezekiel 44; 1 Peter 2:4-25; Psalm 132:1-18
Day 328: Ezekiel 45, Ezekiel 46; 1 Peter 3; Proverbs 28:18-28
Day 329: Ezekiel 47, Ezekiel 48; 1 Peter 4; Psalm 133:1-3

Weekly Reflection:

This week's readings highlight God's promise of restoration and the call to live holy and righteous lives as His people. In Ezekiel, we see God's promise to restore Israel and bring about new life, symbolized by the dry bones coming to life in Ezekiel 37. This restoration is not just a physical return to the land but also a spiritual renewal. Similarly, in 1 Peter, we are reminded of our identity as God's holy people, called to live in holiness and love, drawing near to Christ, the cornerstone of our faith.

James continues to challenge us in our actions, urging us to speak with wisdom and humility, and to submit ourselves to God's will. His letter calls us to recognize the power of our words and to live out our faith with integrity. The psalms this week call us to trust in God's faithfulness and to seek His help in times of distress, encouraging us to live in peace and unity.

For couples, this week's scriptures challenge us to be agents of restoration in our relationship. Just as God promises to restore His people, we are called to help restore and strengthen our marriage, living in holiness and grace. God's work in us is ongoing, and as we seek His strength, we can continue to grow together in love and faith.

Weekly Discussion Prompts:

1. Restoration and New Life: Ezekiel 37:4-6 describes the dry bones being restored to life. How can you as a couple experience spiritual renewal together? What areas of your relationship need God's restoration, and how can you invite Him into those areas?

2. The Power of Words: James 3:5-6 speaks of the power of the tongue to build up or destroy. How do your words impact your marriage? How can you use your words to encourage and strengthen one another rather than tear each other down?

3. Humility and Submission: James 4:7 urges us to submit ourselves to God. What does submission look like in your marriage? How can you as a couple humbly submit to God's will and trust in His guidance in your relationship?

4. Living as God's Holy People: 1 Peter 1:16 says, "You shall be holy, for I am holy." How can you live out God's holiness in your marriage? What steps can you take to honor God in the way you treat each other, especially in challenging moments?

5. Unity and Peace: Psalm 133:1 celebrates the blessing of unity. How can you as a couple work together to build peace and unity in your relationship? What practical steps can you take to foster harmony and resolve conflicts in a healthy way?

6. Suffering for Christ's Sake: In 1 Peter 3:14-17, Peter speaks about suffering for doing what is right. How can you support one another when facing trials or persecution? How can you strengthen each other's faith when you are tested?

7. Pursuing Holiness Together: Ezekiel 43:12 calls for holiness in God's temple. How can you prioritize holiness in your marriage? What can you do to grow in purity and righteousness as a couple, both in your actions and in your hearts?

Joint Couple Activity:

"Restoring and Strengthening Your Marriage": This week, take time to pray together for God's restoration in your relationship. Reflect on areas where you may need spiritual renewal— whether it's communication, trust, or emotional intimacy. Ask God to breathe new life into those areas and restore you both to a stronger, more faithful bond. Consider reading Ezekiel 37 together and discussing how God's restoration power can work in your relationship.

Additionally, write down one area of your marriage where you need to speak more kindly or gently and pray for God to help you grow in wisdom. Spend time each day affirming each other with words of encouragement. Finally, as a couple, commit to pursuing holiness together, whether it's through joint prayer, studying Scripture together, or taking specific steps to live out God's commands in your relationship.

Couple for Week 47: King Ahasuerus and Vashti

King Ahasuerus and Vashti are central figures in the book of Esther, which tells the story of the Persian king's relationship with his queen, Vashti, and the subsequent rise of Esther, a Jewish woman, to the throne. The story of King Ahasuerus and Vashti highlights themes of power, authority, disobedience, and the consequences of a wife standing up for her dignity. It also explores the importance of leadership, humility, and the role of women in times of crisis.

The Story of King Ahasuerus and Vashti:

1. The Royal Banquet: King Ahasuerus (often identified as Xerxes I) ruled over the vast Persian Empire. In the third year of his reign, he threw a grand banquet that lasted for 180 days to display his wealth and power. During this extravagant event, the king commanded that Queen Vashti appear before him and his guests to show off her beauty. She was to wear her royal crown, likely as a symbol of her beauty and status, and display herself as part of his splendor (Esther 1:10-11).

2. Vashti's Refusal: Vashti, the queen, refused to obey the king's command to appear before his guests. While the reasons for her refusal are not explicitly stated in the text, it is clear that she either found the request inappropriate or demeaning, or she simply did not want to be treated as an object of display. Her refusal to appear before the king and his guests was seen as an act of defiance and disrespect to the king's authority.

3. The King's Reaction: King Ahasuerus was furious when Vashti defied him. In his anger, he sought counsel from his advisors about how to handle the situation, fearing that her disobedience might encourage other women in the empire to act similarly. His advisors recommended that Vashti be removed from her position as queen, and a decree was issued to depose her and prohibit her from ever appearing before the king again (Esther 1:12-19).

4. Vashti's Removal: As a result of her refusal, Vashti was deposed, and the king's advisors made it clear that she would no longer be queen. This left the position of queen open, which led to the search for a new queen, eventually bringing Esther, a Jewish orphan, into the king's harem and later into a position of favor (Esther 2:1-17).

5. Aftermath and Esther's Rise: After Vashti's removal, the king eventually chose Esther, a Jewish woman raised by her cousin Mordecai, to become the new queen. Esther's story unfolds as she plays a critical role in saving the Jewish people from destruction. Although Vashti's role is limited in the narrative, her act of defiance sets the stage for Esther's courage and leadership, demonstrating how even a seemingly small event can have profound consequences in God's plan.

Lessons for Couples from the Story of King Ahasuerus and Vashti:

1. **The Importance of Respect in Marriage:** The central issue in the relationship between Ahasuerus and Vashti is respect. While Ahasuerus wielded immense power and authority, his command for Vashti to appear before his guests was not just a request; it was a demand that undermined her dignity. In a marriage, mutual respect is essential. Both partners should respect each other's autonomy, feelings, and dignity. Forced submission, as seen in this case, can lead to resentment and discontent.

2. **The Power of Standing Up for Dignity:** Vashti's refusal to appear before the king was a stand for her dignity, even though it came at great personal cost. She chose not to allow herself to be objectified for the amusement of others, showing that standing firm in one's principles, especially regarding personal dignity, is important. For couples, it's crucial to support each other's dignity and avoid situations that diminish the worth of either partner.

3. **The Consequences of Disrespect:** King Ahasuerus' reaction to Vashti's defiance reveals the consequences of disrespect in relationships. Rather than understanding or discussing the reasons behind Vashti's refusal, the king reacted impulsively and removed her as queen. This highlights that when respect is lost in a relationship, drastic measures are sometimes taken in anger, leading to a breakdown of trust and communication. Couples should address conflicts with respect and patience rather than seeking harsh measures.

4. **Leadership and Humility in Marriage:** While Ahasuerus held significant power, his reaction to Vashti's refusal demonstrated a lack of humility in leadership. A true leader—whether in a marriage or any relationship—leads with humility, patience, and understanding, rather than asserting dominance or expecting blind obedience. A marriage should be a partnership, where both partners lead with love and respect for one another.

5. **Navigating Difficult Situations with Wisdom:** After Vashti's removal, the king sought advice from his counselors. While their advice led to Vashti's removal, it also set the stage for Esther's eventual rise. Couples can learn from this that seeking wise counsel in difficult situations is important. While Ahasuerus' advisers were not always wise, their counsel still led to a turning point in the narrative. Couples should seek advice from trusted individuals when facing challenges, but they should also consider the consequences of the advice they follow.

6. **The Role of Women in Marriage and Society:** Vashti's story highlights the tension between the roles women are expected to play in marriage and society and their right to self-respect and autonomy. Although she was punished for refusing to submit to the king's command, her defiance highlights the importance of women standing up for

themselves in relationships. In a healthy marriage, both partners should recognize and honor each other's individual rights, needs, and desires.

7. God's Providence in Difficult Situations: While the story of Vashti's removal may seem like an unfortunate and unjust event, it paved the way for Esther's rise to prominence, through which God saved the Jewish people. This shows how God can work through difficult or painful circumstances to bring about His greater purpose. Couples can take comfort in knowing that even in challenging times, God's plans may unfold in ways they cannot immediately see.

Week 48

Trusting God in Times of Trial and His Sovereignty

Weekly Readings:

Day 330: Daniel 1, Daniel 2:1-23; 1 Peter 5; Psalm 134:1-3
Day 331: Daniel 2:24-49, Daniel 3:1-12; 2 Peter 1; Psalm 135:1-12
Day 332: Daniel 3:13-30, Daniel 4:1-18; 2 Peter 2; Proverbs 29:1-9
Day 333: Daniel 4:19-37, Daniel 5:1-16; 2 Peter 3; Psalm 135:13-21
Day 334: Daniel 5:17-31, Daniel 6:1-28; 1 John 1, 1 John 2; Psalm 136:1-12
Day 335: Daniel 7, Daniel 8:1-14; 1 John 2:12-27; Psalm 136:13-26
Day 336: Daniel 8:15-27, Daniel 9:1-19; 1 John 2:28-29, 1 John 3:1-10; Proverbs 29:10-18

Weekly Reflection:

This week's readings center on God's sovereignty and His faithfulness to those who trust in Him, even in times of trial. In the book of Daniel, we see how God gave wisdom and favor to Daniel and his friends in the face of danger, showing His power to deliver and His ability to control the course of nations. Daniel's unwavering faith in God's sovereignty serves as a powerful example for us today as we face our own challenges.

The New Testament readings in 1 Peter and 2 Peter continue to encourage believers to stand firm in their faith, resist the temptation to fall away, and recognize God's promise to keep those who are faithful. We are reminded that trials are inevitable, but God has promised His grace and His power to see us through. In the psalms, we see a consistent theme of praising God for His enduring faithfulness and sovereignty.

For couples, this week's scriptures are a reminder that, just as God worked powerfully in the lives of Daniel and his companions, He desires to work in your marriage. When facing trials or difficult seasons, God remains sovereign and faithful, offering His strength and wisdom to navigate through any challenge. Trust in His guidance, knowing that He is always with you.

Weekly Discussion Prompts:

1. Faith in the Midst of Trials: Daniel 3:17-18 speaks of Shadrach, Meshach, and Abednego standing firm in their faith even when faced with the fiery furnace. How can you support each other in staying faithful during times of trial or difficulty? What practical steps can you take to strengthen your faith as a couple?

2. God's Sovereignty: Daniel 2:20-23 highlights God's wisdom in revealing the mysteries of the king's dream. How do you see God's sovereignty in your own life? As a couple, how can you trust God's plan for your future, even when it's unclear?

3. Resisting Temptation: In 2 Peter 1:5-10, Peter encourages believers to add to their faith virtues like self-control and godliness. How can you help each other grow in these virtues, especially in the face of temptation or difficult circumstances?

4. Humility and Pride: Daniel 4:37 speaks of King Nebuchadnezzar humbling himself before God. What role does humility play in your marriage? How can you both practice humility and resist the temptation to let pride get in the way of your relationship?

5. Endurance and Hope: In 2 Peter 3:13-14, Peter encourages believers to look forward to God's new creation and to live in peace with one another. How can you as a couple live in light of the hope of Christ's return? What does living in peace look like in your relationship?

6. Living in the Light: 1 John 1:7 speaks of walking in the light as God is in the light. How can you live transparently in your marriage? How can you be more open and honest with each other, particularly in areas of struggle or weakness?

7. God's Promise of Restoration: Daniel 9:19 is a plea for God's mercy and restoration. How can you as a couple actively seek God's restoration in your relationship? What areas of your marriage need God's healing and grace?

"Standing Firm Together in Faith": Take time this week to reflect on the faithfulness of God in your marriage and the ways He has worked in your lives. As a couple, discuss any areas where you may be facing challenges and pray together for strength to trust God through them. Look back on how God has helped you overcome past trials, and use that as a foundation for facing future ones.

Additionally, choose a passage from this week's readings, such as Daniel 3:17-18 or 1 Peter 5:6-7, and commit to memorizing it together. This will serve as a reminder of God's power and faithfulness, especially in difficult times. Spend time praying for one another, asking God to help you both remain faithful and steadfast in your marriage, and to be a shining example of His grace and sovereignty.

Couple for Week 48: Solomon and Pharaoh's Daughter

King Solomon, known for his wisdom, wealth, and expansive building projects, entered into a political marriage with Pharaoh's daughter early in his reign. This marriage symbolized an alliance between Israel and Egypt, reflecting the peak of Israel's influence. While she was not the only wife Solomon took, Pharaoh's daughter is specifically mentioned, highlighting the importance of the alliance. However, Solomon's marriage to her and later to many other foreign wives introduced influences that eventually led him to idolatry, a departure from his devotion to God that had serious consequences for his reign and Israel's future.

Lessons for Couples:

1. The Impact of Spiritual Unity: Pharaoh's daughter did not share Solomon's faith, which eventually contributed to his drift toward idol worship. Couples can learn from this by understanding the importance of sharing a common faith and supporting each other in spiritual growth to maintain a strong foundation in their relationship.

2. The Influence of Companionship Choices: Solomon's story shows how the people we allow into our lives can profoundly impact our values. Couples can be reminded to surround themselves with relationships that encourage godliness and strengthen, rather than compromise, their commitment to their faith.

3. Avoiding Compromises in Faith: Solomon's marriage to Pharaoh's daughter marked the beginning of a series of compromises that led to Israel's eventual spiritual decline. Couples can take this lesson to heart, being mindful to avoid gradual compromises that could lead them away from their faith and values over time.

4. Understanding the Consequences of Divided Loyalties: Solomon's love for his many wives and their gods led him to a divided heart, impacting his once-strong devotion to God. This teaches couples the importance of keeping God at the center of their relationship and avoiding anything that might divide their attention or devotion.

5. Protecting the Spiritual Integrity of the Home: Solomon's foreign marriages brought idol worship into Israel, leading his people astray. Couples can be inspired to protect their home environment, ensuring it reflects their values and dedication to God and encourages positive spiritual growth for themselves and their family.

6. Recognizing the Purpose of Marriage Beyond Alliances: Solomon's marriage to Pharaoh's daughter was strategic but lacked spiritual depth, showing the importance of marriage as a partnership in both life and faith. Couples can see marriage as not just a bond for mutual benefit, but as a union meant to honor God and support each other's walk with Him.

7. Choosing Faithful Influence Over Cultural Pressure: Solomon's marriage was a symbol of Israel's status, but it ultimately led him away from God's commands. Couples today can learn to prioritize faithfulness to God over the pressures or influences of societal expectations, striving to keep their relationship aligned with His will above all else.

8. Honoring Commitments to God Above All Else: God had warned Israel's kings against taking foreign wives to avoid the lure of other gods, a command Solomon ignored. Couples can learn to honor their commitment to God above all else, ensuring that their relationship decisions honor His word and reflect their devotion to Him.

9. The Power of Influence Within Marriage: Solomon's relationship with Pharaoh's daughter and other foreign wives demonstrates how deeply spouses influence each other. Couples can strive to be positive spiritual influences on each other, fostering an environment of encouragement, growth, and accountability.

10. Leaving a Lasting Legacy of Faithfulness: Solomon's unfaithfulness left a legacy that troubled Israel for generations. Couples can be inspired by this story to leave behind a legacy of faithfulness, teaching future generations the value of devotion to God and the importance of keeping Him at the center of their lives and marriage.

Week 49

God's Sovereignty and His Promise of Restoration

Weekly Readings:

Day 337: Daniel 9:20-27, Daniel 10, Daniel 11:1; 1 John 3:11-24, 1 John 4:1-6; Psalm 137:1-9
Day 338: Daniel 11:2-35; 1 John 4:7-21; Psalm 138:1-8
Day 339: Daniel 11:36-45, Daniel 12; 1 John 5:1-21; Psalm 139:1-10
Day 340: Haggai 1, Haggai 2:1-23; 2 John 1:1-13; Proverbs 29:19-27
Day 341: Zechariah 1, Zechariah 2, Zechariah 3, Zechariah 4; 3 John 1:1-14; Psalm 139:11-16
Day 342: Zechariah 5, Zechariah 6, Zechariah 7, Zechariah 8; Jude 1:1-25; Psalm 139:17-24
Day 343: Zechariah 9, Zechariah 10, Zechariah 11; Revelation 1; Psalm 140:1-5

Weekly Reflection:

This week's readings offer a glimpse into God's sovereign power over nations, His promise to restore His people, and the call to walk in love and truth. In the book of Daniel, we see God revealing future events to Daniel, showing His ultimate control over history. These visions offer hope in the midst of trials, pointing forward to a time when God's kingdom will triumph over evil.

The New Testament readings, particularly in 1 John, emphasize the importance of love, obedience, and the role of the Holy Spirit. We are called to live in love for one another, just as God has loved us, and to remain faithful to His commands. The letters of John remind us that God's love is both a command and a source of strength. When we abide in His love, we are assured of His presence and His promise of eternal life.

The prophetic books of Haggai and Zechariah encourage us to rebuild, restore, and wait expectantly for God's deliverance. Haggai calls the people to rebuild the temple, symbolizing the need for spiritual renewal, while Zechariah speaks of God's future blessings and the coming

Messiah. In Revelation, we are reminded that despite present struggles, the final victory belongs to God, and He will restore all things.

For couples, this week's scriptures are an invitation to reflect on God's sovereign control over your lives and relationships. Just as God was faithful to restore His people, He promises to restore and strengthen your marriage. As you walk in His love, trust in His promises for the future, knowing that He is faithful to complete the good work He has begun in you.

Weekly Discussion Prompts:

1. Trusting God's Sovereignty: Daniel 9:20-27 speaks of God's plans for Israel, even in the midst of judgment. How can you as a couple trust in God's plans for your marriage, even during difficult or uncertain times?

2. Living in Love: 1 John 3:16 says, "By this we know love, that He laid down His life for us." How can you as a couple live out this sacrificial love in your relationship? What are practical ways to show love to each other daily?

3. Overcoming Trials: In Daniel 11, we see the people of Israel facing great opposition. How can you support each other in times of trial? What role does faith play in overcoming challenges in your marriage?

4. Restoring God's Temple: Haggai 1:4-8 calls the people to rebuild God's house. As a couple, how can you rebuild your spiritual life together? What practices can you implement to strengthen your relationship with God and each other?

5. God's Promise of Blessing: Zechariah 2:10-13 speaks of God's promise to dwell among His people. How can you invite God's presence into your marriage and home? What changes can you make to ensure that God is central in your relationship?

6. Walking in Truth: 2 John 1:4 says, "I rejoice greatly to find some of your children walking in the truth." How can you both ensure that you are walking in truth together? Are there areas in your marriage where honesty and transparency need to be strengthened?

7. Hope in Christ's Return: Revelation 1:7 reminds us that Christ will return in glory. How can you as a couple live in light of the hope of Christ's return? What does it mean to "live expectantly" in your marriage?

Couple for Week 49: King Saul and Ahinoam

King Saul and Ahinoam are mentioned in the Old Testament, particularly in the books of 1 Samuel, where their story is intertwined with the rise and fall of Saul as king of Israel. While their relationship is not extensively detailed, there are some key points about their marriage and the broader implications for couples.

The Story of Saul and Ahinoam:

- Saul's Early Reign: Saul, the first king of Israel, was anointed by the prophet Samuel. He initially displayed humility and leadership potential, but over time, his disobedience and reliance on his own strength led to his downfall. Ahinoam was his wife, and she is mentioned several times in the context of Saul's reign.

- Ahinoam's Role: Ahinoam is described as the daughter of Ahimaaz (1 Samuel 14:50). She is the mother of at least two of Saul's sons: Jonathan and Ishbosheth (1 Samuel 14:49). Though Ahinoam is mentioned only briefly in the biblical narrative, her role as the wife of Saul places her in the background of some key events during Saul's reign.

- Saul's Decline and Ahinoam's Tragedy: The latter part of Saul's life was marked by increasing paranoia, jealousy, and his downfall due to his failure to obey God's commands. Saul's relationship with Ahinoam appears to be impacted by his own spiritual struggles, and the Bible doesn't provide much about their emotional or personal life. One of the most tragic events for Ahinoam occurred when her husband Saul died. After Saul's death, Ahinoam's family faced further tragedy, as her son Ishbosheth, the last remaining son of Saul, was murdered (2 Samuel 4:5-7).

- **Saul's Final Years:** During the time when Saul was battling David, Ahinoam's position as queen would have been fraught with tension, as David, whom Saul viewed as a threat to his throne, was gaining increasing popularity. Saul's obsession with pursuing and killing David left little room for peace or stability within his family.

- **Saul's Death and Ahinoam's Fate:** When Saul died at the battle of Mount Gilboa (1 Samuel 31), Ahinoam was left without her husband. Saul's death also marked the collapse of his dynasty. Ahinoam's final fate is not detailed in the Scriptures, but her life was undoubtedly filled with hardship due to her husband's poor decisions and the tumultuous times in which they lived.

Lessons for Couples:

1. **The Impact of Spiritual Integrity in Marriage:** Saul's relationship with Ahinoam provides a glimpse into how a leader's spiritual integrity (or lack thereof) can affect the marriage. Saul's disobedience to God led to personal and national consequences, and his lack of spiritual alignment with God affected his relationships, including his marriage. For couples, this highlights the importance of staying spiritually grounded in faith. A lack of spiritual discipline and obedience can disrupt peace and stability in marriage.

2. **The Role of Mutual Support:** Although the Bible doesn't give much insight into Ahinoam's actions or thoughts, we can infer that, as the wife of the king, she likely had a role in supporting her husband during his reign. A strong marriage requires mutual support, especially during difficult times. Ahinoam's support of Saul, even during his spiritual decline, serves as a reminder that couples need to stand by each other through challenges, but also help one another stay true to their values and convictions.

3. **The Consequences of Disobedience:** Saul's downfall is marked by his repeated disobedience to God. His failure to lead with godly wisdom and his decisions, driven by jealousy and fear, had tragic consequences for his family. For couples, this story underscores the importance of living according to God's will, as disobedience can lead to long-term negative consequences. Marriage should be built on mutual respect for God's commands and a shared commitment to following them.

4. **Dealing with Tragedy and Loss:** Ahinoam's story includes the suffering of losing her husband and later, her son. For couples, this highlights the inevitability of hardship and loss in life. But it also teaches the importance of relying on God through times of grief. Couples should strengthen each other during difficult times, supporting one another as they navigate pain and loss, and lean on God for comfort and healing.

5. **The Importance of Legacy:** Saul's legacy was one of failure, and this negatively impacted his family, including Ahinoam and their children. For couples, this serves as a reminder to build a legacy that reflects faith, obedience, and righteousness. The choices made in

marriage, particularly those that affect children and the future, can shape the legacy a couple leaves behind.

6. Emotional and Spiritual Communication: Though we do not hear much about the emotional dynamics of Saul and Ahinoam's marriage, we can infer that the tumult of Saul's reign likely affected their relationship. The importance of emotional and spiritual communication is critical in marriage. Couples should prioritize open communication, emotional support, and mutual growth in faith, especially when facing external pressures.

7. Trusting God in Times of Conflict: With Saul's increasing paranoia and obsession with David, the family would have been under constant tension. Ahinoam's position as the wife of a troubled king teaches couples that, even in times of conflict, the foundation of a strong marriage is trust in God. Trusting God through conflict can provide stability and peace in the midst of uncertainty.

Week 50

God's Faithfulness and the Triumph of His Kingdom

Weekly Readings:

Day 344: Zechariah 12, Zechariah 13, Zechariah 14; Revelation 2:1-17; Proverbs 30:1-10
Day 345: Esther 1, Esther 2:1-18; Revelation 2:18-29, Revelation 3:1-6; Psalm 140:6-13
Day 346: Esther 2:19-23, Esther 3, Esther 4, Esther 5; Revelation 3:7-22; Psalm 141:1-10
Day 347: Esther 6, Esther 7, Esther 8; Revelation 4; Psalm 142:1-11
Day 348: Esther 9, Esther 10; Revelation 5; Proverbs 30:11-23
Day 349: Malachi 1, Malachi 2:1-16; Revelation 6; Psalm 143:1-12
Day 350: Malachi 2:17, Malachi 3, Malachi 4; Revelation 7; Psalm 144:1-8

Weekly Reflection:

This week's readings offer a compelling look at God's faithfulness in the face of trials and His ultimate victory over evil. Zechariah paints a powerful image of God's deliverance and the future triumph of His kingdom, when all nations will recognize His sovereignty and worship Him. The Book of Esther shows how God's providence and timing work behind the scenes to bring deliverance to His people, even when His name is not explicitly mentioned. Through Esther's courage and faithfulness, we see God's hand at work, orchestrating events for the good of His people.

The letters to the churches in Revelation challenge us to evaluate our faithfulness to God. The letters highlight the strengths and weaknesses of each church, calling believers to repent where they have fallen short and to remain faithful to the truth of the gospel. In the same way, God calls us as couples to remain steadfast in our faith and to work together in obedience to His commands.

The Book of Malachi calls Israel to return to faithfulness in their worship and relationships with God. Despite the people's unfaithfulness, God promises to send His messenger to prepare the way for His ultimate redemption. In Revelation, we see glimpses of the victory Christ has already secured, assuring us that He will return to bring about the full restoration of His kingdom.

For couples, these readings remind us that God's plans are always for our good, and even when we cannot see His hand at work, we can trust in His providence. Just as Esther had to trust in God's timing, so must we trust in His perfect plan for our marriages and our lives.

Weekly Discussion Prompts:

1. Trusting God's Timing: Zechariah 14 speaks of a future day when God will reign over all. How do you as a couple trust in God's timing, even when things do not seem to be going according to your plans? How can you encourage each other to remain faithful in times of uncertainty?

2. Living with Integrity: Esther shows how integrity and courage can bring about great change. What does integrity look like in your marriage? How can you work together to maintain transparency and honesty in your relationship?

3. Repentance and Renewal: Revelation 2:5 urges the church in Ephesus to "remember, repent, and do the works you did at first." Are there areas in your marriage where you need to return to your first love—God? How can you restore passion for God's work in your relationship?

4. Obedience to God's Call: In Esther 4:14, Mordecai says to Esther, "Who knows whether you have come to the kingdom for such a time as this?" How can you both see your marriage as part of God's greater plan? How do you discern God's calling for your relationship and serve Him together?

5. Faithfulness in Difficult Times: Revelation 3:10 speaks of God's promise to keep His people from the hour of trial. How can you as a couple support one another during difficult seasons? What role does faithfulness play in maintaining a strong marriage when facing external challenges?

6. Living with Hope: Malachi 3:16-18 speaks of those who fear the Lord being treasured by God. How can you as a couple live in hope of God's promises, even when the world around you may seem uncertain or difficult? How can you build a strong foundation of hope together?

7. Looking Forward to Christ's Return: Revelation 7 gives a picture of the saints before the throne of God, worshiping Him. How does the hope of Christ's return shape your marriage? How can you live in such a way that your relationship reflects the anticipation of His glorious return?

"Reflecting God's Providence Together": This week, take time to reflect on the ways God has shown His faithfulness in your relationship. Write down specific moments where you have seen God's hand at work, whether it's through provision, guidance, or protection. Share these moments with each other and thank God for His faithfulness.

As you look ahead to the future, consider areas in your marriage where God may be calling you to step out in faith. Are there ways you can support each other in trusting God's timing or in making courageous decisions for your family or your relationship with Him? This week, commit to praying for each other's growth and for the fulfillment of God's plan in your marriage. Lastly, engage in an act of service together, as a way of reflecting God's love to others. Whether it's helping a neighbor, serving at church, or giving to those in need, let this act of love and service be a tangible reminder of the ultimate service Christ has shown to us.

Couple for Week 50: King Solomon and Naamah

King Solomon, the son of David and Bathsheba, is widely known for his wisdom, wealth, and the building of the First Temple in Jerusalem. His reign was a time of great prosperity and peace for Israel, but also marked by a complex and sometimes troubled personal life, particularly his many marriages. One of these marriages was to Naamah, an Ammonite woman who became one of his wives.

The Story of Solomon and Naamah:

- Naamah's Background: Naamah is described as the daughter of an Ammonite king (1 Kings 14:21). The Ammonites were often in conflict with Israel, and this marriage likely served as a political alliance between Israel and Ammon, as was common in royal marriages at the time.

- Solomon's Polygamy: Solomon had many wives—700, according to 1 Kings 11:3—and Naamah was one of these wives. While Solomon's wisdom and wealth made him renowned throughout the ancient world, his numerous marriages led him into spiritual compromise. Solomon's marriages, including his union with Naamah, are often seen as part of the reason for his eventual downfall. Many of his wives led him to worship foreign gods, which ultimately caused God to become angry with Solomon (1 Kings 11:1-13).

- Naamah's Role and Legacy: Although Naamah is only mentioned briefly in the Bible, her role as the mother of Rehoboam, Solomon's successor, is significant. Rehoboam would later become king of Judah after Solomon's death. His reign marked the division of the united kingdom of Israel into two separate kingdoms: Israel and Judah. Rehoboam's reign was marked by poor decisions and his inability to unite the tribes, which led to a long-lasting split in the kingdom.

- **Naamah's Influence:** Naamah's influence as the mother of Rehoboam may have played a role in the way her son ruled. While the Bible does not give much insight into her personal character or influence, the fact that she was the mother of the king suggests that she may have had some influence in the royal court. Some scholars speculate that the Ammonite heritage could have been a factor in Rehoboam's decisions, though this is not explicitly detailed in the text.

- **The Consequences of Solomon's Marriages:** Solomon's marriages to foreign women, including Naamah, were in direct contradiction to God's command in Deuteronomy 7:3-4, which warned Israel not to intermarry with the surrounding nations because it would lead them away from God. Unfortunately, this is what happened in Solomon's life. The marriages were not just political; they involved the introduction of foreign gods into Israel. Naamah, though not a major figure in the Bible, represents one of the many foreign wives who influenced Solomon's spiritual decline.

Lessons for Couples:

1. **The Dangers of Compromise in Marriage:** Solomon's marriage to Naamah, as with his other marriages to foreign women, was a compromise that ultimately led him away from God. For modern couples, this story serves as a reminder that compromising on faith, values, and beliefs within a marriage can lead to serious consequences. A marriage should be built on mutual respect and shared values, especially when it comes to spiritual beliefs.

2. **The Importance of Prioritizing Faith:** Solomon's story is a cautionary tale about the importance of prioritizing faith in marriage. Solomon allowed his foreign wives to turn his heart away from God (1 Kings 11:4). For couples, it's crucial to maintain a strong relationship with God, both individually and as a couple, to prevent outside influences from leading one away from their spiritual path. A strong, faith-centered marriage can withstand external pressures and challenges.

3. **The Influence of Parents:** Naamah, as the mother of Rehoboam, had the potential to influence her son's reign. The influence of parents—especially mothers—on children is undeniable. Parents, particularly mothers, have a significant role in shaping the values, character, and spiritual direction of their children. Naamah's influence on Rehoboam's reign, though not clearly outlined in Scripture, can be seen as a reminder that the values and beliefs passed down from parents play a critical role in a child's future decisions.

4. **The Risk of Political or Strategic Marriages:** Solomon's marriage to Naamah was likely politically motivated. While political or strategic marriages may offer short-term benefits, they can have long-term spiritual and personal consequences. Couples should

be cautious about entering into relationships for reasons other than mutual love, respect, and shared values. A marriage built solely on external considerations may not be stable or fulfilling in the long run.

5. Wisdom in Marriage Decisions: Solomon's wisdom in many areas was well-known, but he faltered in his personal life. His many marriages were not wise decisions, especially when they led him away from God. For couples, this teaches that wisdom should guide marriage decisions. Wisdom in choosing a partner, nurturing the relationship, and managing the challenges of marriage can help couples avoid the pitfalls that Solomon faced.

6. The Consequences of Misaligned Priorities: Solomon's marriages to foreign women led to a divided kingdom, and his spiritual decline resulted in God's judgment. Couples should be aware that misaligned priorities—such as neglecting spiritual health, family, or integrity for personal gain—can lead to broader consequences. A marriage should align with God's will to build a lasting, fruitful partnership.

7. Building a Legacy: Solomon's legacy, particularly through his son Rehoboam, reflects the impact that decisions in marriage can have on future generations. Couples have the ability to shape their family's legacy, especially through the upbringing of children. A marriage centered on faith, love, and wisdom has the potential to create a strong and positive legacy for future generations.

Week 51

Returning to God's Presence and the Victory of Christ

Weekly Readings:

Day 351: Ezra 1, Ezra 2:1-67; Revelation 8, Revelation 9:1-12; Psalm 144:9-15
Day 352: Ezra 2:68-70, Ezra 3, Ezra 4:1-5; Revelation 9:13-21, Revelation 10; Proverbs 30:24-33
Day 353: Ezra 4:6-24, Ezra 5; Revelation 11; Psalm 145:1-7
Day 354: Ezra 6, Ezra 7:1-10; Revelation 12, Revelation 13:1; Psalm 145:8-13
Day 355: Ezra 7:11-28, Ezra 8:1-14; Revelation 13:1-18; Psalm 145:13-21
Day 356: Ezra 8:15-36, Ezra 9:1-15; Revelation 14:1-13; Proverbs 31:1-9
Day 357: Ezra 10; Revelation 14:14-20, Revelation 15; Psalm 146:1-10

Weekly Reflection:

This week's readings focus on the themes of restoration, faithfulness, and the ultimate victory of God over evil. In the Book of Ezra, we witness the return of the exiles to Jerusalem and their efforts to rebuild the temple. This is a powerful image of God's faithfulness to His promises and His desire to restore His people. Even though there are challenges, opposition, and delays, the people are called to remain committed to God's work, trusting that He will complete what He has started.

The Book of Revelation, by contrast, reveals the cosmic battle between good and evil, as well as the triumph of Christ over all forces of darkness. The trumpets and bowls signal God's righteous judgment, but also the ultimate victory of His kingdom. Through the visions of Revelation, we see that even in the midst of trials and tribulation, Christ's victory is assured. His return will bring about the fullness of God's kingdom.

For couples, these readings remind us that no matter the challenges or opposition we may face in our relationship, God's faithfulness and His victory over sin and death give us hope. Just as the exiles rebuilt the temple despite opposition, we too can build strong marriages when we rely on God's strength, trusting in His faithfulness to finish the work He has started in us.

Weekly Discussion Prompts:

1. God's Faithfulness in Restoration: In Ezra 1:1-2, we see God stirring the heart of King Cyrus to allow the Israelites to return to their land. In what ways have you seen God restore your relationship with Him and with each other? How can you trust in His faithfulness to continue restoring and strengthening your marriage?

2. Overcoming Opposition: Ezra 4:4-5 shows that the rebuilding of the temple faced opposition. As a couple, how do you handle opposition in your marriage, whether from external forces or internal struggles? How can you support each other when you face challenges in your relationship?

3. The Victory of Christ: Revelation 9:11 speaks of the "angel of the abyss." What does it mean for you as a couple that Christ has already defeated the ultimate enemy? How does knowing that Christ has won the victory over sin and death impact your daily life and your marriage?

4. Faithfulness in the Midst of Trials: In Ezra 3:3, the people of Israel offered sacrifices despite the challenges. How can you both remain faithful to God, even when times are difficult? How can you encourage one another to persevere in prayer, worship, and service, even when things feel uncertain?

5. The Call to Holiness: Revelation 14:4 describes those who are "pure" and "redeemed." How can you as a couple live in a way that reflects purity and holiness? What steps can you take to strengthen your spiritual lives and grow closer to God together?

6. God's Judgment and Mercy: Ezra 9:6-7 describes how Israel had fallen short of God's commandments but found mercy through repentance. How does repentance play a role in your marriage? How can you support one another in turning to God for mercy and grace, especially when you fall short?

7. Living with Hope of Christ's Return: Revelation 15:3-4 gives us a picture of the saints praising God for His victory. How does the anticipation of Christ's return affect the way you live your life and your marriage? How can you live with a sense of hope and joy, knowing that Christ will return to bring about ultimate restoration?

"Building a Strong Foundation Together": This week, take some time to reflect on the areas in your marriage that need restoration or strengthening. Just as the Israelites had to rebuild the temple, you may have areas in your relationship that need attention and care. Take time to pray together, asking God to guide you as you work to restore those areas in your marriage.

Create a list of things you can both do to strengthen your relationship, whether it's through more intentional time together, regular prayers, or seeking support from a trusted mentor or counselor. Reflect on the hope you have in God's faithfulness to complete the work He has begun in your marriage.

Finally, spend time praising God together for His mercy and grace. Consider reading Revelation 15:3-4 aloud and discussing how it speaks to your hope in God's ultimate victory and the restoration He is bringing about in your lives.

Couple for Week 51: Tamar and Er

Tamar and Er's story is one of tragedy, family duty, and ultimately, redemption, found in the Old Testament book of Genesis 38. It centers on Tamar, the widow of Er, and the complex and challenging circumstances she faced in fulfilling her levirate duties and ensuring the continuation of her husband's lineage.

The Story of Tamar and Er:

- Er's Sin and Death: Tamar was married to Er, the firstborn son of Judah, one of the twelve sons of Jacob. Er, however, was wicked in the sight of the Lord, and because of his sin, God struck him dead (Genesis 38:7). In the ancient Near East, it was customary for a widow to marry her deceased husband's brother in order to continue the family line, a practice known as levirate marriage. Judah, Er's father, instructed his second son, Onan, to fulfill this duty by marrying Tamar and providing offspring to carry on his brother's name.

- Onan's Refusal and His Death: Onan, however, was unwilling to father children for his brother, as it would not be considered his own legacy, and he practiced a form of birth control. God was displeased with his actions and struck him dead as well (Genesis 38:8-10). This left Tamar in a difficult and precarious position, as she had now lost both her husbands and had no children to carry on the family name.

- Judah's Promise and Tamar's Action: Judah then promised Tamar that when his youngest son, Shelah, came of age, he would marry her and fulfill the levirate duty. However, Judah did not keep his promise, possibly fearing that Shelah might also die like his brothers. Tamar, aware that Judah had no intention of honoring his word, took matters into her own hands. She disguised herself as a prostitute and waited by the roadside where Judah would pass by. Judah, not recognizing her, solicited her services, and Tamar became pregnant by him.

- The Revelation and Judah's Acknowledgment: When Tamar's pregnancy became known, Judah was initially angered and ordered her to be burned to death for her perceived immorality. However, Tamar revealed that the father of her child was Judah himself, showing him the items (a signet ring, cord, and staff) he had left with her as a pledge for payment. Judah, realizing that he had failed to provide for her as he should have, acknowledged that she was more righteous than he (Genesis 38:26). Tamar gave birth to twins, Perez and Zerah, and through Perez, the line of Judah continued.

Lessons for Couples:

1. The Importance of Keeping Promises: Judah's failure to honor his promise to Tamar was a significant part of the tragedy in her story. Couples can learn from this that keeping promises, especially those made in marriage or family obligations, is essential for maintaining trust and integrity. When promises are broken, they can lead to serious consequences.

2. The Value of Justice and Righteousness: Tamar's actions, while unconventional, were driven by a desire to fulfill her responsibility and continue her deceased husband's lineage. She is ultimately recognized for her righteousness, not for the way she went about it, but for her commitment to family and justice. Couples can reflect on the importance of acting with justice and integrity, even when faced with difficult and unfair situations.

3. Taking Responsibility in Difficult Circumstances: Tamar's story teaches the importance of taking responsibility and initiative in challenging situations. Rather than passively waiting for others to act, she took matters into her own hands when Judah failed to fulfill his promise. Couples can learn the importance of standing up for what is right, taking action when necessary, and not relying solely on others to solve their problems.

4. Redemption and Grace: Although Tamar's actions could have been seen in a negative light, the story ultimately ends in redemption. God used Tamar's actions to continue the line of Judah, which eventually leads to the birth of King David, and ultimately, Jesus Christ. This shows that God's grace can work through imperfect situations and individuals. Couples can be reminded that even when they make mistakes or face challenging situations, God can still bring redemption and blessing from them.

5. The Significance of Family: Tamar's primary concern was ensuring that her husband's family line continued. This reflects the importance of family relationships and legacy in the biblical worldview. Couples can take away the importance of nurturing their family relationships, supporting each other in difficult times, and honoring family duties.

6. The Consequences of Neglecting Responsibility: Judah's neglect of his responsibility to Tamar had negative consequences for him and his family. Couples should be aware that neglecting responsibilities to each other, especially in marriage or family matters, can lead to harm. It's essential to fulfill commitments, be dependable, and prioritize family welfare.

7. The Power of Integrity: Despite the unconventional nature of Tamar's actions, her integrity was evident in her desire to do what was right, which was to secure her future and fulfill her levirate duties. For couples, this serves as a reminder that integrity—doing what is right in the eyes of God—is vital, even when it requires great personal sacrifice.

Week 52

A Year of Restoration and Hope in Christ's Return

Weekly Readings:

Day 358: Nehemiah 1, Nehemiah 2; Revelation 16; Psalm 147:1-11
Day 359: Nehemiah 3, Nehemiah 4; Revelation 17; Psalm 147:12-20
Day 360: Nehemiah 5, Nehemiah 6, Nehemiah 7:1-3; Revelation 18:1-17; Proverbs 31:10-20
Day 361: Nehemiah 7:4-73, Nehemiah 8; Revelation 18:17-24, Revelation 19:1-10; Psalm 148:1-6
Day 362: Nehemiah 9:1-37; Revelation 19:11-21; Psalm 148:7-14
Day 363: Nehemiah 9:38, Nehemiah 10, Nehemiah 11:1-21; Revelation 20; Psalm 149:1-9
Day 364: Nehemiah 11:22-36, Nehemiah 12:1-47; Revelation 21; Proverbs 31:21-31
Day 365: Nehemiah 13; Revelation 22; Psalm 150:1-6

Weekly Reflection:

This final week of the year draws together the themes of restoration, rebuilding, and the ultimate fulfillment of God's promises. In Nehemiah, the rebuilding of the walls of Jerusalem symbolizes God's work of restoring His people, offering protection, strength, and renewal after a period of exile and destruction. The people return to the city with a renewed commitment to follow God's commands and live in covenant with Him, showing that true restoration requires not just external rebuilding, but internal transformation through repentance, prayer, and renewal of covenant.

The Book of Revelation offers the triumphant conclusion to the cosmic story of salvation. It reveals Christ's ultimate victory over evil and His return to make all things new. As God restores His people on earth, He also promises to restore all creation, bringing an end to suffering and death. Revelation 21 and 22 provide a vision of the New Jerusalem—a place of eternal joy, peace, and fellowship with God. This final vision is one of great hope, pointing to the day when God will dwell with His people forever.

For couples, this week's readings offer encouragement to continue rebuilding areas of your relationship that may have been broken or neglected. As you reflect on the restoration of Jerusalem and the ultimate restoration in the New Jerusalem, think about how God can restore your marriage, bringing new life, purpose, and joy. Just as Nehemiah and the people of Jerusalem committed to renewing their covenant with God, you too can renew your commitment to one another and to God.

Weekly Discussion Prompts:

1. The Work of Restoration: Nehemiah's efforts to rebuild the walls of Jerusalem represent both physical and spiritual restoration. In what areas of your marriage do you feel called to restore or rebuild? How can you work together to create a stronger foundation for your relationship?

2. Commitment to Covenant: Nehemiah 9:38 shows that the people renewed their covenant with God. How can you both renew your commitment to God and to each other? In what ways can you deepen your relationship with one another and with God in the coming year?

3. Facing Opposition Together: Nehemiah 4:14 talks about standing firm against opposition. As a couple, how do you handle challenges or external pressures? How can you support each other when your relationship is under strain or when life presents difficulties?

4. God's Promise of Restoration: Revelation 21:1-4 speaks of God making all things new. How does the hope of God's ultimate restoration impact your view of your relationship? How can you lean on this promise to help you through tough times in your marriage?

5. Living in Hope of Christ's Return: Revelation 22:20 speaks of the return of Christ. As a couple, how can you live with the anticipation of Christ's return and the fulfillment of God's promises? How does this hope influence the way you treat one another and the way you live out your faith together?

6. God's Provision and Blessing: Nehemiah 12:27-43 describes the people celebrating God's faithfulness with music and thanksgiving. How can you celebrate God's provision and blessings in your marriage? What are some specific ways you can express gratitude to God for the blessings in your relationship?

7. Living for Eternity: Revelation 21:4 speaks of the end of suffering, death, and pain. How can you, as a couple, focus on eternal values and invest in things that will last beyond this life? How does this eternal perspective affect the way you build your marriage today?

Joint Couple Activity:

"Renewing Your Covenant": This week, take time to reflect on the state of your marriage and what God has done in your relationship over the past year. As you look back, consider the areas that need restoration, healing, and renewal. Spend time in prayer together, asking God to continue His work of restoration in your marriage.

Write down a covenant statement that reflects your commitment to each other and to God. Consider including promises of love, support, prayer, and mutual respect. Seal this covenant by reading it aloud to one another and praying together for the strength to live it out in the coming year.

Additionally, spend time in worship by reading Revelation 21:1-4 and praising God for His promises of a new creation. Discuss how the hope of Christ's return and the ultimate restoration of all things impacts your life together, both now and in the future.

Couple for Week 52: Abraham and Hagar

The story of Abraham and Hagar is one of complexity and significant lessons for relationships, faith, and the consequences of acting outside of God's timing. Hagar was an Egyptian maidservant to Sarah, Abraham's wife, and became part of a pivotal moment in the biblical narrative when Sarah and Abraham struggled with infertility. The story of Hagar is primarily found in Genesis 16 and Genesis 21.

The Story of Abraham and Hagar:

- The Initial Situation: Abraham and Sarah had been promised by God that they would have a child who would become the father of many nations (Genesis 17:4-5). However, as they grew older and still had no child, Sarah grew impatient and devised a plan to help God fulfill the promise. She offered Hagar, her Egyptian maidservant, to Abraham as a surrogate to bear a child (Genesis 16:1-2). Sarah believed that if Hagar bore Abraham's child, it would fulfill God's promise.

- The Consequences of the Decision: Abraham agreed to Sarah's plan, and Hagar conceived a child. However, when Hagar became pregnant, she began to despise Sarah, which led to conflict in the household (Genesis 16:4). Sarah, feeling slighted and mistreated, mistreated Hagar, who fled into the wilderness. There, an angel of the Lord appeared to Hagar and instructed her to return to Sarah and submit to her authority. The angel also told Hagar that her son would be named Ishmael, and he would become the father of a great nation (Genesis 16:7-12). Hagar returned, and she gave birth to Ishmael.

- **The Birth of Isaac:** Despite this situation, God's promise to Abraham and Sarah was ultimately fulfilled through Sarah. At the age of 90, Sarah gave birth to a son, Isaac, in her old age (Genesis 21:1-3). The birth of Isaac caused tension between Sarah and Hagar, especially as Isaac grew older. Sarah demanded that Abraham send Hagar and Ishmael away to ensure that Isaac would inherit the promise made to Abraham (Genesis 21:9-10).

- **The Aftermath:** Abraham was distressed by Sarah's request, but God told him to listen to Sarah, assuring him that He would take care of Hagar and Ishmael. Abraham sent Hagar and Ishmael away into the wilderness. When their provisions ran out, Hagar despaired, but God again intervened by showing her a well of water and promising that Ishmael would become a great nation (Genesis 21:14-21). Hagar and Ishmael's story ends on a hopeful note, with God's continued provision for them in the desert.

Lessons for Couples:

1. **The Consequences of Acting Outside God's Timing:** Abraham and Sarah's decision to have a child through Hagar was based on impatience and a lack of trust in God's timing. Although they were promised a son, they sought to fulfill God's promise through their own plan, which led to conflict and hardship. For couples, this serves as a reminder that God's promises will be fulfilled in His timing, and impatience or human intervention can lead to complications and unforeseen consequences.

2. **The Impact of Decisions on Family Dynamics:** The relationship between Abraham, Sarah, and Hagar became strained as a result of their decision to have a child outside of God's plan. Hagar's pregnancy created tension in the household, and Sarah's resentment led to mistreatment. This is a clear example of how decisions made without considering the long-term consequences can affect relationships and cause division in families. Couples can learn the importance of thoughtful decision-making, communication, and seeking God's guidance in all matters, especially those that affect family harmony.

3. **God's Grace and Provision in Difficult Situations:** Even though the situation with Hagar and Ishmael was born out of human error, God's grace and provision were evident. He protected Hagar and Ishmael in the wilderness and promised that Ishmael would become the father of a great nation. For couples, this serves as a reminder that even when they make mistakes or face challenging circumstances, God is faithful to provide, guide, and offer grace. His plans are not thwarted by human failure.

4. **The Importance of Clear Communication and Trust:** The breakdown in communication between Abraham and Sarah regarding their plans for a child caused unnecessary strife. Sarah's initial suggestion was not openly questioned by Abraham, and the situation escalated without the trust and openness needed between a husband and wife. Couples can learn the importance of clear communication, trust, and mutual respect in their relationship, especially when making major life decisions.

5. Trusting in God's Promises: Abraham and Sarah struggled to fully trust in God's promise that they would have a child. By trying to fulfill the promise through their own means, they lacked the faith to wait for God's perfect timing. Couples can learn from this that trusting in God's promises, even when the waiting is difficult, is essential for a peaceful and fulfilling relationship. God's plans for them are better than any plans they can devise on their own.

6. Compassion and Understanding in Difficult Situations: The story of Hagar also teaches couples the importance of compassion and understanding in difficult situations. Hagar's mistreatment by Sarah and her feelings of abandonment when sent into the wilderness show the need for empathy. Couples should be compassionate toward one another, especially when faced with challenges, and seek to lift each other up rather than resorting to harshness or blame.

7. God's Redemptive Power: Even though Hagar's situation was complicated and painful, God intervened to protect her and her son, Ishmael. This demonstrates that God's redemptive power can bring hope and restoration even to challenging and broken situations. For couples, this is a reminder that no situation is beyond God's redemptive touch. God can bring healing and hope to the broken parts of their lives and relationships.

Conclusion

Reflecting on the Journey: A Year of Growing in Love and Faith Together

Dear Couples,

As you reach the final pages of *The Bible in 52 Weeks for Couples*, pause and celebrate this meaningful milestone. You've walked through a full year of exploration, learning, and growth in God's Word, deepening not only your understanding of Scripture but also your commitment to each other. Together, you have embraced the highs and lows of biblical stories, drawn wisdom from God's teachings, and uncovered new depths in your own partnership.

This journey has been one of discovery—a journey that we pray has drawn you closer to God and to each other. Every theme, every reading, and every discussion was designed to help you see your marriage through the lens of faith, encouraging you to strengthen your bond and build a love that mirrors God's love for us. Reflect now on all that you've accomplished as a couple, the new insights you've gained, and the ways in which you've both grown. Each week was a step, each reading a building block, forming the foundation of a love that is resilient, compassionate, and grounded in faith.

Looking Back at What You've Gained

Throughout this year, you've journeyed through diverse themes—trust, forgiveness, unity, patience, and many others—that have shaped your relationship in lasting ways. Here are some of the highlights of your journey:

1. Strengthened Communication: By exploring weekly discussion prompts and engaging in heartfelt conversations, you've likely found new ways to share openly and listen with greater empathy. These skills are invaluable, strengthening the foundation of your marriage.

2. Deepened Spiritual Connection: Reading Scripture together and taking time for shared prayer has enriched your bond with God as a couple. By cultivating this spiritual intimacy, you've built a marriage that is grounded not only in love but also in shared faith and values.

3. Enduring Commitment: Each activity and reflection helped to reinforce your dedication to one another. You've committed to growing together, through challenges and joys, with God as the center of your union.

4. Faithful Legacy: Whether it's in your words, your actions, or the promises you've renewed, you're leaving a legacy of faith for those who look up to you. Each step you've taken this year contributes to a foundation that will last well beyond these pages.

Moving Forward: How to Continue Nurturing Your Faith and Marriage

While this book may be concluding, your journey of faith and growth as a couple continues. Here are a few suggestions for carrying forward the lessons and habits you've cultivated this year:

- Make Scripture a Part of Your Life: Continue reading the Bible together, perhaps choosing a new book or theme that speaks to you. Whether it's Proverbs for wisdom, Psalms for encouragement, or the Gospels for inspiration, keep the Word alive in your home.

- Stay Connected in Prayer: Let prayer remain central to your relationship. Pray together, for each other, and over the dreams and challenges you face as a couple. When prayer is a regular part of your lives, you invite God's presence and wisdom into every aspect of your relationship.

- Regular Check-Ins: Just as you took time each week to discuss, reflect, and connect, create a rhythm of weekly or monthly check-ins where you intentionally talk about your relationship. Discuss your goals, challenges, and the ways you can continue to grow together.

- Renew Your Commitment to Each Other: Occasionally, revisit the promises and commitments you made in the early weeks of this journey. Remind each other of your love, your shared goals, and your dedication to building a marriage rooted in faith.

- Serve Together: Whether it's within your church, your community, or even in small acts of kindness, look for ways to serve others together. Acts of service strengthen your bond, build compassion, and remind you of your shared purpose as a couple.

Closing Blessing

As you close this chapter, may you carry forward the peace, strength, and love that God has cultivated in your hearts this year. May your marriage continue to be a beautiful reflection of His love—a partnership that grows richer and deeper with time. May you find joy in each other, grace in your struggles, and courage in your journey ahead.

Thank you for allowing *The Bible in 52 Weeks for Couples* to be part of your story. May God bless your marriage abundantly and lead you into a future filled with love, faith, and enduring partnership.

With love and blessings,

Esther W. Dawson

Made in the USA
Las Vegas, NV
02 January 2025

15663420R00136